Sharing the Earth

Studies in Rhetoric/Communication
Thomas W. Benson, Series Editor

Sharing the Earth
The Rhetoric of
Sustainable Development

Tarla Rai Peterson

UNIVERSITY OF SOUTH CAROLINA PRESS

338.927
P48 e

H   © 1997 University of South Carolina

Published in Columbia, South Carolina, by the
University of South Carolina Press

Manufactured in the United States of America

01 00 99 98 97 5 4 3 2 1

Library of Congress Cataloging-in-Publication Data

Peterson, Tarla Rai.
  Sharing the earth : the rhetoric of sustainable development /
Tarla Rai Peterson.
    p.   cm. — (Studies in rhetoric/communication)
  Includes bibliographical references and index.
  ISBN 1–57003–173–8
  1. Sustainable development. I. Title. II. Series.
HC79.E5P474 1997
338.9'27—dc21   97–4737

50% recycled
10% post-consumer waste

For Markus

Contents

Contents

Editor's Preface

In this latest contribution to the series in Rhetoric/Communication of the University of South Carolina Press, Tarla Rai Peterson invites readers to cross boundaries of nation, class, culture, ethnicity, academic disciplines, and taken-for-granted conceptual categories.

Professor Peterson's book explores the ways in which a rhetoric of "sustainable development" might break through a political and conceptual stalemate between two either-or models of ecological integrity—an "ecocentric" view that sacrifices human interests for the sake of "nature," and an "anthropocentric" view that would value nature only for human use. Although "sustainable development" might offer a newly progressive consensus, argues Professor Peterson, it could as easily be coopted by the powerful and used as a mystifying slogan to stifle needed debate.

As a way of exploring the promises and perils of "sustainable development," Professor Peterson examines the term in the light of rhetorical theory and through the lens of rhetorical criticism in a series of three remarkable case studies—of the Rio Earth Summit of 1992; of the debate over the fate of the wood bison in Canada's Wood Buffalo National Park; and of the environmental politics of Cameron County in southern Texas.

Professor Peterson's tough-minded analysis of the rhetoric of sustainable development should be of immediate and lasting use to policy planners and environmental advocates. Her deft combination of theory, critical analysis, and cross-disciplinary fieldwork will be an inspiration and a model for her colleagues in rhetoric and communication.

Thomas W. Benson

Acknowledgments

Numerous colleagues, students, friends, and institutions contributed to this book through critical readings, stimulating conversations, suggestions, financial support, and less tangible forms of encouragement.

First, I would like to thank a special group of people who assisted me with the unique challenges presented by cross-disciplinary research. Among those to whom I am indebted special thanks go to Markus J. Peterson. His willingness to share his knowledge of ecological processes significantly improved the substance of this book. Additionally, he read several drafts of the manuscript, helping immeasurably with corrections, reactions, and friendly encouragement. Dean Wayne Esplin's far-ranging discussions of sustainable development refused to recognize disciplinary boundaries long before either *sustainability* or *cross-disciplinary* became popular terms. Although I have never met him, I am indebted to Daniel Botkin; his book *Discordant Harmonies* persuaded me that it was reasonable to attempt a book that spoke to both social critics and biologists. Becca Esplin helped me understand the significance of locating humans within, rather than beyond, the biosphere. Discussions with Paul Thompson helped me understand more incisively the social history and technical intricacies of various perspectives toward ecological questions. Participation in the sustainability discussion group sponsored by the Center for Biotechnology Policy and Ethics at Texas A&M University improved my abilities to communicate across disciplines. Marion Christensen provided me with invaluable editorial assistance in writing a book that was accessible to that broad audience.

Examination of environmental policy suggests that, in addition to crossing disciplinary boundaries, productive criticism must breach the boundaries that have developed between the academy and the "real world." I learned much about rhetorical studies, humanistic inquiry, and their potential contribution to living well in the world from Robert L. Ivie. Robert Cox contributed a sense of urgency and showed me how to apply this understanding to environmental policy. Cox, Dennis Jaehne, and John Lange read portions of the manuscript and provided critical commentaries that contributed to making it both more insightful and

Acknowledgments

accessible. Discussions with James Cantrill, Jimmy Killingsworth, Kai Lee, Chris Oravec, Mike Salvador, Sue Senecah, Greg Walker, and several participants in the conferences on communication and the environment held in Alta, Utah; Big Sky, Montana; and Chattanooga, Tennessee, deepened my understanding of the critical perspectives from which one could profitably approach ecological questions.

I am indebted to many other individuals and institutions for providing the support needed to write this book. Texas A&M University granted me a Faculty Development Leave, during which I conducted fieldwork and wrote much of the manuscript. Ed and Ellen Peterson assisted in creating the research environment needed to complete this book. I would like to thank Warren Slesinger for his unparalleled patience and encouragement. The Biotechnology Policy and Ethics Center at Texas A&M University provided a news clipping service and partial funding for obtaining documents analyzed in chapter 3. Conversations with Joanne Carmin were crucial to final revisions for that chapter. Markus J. Peterson obtained the transcripts analyzed in chapter 4 from Canada's Federal Environmental Assessment Review Office in Hull, Quebec. G. Thomas Goodnight provided valuable feedback on this chapter. The fieldwork on which chapter 5 is based was funded by a grant from the U.S. Environmental Protection Agency (ID# MX822144-01-0). This chapter could not have been written without Susan Gilbertz, Kathi Groenendyk, Jay Todd, Gary Varner, and Jill Webb, who devoted countless hours to collecting and interpreting interview texts in south Texas. Additionally, I wish to thank the residents of this region, who were willing to teach us what sustainable development meant to them.

Sharing the Earth

Chapter 1

Introduction

Scientists and social activists have attempted to explain the normative significance of ecological integrity since the earliest days of the environmental movement. The question often has been framed in terms of duties to either nature or to future generations of humans. These two ways of approaching the ethics of environmental issues have led to a debate between ecocentric and anthropocentric environmental theories which presents two alternatives for expressing the normative significance of ecological integrity: (1) nature is valuable in itself, entailing some instances in which human interests should be sacrificed to ecological values; or (2) ecological integrity is important because of its instrumental value for human use. While this way of framing the issue has proven relatively fruitful in discussing reasons for preserving rainforests or protecting the ozone layer, it has proved singularly unhelpful as applied to implementation of environmentally sensitive development policies because it promotes dichotomous approaches that encourage competitive scenarios wherein some participants win, while their opponents lose.

The term *sustainability* offers an alternative to the ecocentric/anthropocentric dichotomy for framing ethical questions about natural or ecological integrity. Ecocentric language can specify duties to preserve nature but presents little guidance for interacting with environments in which the technologies of civilization already have displaced the natural order. Anthropocentric language can specify duties to conserve resources for use by future generations of humans but fails to build any concept of ecosystem integrity into that obligation. Sustainability, on the other hand, offers a conceptualization of ecological integrity which includes humanity. Rather than attempting to displace anthropocentric perspectives with ecocentric perspectives (or vice versa), it suggests integrating human concerns into the larger biosphere. It is at least superficially attractive to say that it is the sustainability of human development practices which is the object of our moral duty. During the past decade the concept of "sustainable development" has become widely celebrated as a public policy goal to be supported and furthered on the basis of scientific research, as members of diverse interest groups have advocated shifts to more sustainable economic development. While the meaning of sustainable development remains contested by divergent political interests, it promises to promote a philosophical unity that could streamline implementation of specific environmental policies. The risk is that both frustrated scientists and environmental activists may grasp this tantalizing possibility for resolving social conflict without attending to the dangers inherent in any such totalizing construct. Although moving away from an artificially dichotomized view of environmental policy is useful, the danger is that real diversity in perspectives may be swallowed up in an attempt to promote consensus. Sustainable development enables efficient policy implementation partially by mystifying internal contradictions that may undermine both nature and future generations of human society.

Clearly, the concept of sustainable development presents many challenges. One is to explore how the current interpretations and political practices associated with the term lead to constraints upon the future evolution of sustainable development discourse. A second challenge is to analyze how social and scientific norms interpenetrate one another with respect to the concept of sustainable development. Another is to promote multidisciplinary dialogue that recognizes the intellectual significance as well as the immediately practical utility of sustainable development. There have, however, been few attempts to examine the content of different meanings for sustainable development and, therefore, few interpretive discussions of how the politics and ethics of environmentally sensitive development are framed by the concept of sustainability and mediated by its rhetoric.

This book is an attempt to analyze critically the language surrounding the concept of sustainable development. It is based on a humanistic commitment to the proposition that resolving conflicts by means of words usually is preferable to resolving them by physical means and grounded in Kenneth Burke's theory of criticism, which proceeds from the belief that community is an elusive yet essential part of civilized life and that rhetoric, or the use of language to secure a sense of identification among individuals, is basic to creating community. The book deals specifically with the rhetorical question of how to utilize the human capacity for language to understand better and reflect upon technologized conditions of our own making but not necessarily to our liking. It follows from Burke's suggestion that criticism can serve as a corrective for humanity's hypertechnologized state if the critic adopts a skeptical yet hopeful stance toward the social constructions that influence, and are influenced by, our material conditions.

A productive criticism of environmental dilemmas and their proposed solutions (such as sustainable development) must be accompanied by a heightened awareness of the interrelationship between verbal and natural systems. Nature, in and of itself, is not a rhetorical text. The acts of sustaining and / or developing it and the discussion surrounding those acts, however, do function rhetorically. Humans add language to nature, thus enabling themselves to manipulate and transform their origins. Rhetoric, then, is grounded in the speechless human body, which in turn is grounded in the pre- or extraverbal realm of nature. Rhetorical criticism must maintain the integrity of both verbal and natural systems, since both are essential: our existence depends on nature, and we need language to conceptualize and discuss the natural systems on which we rely. The danger is that, in the headlong rush toward progress, humans may destroy their grounding in nature under the delusion that natural and verbal systems are the same and that they have the same freedom with, and power over, both. Rhetorical criticism provides a means for turning the verbal system on itself, providing greater reflexivity regarding the covert dogmas and orthodoxies of our language and thus of the resulting technologies that impact natural systems. The point of such criticism is to humble without humiliating, or to protect us from our own hubris.

I do not mean to suggest that sustainable development is wholly, or even primarily, rhetorical but, rather, that examining the discourse of sustainable development can reveal dimensions of this provocative concept which might otherwise remain concealed. I offer rhetorical criticism as a means of enhancing the productive tension within the term *sustainable development* by displaying possibilities that current interpretations of the term have closed off. Reframing *sustainable development* to include those possibilities enables the concept to provide a powerful center around which environmental and human development advocates can unite. The book analyzes three disputes over the appropriate relationship between humans and their environment as a means of furthering our understanding of how the global concept of sustainable development is formulated, discussed, and implemented within specific communities. By analyzing the communicative performances whereby participants in environmental conflicts invent definitions for and advocate implementation of sustainable development, each chapter identifies points of tension between alternative definitions.

I begin in chapter 2 with a brief historical narrative of the process whereby the term *sustainable development* has achieved public currency. Chapter 3 provides a description of the book's theoretical grounding. This chapter represents a somewhat unsatisfactory compromise. I have written it for the reader who is familiar with rhetorical and communication theory but is not an authority on the theoretical contributions of Kenneth Burke and/or Niklas Luhmann. Readers whose expertise includes these perspectives may find much of this chapter overly elementary and simplistic, and these readers may want to skim the chapter briefly. On the other hand, those who are unfamiliar with rhetorical and communication theory may find it rather dense reading. For this reason I have constructed the case studies that follow in such a way that the reader is not overly dependent on the information provided in chapter 3.

Chapters 4, 5, and 6 are case studies in which I analyze the ways that language developed out of various rhetorical frames and social systems constrain the possible interpretations of sustainable development. Participants' concerns with sustainability and development move from the global in the first episode to the local and particular in the third. Conversely, my interpretation of what counts as a rhetorical text grows more expansive as I move through the three episodes.

The first case study relies exclusively on traditional, published texts to explore the construction of sustainable development at the 1992 Earth Summit Meeting in Rio de Janeiro. The model of sustainable development discovered in this analysis results from examining the written texts of formal presentations, newspaper articles, and official conference documents. While this analysis captures a global perspective toward environmental conservation and development, it cannot tell us what sustainable development means to the local communities in which it will be implemented.

The second case study uses the public forum as the primary text, relying on more traditional texts such as speeches and newspaper articles only to supplement the principle analysis of testimony presented at community hearings. The detailed analysis of public hearings designed to allow community members to comment on a development policy proposed by Agriculture Canada provides a window on the contrast between a development model grounded in the culture of technical expertise and a model grounded in everyday, localized practices. This analysis helps turn our attention to the struggle entailed in deciding who gets to participate in setting the agenda for sustainable development.

The final case study relies primarily on transcripts of interviews I conducted with residents of the Texas (U.S.)–Mexico border who are in the midst of a bitter controversy regarding the influence of local industrial development on birth defects and other aspects of human health. This analysis provides a detailed picture of how differently members of a single community view sustainable development. In addition to disclosing practices involved in the struggle for participation, it clarifies the communication dynamics involved when community members choose which elements of their world are most essential to sustain, which are most essential to develop, and how the two interrelate.

Chapter 7 concludes the book with an examination of pathways whereby ethical and political norms that have been associated with sustainable development can be brought to bear upon political solutions that resolve conflict, permit research, and sanction an acceptable course of public policy.

Chapter 2

Sustainable Development Comes of Age

We have not inherited the world from our forefathers—we have borrowed it from our children.

Kashmiri proverb

Sustainable development is a banner under which transformed environmentalism has marched into the public consciousness. Rather than being a radically new idea, it is an old philosophy that is being revived to cope with new problems. It says that care for the environment is essential to economic progress; that the natural resources of our planet are the base of all agriculture and industry; and that only by sustaining that base can we sustain human development. In this chapter I trace the growing concern with sustainability, briefly discuss the landmark publication entitled *Our Common Future,* and, finally, examine some of the problems associated with the idea of sustainable development.

Environmentalists were the "others" of popular culture throughout the 1970s and early 1980s. Now there are signs of a broad, popular identification with what was once a movement of radical resistance. These signs include Republican U.S. presidential candidate George Bush's decision to adopt the label "environmentalist president" during his first run for the presidency in 1988 and the selection of Albert Gore, author of *Earth in the Balance* (1992), as a running mate for Bush's Democratic opponent four years later. The rush of schools and universities to add interdisciplinary programs and courses in environmental studies, the eagerness of commercial publishers to bring out books on environmental topics, the use of environmentalist themes in advertising, the increased coverage of environmental issues in periodicals and electronic media, and the emergence of "environmentally sensitive" investment funds all point to the increasing cultural centrality of environmentalism. Yet it is a transformed environmentalism, which dialectically embraces a number of values from the developmentalist program, including an ideological commitment to achieving universal prosperity by addressing poverty in third world countries and a worldwide market economy (Killingsworth and Palmer 1992). Support of sustainability implies a criticism of past practices whereby science and technology were employed to increase the production of consumable goods, with little regard for long-term or easily externalized costs, yet it maintains support for the general goals toward which science and technology are directed. The call for sustainable development is a central component of the transformed environmental consciousness.

History of Sustainable Development

Research on tribal cultures provides sufficient evidence to indicate a widespread human capacity to determine, and live safely within, limits of sustainability characteristic of the ecosystems that they occupy (Goodland 1982). Yet human societies appear to have drawn on that capacity only rarely. Although the need to achieve sustainability in the use of land and biotic resources has been referred to in writings dating back at least to ancient Greece (Glacken 1973), human civilizations appear to have been plagued by environmental collapse (Lowdermilk 1953; Osborn 1948; Thomas 1956). Sustainability has been stressed during the twentieth century by the use-oriented conservation movement in the United States as exemplified in the efforts of Gifford Pinchot (1910) in forestry and Aldo Leopold (1933, [1949] 1968) in wildlife management. Publicity (both pro and con) surrounding *The Global 2000 Report to the President* (Barney 1981) injected the concept of sustainability into the U.S. environmental debate. On the international scene the "World Conservation Strategy," at the 1981 meeting of the International Union for the Conservation of Nature and Natural Resources (IUCN 1983), promoted the idea of ecological sustainability in development, while the publication of *Our Common Future* (World Commission for Environment and Development [WCED] 1987) propelled it into mainstream discourse.

Sustainable development was addressed by Gifford Pinchot (1910), a U.S. leader of the conservation movement during the early 1900s. He advocated development of resources and prevention of waste for the benefit of the largest possible number of people (42–50). Conservation referred only to these three principles and was an economic issue. His perspective toward environmental science ensured that he defined nature solely as a resource to facilitate human progress. The benefits he sought to provide through environmental conservation were relatively short term, and those for whom he sought benefits were humans living at the time the decision was made and as near as possible to the location of the natural resource (a river, forest, etc.) in question. Alternately, Aldo Leopold ([1949] 1968) began calling for a revolution in human consciousness with his "land ethic," which proposed an "ecological conscience" as a basis for collective responsibility. This ethic extended the human community to include the land and all that live on it. Accordingly, Leopold's land ethic goes beyond economic exploitation of natural resources and extends natural rights doctrine to the land, including a recognition of the intrinsic value of life that has no economic worth.

Leopold believed the "land ethic" had to reside in the souls of citizens so that they would act freely in ecologically responsible ways. He wrote that once human consciousness was raised it could transcend the limits and shortcomings of largely ineffective environmental conservation laws. Leopold, who spent much of his professional career helping craft a body of conservation legislation which has provided a model for late-twentieth-century environmental policies throughout the world, was not opposed to such legislation. He preferred not to resort to institutional coercion, however, because he believed its results were too limited. He wrote, "In our attempt to make conservation easy, we have made it trivial" ([1949] 1968, 246). For Leopold the science of ecology served as moral instruction for his fellow citizens. The passionate public response to Rachel Carson's *Silent Spring* ([1962] 1966) dramatized the political power of this combination of moral, ethical, cultural, political, and scientific concerns. Her carefully documented attack on the use of nonselective chemicals did more to rally the public outrage behind environmentalism than any previously written statement (Killingsworth and Palmer 1995). Leopold's and Carson's work provides a foundation upon which sustainable development discourse has built.

Contemporary advocates of sustainable development argue that humanity must move toward a new paradigm supportive of sustainable resource management and environmental improvement, equitable economic development, and an integrated sense of the biosphere. Only when these ideas gain mainstream legitimacy will human society implement measures to conserve biological diversity. Practices integral to this move include stabilizing the world human population; safe use of renewable resources; and development and application of appropriate technologies, especially those that enable energy use that is efficient and nonthreatening to the biosphere (Talbot 1989, 26). Of course, sustainable development has not earned the support of all environmentalists. Many deep ecologists adopt an "ecocentric" position that emphasizes respect for the rights of nature above and beyond human interests in "development." From this perspective the term *natural resource* is itself offensive (for an example, see Devall and Sessions 1985). Others view the earth as a living organism and question the relative importance of the survival of the human species when compared with the survival of the planet (Lovelock 1979). Parfit (1990) has summarized several varieties of radical environmentalism which do not subscribe to the tenets of sustainable development.

The centrality of human development issues in sustainable development discourse turns environmentalism toward common interests with other political and social causes and differentiates globally oriented environmentalists from many reform and radical environmentalists of the past. Since the primary enemies of the "greens" always have been "developers" and advocates of unlimited growth, any concession in the direction of development is looked upon with suspicion. The concern with development, however, provides a point of linkage between two rapidly growing branches of the environmental movement, the globalists and the grassroots activists.

Although globalists such as Herman Daly (through the World Bank) and Lester Brown (through the Worldwatch Institute) argue for positive and sustainable human development, they do not ignore, indeed they have contributed to, an ecologically based critique of standard economics. Both Daly (1989, 1991), the theorist of "steady-state economics," and Brown (1984–95), a leading mentor of the sustainability movement, have become powerful critics of high-growth economics and have lambasted the old liberal "illusion of progress." They call, instead, for a revision of liberalism toward a social ecology in which institutions, communities, and individual people promote forms of development rooted in scientific understanding, ecological wisdom, small-scale production, environmentally conscious consumption, community-based ethics, and participatory rights for impacted communities and peoples. Brown has used his World Watch publications to highlight grassroots activities that focus on establishing links between human health and environmental conditions. For example, the Right-to-Know Computer Network (RTK

Net), which is operated by two nonprofit groups, offers on-line access to the U.S. government's Toxics Release Inventory (TRI), a database covering industrial releases of toxic chemicals. RTK Net was created because, although TRI data is public information, the National Library of Medicine charges $18–20 per hour for access to the computer network in which it is stored. Although many corporations utilize the system, few community-based activists have the necessary financial base. The globally oriented Worldwatch Institute has publicized the RTK Net's grassroots activities, including its use of TRI data, to demonstrate that low-income and minority communities in the United States are subjected to disproportionately high levels of pollution (Brown 1994, 106–7). As grassroots activities such as these confirm the environmental health risks endured by minority communities, traditional civil rights groups also have turned their attention toward environmental justice (Suro 1993). The working papers series published by the Worldwatch Institute illustrates the synergy developing between globalists and grassroots activists, as do the institute's annually published *State of the World* volumes (since 1984), all of which are subtitled *A Worldwatch Institute Report on Progress toward a Sustainable Society.*

Sustainable Agriculture

The related sustainable agriculture movement emerged in the late 1970s as a challenge to conventional agriculture. Esbjornson (1992) notes that, throughout the 8,000 to 10,000 years of human agricultural history, sustainable agricultures have existed primarily "on the margins of human civilization and on marginal land" (21). The Chinese and Japanese rice farmers who farmed the same fields for 40 centuries and the agriculture in the bottomlands of the Nile River, which thrived from the time of the pharaohs to the time of the Aswan Dam, are well-known exceptions to this rule. Agriculture, however, is more accurately characterized as "a scant trail of human-aided ecological blunders, to be distinguished from periodic natural catastrophes, including clearcutting the cedars of Lebanon, overgrazing in the Mideast and north Africa, exhausting soil on Greek and Roman agricultural lands, and the American Dust Bowl of the 1930s" (21) than as a sustainable enterprise.

The sustainable agriculture movement focuses on environmental problems associated with production of food and fiber, particularly pesticide use, and the increasing power of agribusiness. A related concern is overspecialization and declining biological diversity at the regional, farm, and field levels. It is significant that, among the rhetorical alternatives for designating the trend toward environmentally sensitive agriculture, *sustainable,* rather than *alternative* or *low-input,* agriculture has emerged as the term of choice. Everyone can support sustainable agriculture, while those who have been most closely associated with past practices express resistance to characterizing agriculture as something that is "alternative" or "low input." Over time sustainable agriculture has been appropriated by members of the agricultural establishment ranging from the World Bank to the California Cotton Growers Association. U.S. agricultural agencies, including the Forest Service, Soil Conservation Service, and Bureau of Land Management, have renamed programs and revised priorities to indicate their concern with sustainability. In all cases policy makers have reassured their constituencies that sustainable development does not entail radical reorientation. For example, the Australian Forest Service has launched a nationwide research program to determine "the effectiveness of ecologically sustainable forest management." John Turner, chairman of the Standing Committee on Forestry's Research Priorities Co-ordinating Committee for Australia, explained that "sustainable forest management as a concept has been around for a long time and is the fundamental, primary aim of all State Forests' forest planning" ("National Search" 1995, 5). Thus, *sustainability* has become a buzzword whereby conventional agriculture policy makers indicate their concern with ecology and the environment. Allen and Sachs (1991) have argued that in these contexts the agenda for sustainable agriculture has been narrowed to technical approaches for reducing the environmental impacts of agricultural practices without questioning social relations in agriculture.

Further, while the discourse of sustainability potentiates, it does not guarantee, the ability to transcend the anthropocentric-ecocentric divide of previous conflicts regarding environmental management. Many authors who have taken up the banner of sustainability seem quite content with language limited to avoiding unwanted technical consequences for humans. Pearce, Barbier, and Markandya (1989), for example, define sustainable development as "a situation in which the development vector D does not decrease over time" (3). Their "development vector" emphasizes objectives such as increasing per capita income, improving human health and nutrition, and bolstering levels of education and distributive justice. It is easy to think of declines in the development vector as unwanted consequences to human society and to direct environmental policy toward an attempt to reverse these declines. When unwanted consequences impact upon society as a whole, there may well be an ethical imperative to avoid or mitigate them. Introducing the language of sustainability, however, adds nothing to the discussion. Rather than offering any conceptual enrichment, this use of the term *sustainable development* serves only to mask traditional practices.

Douglass (1984) discussed three approaches to the idea of sustainable agriculture. The most limited is a technical definition that refers to stability of a desirable trait (such as crop yield), either over several generations of seed or under different climatic conditions. A second interpretation of sustainable agriculture describes production systems that rely on renewable resources. The most broad definition includes social goals within the framework of traits deemed necessary for sustainable agriculture, thus encompassing small farms and rural communities. Each of these definitions represents a focus of criticism for existing agricultural research and production practices. The more narrow interpretations, which are exemplified by Pearce, Barbier, and Markandya's (1989) definition, easily can be limited to discussions of what type of plow is most appropriate for soil type X in location Y and add little to the discussion of environmental policy. The third approach, however, provides the most telling critique and positions the sustainable agriculture movement as fundamental to the broader sustainable development literature.

The sustainable agriculture movement also can be seen as a contemporary expression of agrarian idealism. Yet "what distinguishes it from the other forms of agrarian idealism is the priority it gives to its legitimate awareness of the ecological devastation caused by agriculture" (Esbjornson 1992, 23). Wendell Berry (1977, 1981, 1990), one of the movement's most well-known voices, writes that the loss of community and the removal of local wisdom necessary to sustainable local practices and a healthy culture are fundamental to the "unsettling of America" and suggests that this problem is now occurring around the globe. Wojcik (1984) argues that the most significant contribution of Berry's work is its insistence that "for the first time in history how to use farming technique has become a moral question" (35). Both Berry and Wes Jackson (1987, 1990) exhibit an almost evangelical fervor in their attempts to persuade audiences of the error of Cartesian dualism (which encourages the assumption that humans are largely separate from nature). They claim that sustainability only can be achieved when society understands that nature and humans are fundamentally and inextricably linked.

Yet, despite the popularity of Berry's writing among both professional and amateur critics of culture, most producers remain oblivious to these ideas. Agricultural development practices remain firmly based on the belief in unlimited resources, unbounded technological advance, and the existence of a bottomless sink into which toxic wastes can be poured. For example, industrialized nations that would not consider using such practices at home, and may in fact take great care in managing their own resources, often advocate and support rapacious development practices in third world countries. This leads to forecasts such as the Council of Environmental Quality's *U.S. Global 2000 Report* (Barney 1981), which predicts that, at the same time the forested area of the industrialized world will stabilize, the area of tropical forests will experience a catastrophic decline. The widespread belief that the concept of sustainability exists outside the limitations of human understanding exacerbates such disparities within national environmental policies. Because advocates of sustainable development have drawn the concept of sustainability from the context of scientific ecology, a brief description of the concept of sustainability as it has developed within ecology can help explain how sustainable development provides a reference that appears to exist outside the subjective confines of human experience yet remains relevant to that experience.

The Concept of Sustainability in Ecology

The science of ecology has provided ideas about the way natural systems work, at the same time highlighting the point beyond which such systems are no longer "sustainable." Within plant ecology sustainability is related to the successional changes in plant communities, which serve as models for managing the environment. The principle of "maximum sustainable yield" (MSY) has become well established in certain fields of applied ecology such as fisheries management, range management, and forestry. Yet most fisheries biologists concur that reliance on this concept has legitimized exploitation to the point of eliminating important substocks (Botkin 1990; Ludwig, Hilborn, and Walters 1993). While this does not invalidate MSY's underlying assumption that environmental management can benefit from understanding and utilizing population recruitment curves and succession patterns found in natural, ecological systems, it does encourage critical reevaluation of the methods used to assess sustainability. Ludwig (1993, 556) suggests that MSY fails to achieve sustainability because its objective is "*maximum* sustained yield rather than a yield that [is] sure to conserve the stock." His claim suggests that, although MSY and sustainable development may have compatible goals, they differ significantly: sustainable development's focus forms MSY's periphery, and vice versa. Alternatively, sustainable development may be the logical extension of MSY. Sustainable development potentiates a move beyond disciplinary science to integrate issues central to the humanities and social sciences (such as justice, freedom, and motive) into discussions of environmental policy.

Both *sustainability* and *sustainable development* remain contested terms among ecologists and environmental scientists, despite their history as management tools. An article published in *Science* (Ludwig, Hilborn, and Walters 1993) and a forum that *Ecological Applications* (1993, 3) published in response to the article illustrate the sometimes conflicting assortment of available definitions. Although they do not explicitly define *sustainability*, Ludwig, Hilborn, and Walters (1993, 17) begin the debate by suggesting that *sustainable development* refers to "optimum levels of exploitation," which is nearly synonymous with the traditional concept of optimal sustained yield (OSY). Holling (1993, 554), who claims that Ludwig, Hilborn, and Walters' definition is "not useful," suggests including "the social and economic development of a region with the goals to invest in the maintenance and restoration of critical ecosystem functions, to synthesize and make accessible knowledge and understanding for economies, and to develop and communicate the understanding that provides a foundation of trust for citizens." Meyer and Helfman (1993, 569) prefer the definition of *sustainability* adopted by the Ecological Society of America: "management practices that will not degrade the exploited system or any adjacent systems." Ludwig's (1993, 556) forum article maintains his original focus on use, adding that, because ecological systems are bounded, human extraction rates also must be bounded, and the bounds "must be low enough to ensure long-term survival." He suggests that sustainability is impossible to achieve without appropriate limits on the critical problems of human population growth and consumption.

Lee (1993b, 560) defines *sustainability* as "a regime of stable use," which is frustrated by "mismatches of scale between human responsibility and natural interactions." He argues that spatial mismatches of scale occur because discontinuous resource availability encourages widespread unsustainable use of resources which, while scarce on a worldwide scale, are abundant in specific regions. Technological developments that allow us to substitute one material for another (such as petroleum for coal as an energy source) intensify this tendency by discouraging people from considering possible consequences of resource loss. Functional mismatches occur because the natural world is complex and interconnected, whereas human action is specialized. Attempts to realign functional mismatches are complicated by institutional structures that are resistant to change, such as federal or state natural resource agencies. Finally, economic structures encourage temporal mismatches because the earnings from natural resource harvest appreciate more rapidly than does the resource—for example, interest earned on dollars grows faster than trees.

While the previous contributors explored the range of sustainability, others focused on the more internally oppositional concept of sustainable development. Mangel, Hofman, Norse, and Twiss Jr. (1993) offer a dichotomous definition that specifies a choice between use or growth. In the first case *sustainable development* refers to the use of "living components of ecosystems (renewable resources) in ways that allow natural processes to replace what is used" (573). In the second *sustainable development* refers to "sustainable growth of population and resource consumption" and is "impossible" (573). Robert Socolow (1993) writes that sustainable development must ensure that "(1) within a small fraction of the total time under consideration (say, 50 yr out of 500 yr) nearly all the earth's human beings achieve a lifestyle of considerable vigor and quality, and (2) during the time under consideration the survival of the human population and the populations of nearly all other species sharing this planet is not put in jeopardy as a result of life-threatening changes in the natural environment" (581). Daniel Rubenstein (1993) defines *sustainable development* most broadly as a condition in which "the abundance and the genotypic diversity of individual species comprising an ecosystem, as well as the species composition of the overall ecosystem itself, are not significantly reduced by human intervention" (585). Eduardo Fuentes (1993) rejects the more common conceptualization of sustainable development as an end state, preferring to focus on activities and processes. He prefers defining the bounds of sustainable activity over defining a desired end state because the former is more conducive to both human liberty and ecological change. He defines *sustainable development* "as a trajectory in a hyperspace, whose attributes have strong geographical, historical, and cultural components, and it is accepted that the trajectory should be modified according to future, still unknown, events" (576).

Whichever definition for *sustainable development* one chooses to adopt, there is general agreement that more mature ecological systems also are more sustainable (not necessarily stable) than less mature systems. This occurs because the most mature natural systems are those in which energy shifts away from production toward system maintenance. The best examples of such systems are tropical forests, which exhibit all the features of a mature system, as well as enormous biodiversity (Begon, Harper, and Townsend 1990; Odum 1971). In agricultural and urban systems, on the other hand, humans have altered the natural system to enhance productivity at the expense of system maintenance (or sustainability). The lesson from ecology, then, is that to create sustainable societies humans must focus more on a system's abilities to resist or recover from disturbances, stresses, and shocks than on its ability to produce goods.

The Brundtland Commission Report

Although it would be impossible to pinpoint the moment when sustainability was first proposed as a social goal, there is little question that expressions of support for sustainable development have become widespread only after the 1987 publication of the United Nations report entitled *Our Common Future*. This watershed publication, which was produced by a UN special committee formally titled the World Commission on Environment and Development (WCED), marked a turning point at which the concept of interests became central to conservation and development issues and at which sustainability ceased to be a concept strictly for critics of established practices. The commission involved political leaders from around the world, including chairman Gro Brundtland, prime minister of Norway. Much of the WCED's (commonly referred to as the "Brundtland Commission") prestige relied on its chairman's unique political career. "No other political leader had become Prime Minister with a background of several years of political struggle, nationally and internationally, as an environment minister" (WCED ix–x). Members of the Brundtland Commission sought to expose barriers of tariffs, subsidies, bureaucratic infrastructure, and economic and political power. They proposed actions that the members believed would lead to sustainability in development and protection for the environment. Commission members examined global problems of human development and proposed solutions and a direction toward sustainability, with special attention to human interests in environmental conservation.

The resulting report attempts to circumvent the terms in which debate over development had taken place during the preceding decade by linking environmental degradation to processes of economic growth. It focuses on political (rather than philosophical, historical, and cultural) parameters of development. Although the publication has been criticized as a "sellout" by some environmentalists, it did provide the impetus for a variety of institutional reforms within organizations such as the World Bank, the U.S. Agency for International Development, and the U.S. Department of Agriculture. As a group, these reforms have created a research base on sustainability, with the expectation that science can be applied to the promotion of more sustainable development practices.

The Brundtland Commission report, which extends environmental themes across industrialization, agriculture, energy, and public health, marks the symbolic introduction of sustainability to the world development literature. While the report is written in the bland and neutral language of an international committee, interpretive study reveals many significant elements. Its central theme is that environmental issues represent a framework in which developed and developing countries have common interests. Previous examinations of international development tended to describe the world as a division between North and South and to portray international programs as claims of justice owed from North to South. The Brundtland Commission chose, instead, the language of common interests to describe a sustainable course of future development. While the report emphasizes common interests rather than sustainability, the idea of sustainable development becomes a theme for future thinking on international environmental relations.

Prior to the Brundtland report development goals had been based on one of two general perspectives, which can be summarized as the *modernization* and *dependency* views. Advocates of modernization saw development as a process of economic expansion and assumed that the fastest means to increasing the amount and rate of production in any given economic system was the best way to create conditions conducive to development. Development aid within this conceptual framework was intended to increase the recipient nation's available capital for industry. Modernization development policies are patterned after the historical development of capitalism in Western Europe, and Western, or capitalist, development policy has focused on the growth of a developing country's gross national product (GNP).

Critics of this approach have stressed how it would consign nations whose economic growth was at stake to unending dependency upon the developed North. For example, the Marxist critique of development focuses on the exploitative nature of foreign investment in developing countries and thus characterizes foreign capital as counterproductive to the ends of a just state. Foreign investment is seen as exploitative in that the wealthy nations are able to use the power of their capital to extract resources from the developing nations at low cost. From this perspective the phenomenon of cheap oil, for example, arises because the developed nations buy oil at a lower cost in the developing world than in domestic markets. Because the wealthy nations have the initial capital necessary to begin extraction of resources (such as oil) and subsequent influence to control price, the cost of raw materials remains cheap in developing nations as compared to the developed nations.

The distinction between these two perspectives, however, should not be reduced to the distinction between the dominant economic paradigms espoused by the United States and the former Soviet Union. Third world economic development has been a major element of the developed countries' foreign policy since the end of World War II. Regrettably, cold war politics have dominated development policy making until recently. As a result, competition between cold warriors for third world allies has skewed development aid, whether shrouded in Marxist or free market ideology, toward the modernization view, with concomitant expansion of the military sector in third world nations.

Both the modernization and the dependency approach to development provide convenient excuses for governments to portray the goals of development in ways most favorable to their own immediate interests. The dependency view suggests that simple redistribution of wealth concentrated in the North would serve development best, a view attractive to the political elite within many developing countries. Alternately, the modernization view suggests that transfer of technology and expertise is the answer, but this strategy means that a high percentage of development assistance is actually spent within the scientific and technological sectors of developed countries, an outcome that gives development aid a constituency that ensures support of the moderniza-tion strategy in the United States and Western Europe. The problem, of course, is that U.S. and Western European governments oppose the re-distribution preferred by those requesting assistance because they claim that international aid too often finds its way into the pockets of ruling elites, rather than into truly *sustainable* development for the recipient nation. At the same time, they offer technologies and programs that, while beneficial to the donor economies, may be useless to the recipient nations. Leaders of developing nations are understandably wary of the strings attached to the technologies (usually not quite the latest) offered by more wealthy nations. The Brundtland report proposes a paradigm shift that defines development against a background in which the com-mon interests of developed and developing countries are put forward as the central goals. Environmental quality is advanced as first among several such common interests, and both the modernization and depen-dency views are criticized as being insensitive to the environmental impact of development processes.

A cursory reading of the Brundtland report might overlook its at-tempt to supersede the language adopted in the previous Brandt Commission report, published under the title *North-South: A Program for Survival* (1980). Both reports identify similar needs and strategies for more productive relations among relatively more developed countries such as the United States, countries that have made relatively little progress on traditional development indicators such as Bangladesh, and the emerging group of countries such as Mexico and Brazil which have made significant progress but which continue to be plagued by high levels of poverty and population growth (neither report discusses de-velopment problems in Eastern Europe). While the Brandt Commission chose to describe the world as a division between North and South, how-ever, and to portray its programs as claims of justice owed from North to South, the Brundtland Commission chose the language of common interests in a sustainable course of future development. Replacing "jus-tice" with "sustainability" as the key normative concept facilitates a move toward shared interests, rather than competing rights. This rhetorical shift enables political leaders of developed countries to advocate inter-national policies on the basis of national interests, rather than domestically unpopular claims alleged to be owed to noncitizens. The new rhetoric also places citizens of developing countries in a position of equality to those in developed nations. All people base their claims upon a common interest, rather than citizens of the South claiming rights against the North. Although the Brandt Commission characterized these claims as just, the rhetoric of a divided world nevertheless placed the South in a position of dependency upon northern willingness to do the right thing.

The Brundtland report discusses several concerns that threaten the future of all people. Notably, the report describes poverty as a major cause, rather than an effect, of environmental degradation and underdevelopment. It argues that the poor, in a desperate struggle to survive, clear forests, overuse marginal lands, and move into already overpopulated cities—all activities that exacerbate existing environmental and development problems. The report claims that the problem of poverty and its effects are most favorably approached with a view to sustainable development which "in the broadest sense . . . aims to promote harmony among human beings and between humanity and nature" (WCED 1987, 65). The report also discusses the need for international cooperation in preserving the commons. The oceans, for example, provide vital resources for all nations, yet no comprehensive management scheme has been implemented to protect the world's marine resources. Ocean pollution has become a threat to the very survival of oceanic life, and, unless this trend is reversed, the oceans will literally die. The commission reported a similar need for management of Antarctica and space.

The Brundtland report highlights the following six challenges to sustainable development:

1. It discusses population growth. The strain of exponential population growth in the Third World not only frustrates economic growth but also tends to destroy the environment upon which that population depends.

2. It argues that, although food production has increased dramatically in the past few decades, agricultural methods have begun to affect the environment adversely. Examples include increased erosion, water depletion and contamination, and the expanding problem of production in marginal areas. The report suggests several means to combat this problem, including an increased role for biotechnology, matching appropriate crops to local ecosystems, less reliance on chemicals, and diversification of crops produced in the Third World.

3. The report examines the loss of habitat and the consequent loss of species (both plant and animal). The report suggests that such exploitation need not continue and points to examples such as the 1986 formation of the International Tropical Timber Organization as hopeful steps in the direction of conservation conjoined with production.
4. It discusses energy sources. The report claims that the quest for a sustainable energy program must include a trend toward reliance on renewable sources, especially solar energy, combined with energy conservation.
5. The report considers the issue of industrial development. It discusses the pollution and additional environmental degradation traditionally associated with industrial development. It points out that, while the usual way to avoid this problem is with available technical knowledge, developing countries seldom have access to either the knowledge or the technology.
6. It discusses the problems of urban growth in the developing world. The human population of cities in developing countries is growing faster than are the cities' infrastructures. Given current trends, these cities will become increasingly unable to cope with the needs for employment, housing, social services, and sanitation

Our Common Future, thus sets the context for the key problems associated with sustainable development. Although often expressed as critical of science, the goal of sustainability is an outgrowth of ecology and environmental science. Sustainable development thus functions both as an extension and a critique of scientific knowledge. One problem with the Brundtland report's discussion of sustainable development, however, is that, despite its introduction of human interests into the conservation and development debate, the analysis remains grounded in the assumption of a conflict-free social climate wherein scientists can evaluate the sustainability of development and agriculture practices, propose "more sustainable" alternatives, then preside over their introduction. The report does not deal in any significant way with the possibility of culturally based resistance to change. Further, despite the disregard for cultural dimensions involved in implementing sustainable development, sustainability is put forward as something that is at least desirable, and perhaps an imperative, for society to pursue in an organized and publicly supported fashion.

Though seemingly unexceptionable, these characteristics conjoin in definitional problems as well as in conflicts over implementation.

Problematics of Sustainable Development

The concept of sustainable development, since the publication of *Our Common Future,* has become widely celebrated as a public policy goal to be supported and furthered on the basis of scientific research and management. In an age when many have come to question whether technologically defined social progress can continue indefinitely, sustainable development has emerged as a substitute. As with progress, there is a frequent assumption that sustainable development can and should be determined and measured in scientific terms, rather than by ethical or political traditions. Yet there are philosophical problems inherent in any concept that purports to express both an objective, scientifically determinable characteristic and a social goal to be accepted and advocated on normative grounds.

To begin with, the fragmented character of modern society makes the achievement of a single, objective standard of judgment nearly impossible and perhaps inadvisable. As Luhmann (1989) cautions, the attempt to derive the near totality of other sociological phenomena from any one sphere is hopelessly reductionistic. When the criteria of one system are privileged over all others, the number and variety of experiences that count as information in a society are sharply reduced.

Second, it entails that there is a single scientific truth of the matter with respect to sustainability. If scientists are expected to evaluate the sustainability of given practices, then claims about the sustainability of practices are, at least in principle, capable of being shown to be true or false. Given the fact, however, that each scientific discipline has its own way of establishing these parameters, settling cross-disciplinary disputes raises a fundamental epistemological problem (Prelli 1989).

Third, because some of the values that recommend sustainability as a social goal are regarded commonly as extrascientific, there is at least the possibility that what is ultimately found to be sustainable (based on scientific claims of truth or falsity) in fact diverges from that which sustainability is thought to mean as a social goal. For example, some advocates of sustainable development envision it in terms of aboriginal tribes relying primarily on local flora to produce Rainforest Crunch candy or tagua nut buttons. For such advocates support of sustainable development is rooted in the moral, political, or aesthetic value associated with this form of development. Perhaps they think that maintenance of aboriginal tribal culture is just what sustainability means, but, if so, then it is simply a tautology to say that "maintenance of aboriginal people and their environment is sustainable development." Such a view expresses a value, clearly, but undercuts any scientific attempt to hypothesize the truth or falsity of their claims regarding sustainability. Alternately, natural science provides no justification for preferring maintenance of aboriginal tribal culture over an arrangement in which a transnational corporation headquartered in Japan establishes a "sustainable" industry using the same resources in the same location. If the corporation employs local labor to manufacture finished products, rather than displacing the current inhabitants, economic concerns also are alleviated. It becomes quite unclear what science can contribute in the way of empirically validating the sustainability claim. Instead, an extrascientific conceptualization of sustainable development, which calls for analysis of culturally grounded symbol systems, drives decision making. As these somewhat contradictory strands of thought intermingle, sustainability is socially constructed through a combination of discipline-based research concepts drawn from the natural sciences and politically motivated arguments expressing and defending ethical norms. That is, although disciplinary concepts might form a basis for deciding what sustainability is, relatively unexamined cultural norms are used to determine which systems or characteristics it is important to sustain.

It is relatively obvious how extrascientific values provide normative accounts of sustainability, but scientific accounts are no less embedded with norms. The key to different descriptive accounts of sustainability often lies in which questions scientists in a given discipline define as within their disciplinary scope (Prelli 1989; Ludwig, Hilborn, and Walters 1993). These boundaries can be understood as norms that define good disciplinary practice. They reflect a consensus judgment of what factors are most crucially relevant to explanation and prediction of phenomena that are of interest to the discipline. Such judgments function as norms because they stipulate which data, which experiments, and which explanatory concepts may and may not be used in constructing theory or in explanation and prediction. These norms are key to enforcing disciplinary practices through rewards such as publication, tenure, promotion, and competitive grants. As such, the way disciplinary boundaries determine a research orientation toward sustainability blocks progress on integrated and comprehensive accounts of sustainable development. The concept of sustainable development implies a scientifically grounded and empirically robust account of how development is to be sustained. The research practices of different disciplines, however, have vastly different ways of determining the borders, the temporal and spatial scale, or the ontological status, for example, for data relevant to the validity of empirical claims.

Michael Redclift (1987) echoes one theme of the Brundtland report in calling for emphasis upon the social context of development programs. In his extensive theoretical discussion of sustainable development he advocates rethinking the notion of development, arguing that conventional development strategies have proven inadequate because the goal of accumulation is contradictory to the maintenance of sustainable human/environmental relations. For example, precisely because accumulation in agriculture relies on maintaining low-diversity/low-stability agro-ecological relations, capitalist agricultural strategies are unlikely to be sustainable.

Redclift maintains that conventional development strategies focus on sustaining high levels of production at the expense of understanding whether a given development program will sustain a human population that adopts it. This feature of conventional development follows not only from the conceptual perspective of Enlightenment science and economics (which views the environment as a resource to control and use, rather than as an object to be understood on its own terms) but also from a failure to view sustainability in developing counties as a function of the internationalization of capital, labor, and markets and with them the environment. Hence, sustainability in the developing South is structurally incompatible with an international context dominated by capitalist concepts and economic institutions that thrive at least partly because they pass on the developmental costs of environmental destruction to less powerful people (such as the third world poor and future generations). Thus, a useful definition of *sustainable development* requires us to recognize "that the limits of sustainability have structural as well as natural origins" (199). In turn, it is necessary to reassess the conceptual basis with which we approach development and the environment, including taking more systematic account of extrascientific knowledge systems.

Although there is broad acceptance of the normative value of sustainable development, that acceptance constitutes neither agreement regarding the meaning of sustainability nor its appropriate implementation. One reason for the diverse literature attempting to define sustainability is that divergent political interests are at stake. For example, some corporate officers would consider it rational to define sustainability in such a way that market acceptance of their products also serves as criteria for their sustainability. Political interests deeply influence development literature, as sustainable development becomes integrated into the ongoing debate between free market development theory and its Marxist critics. Even the assumption that natural science is immune to political interests has been exposed as a fiction (Beck 1992; M. J. Peterson 1991; Taylor, forthcoming).

Nevertheless, the existence of political interests is not, in itself, sufficient explanation of the failure of *sustainability* definitions to converge. Rather, it is a symptom of an underlying epistemological ambiguity. Each interest is able to make plausible (if mutually contradictory) claims about *sustainability* because the grammar of the term is contingent upon factors that are specific to particular locations and disciplinary specializations. For example, a cropping system that is sustainable in one location, according to one set of criteria, is unsustainable in another. A sustainable system may occur in an unsustainable village, and villages practicing "sustainable" agriculture may depend upon a broader context of unsustainable political practices. Because scientific disciplines tend to choose one or two of these hierarchical levels as their scope of inquiry, the multiplicity of hierarchies that define sustainable development leaves the door ajar for political interests to adopt whichever definition favors their political ends.

Sustainability as Primary or Secondary Goal

The recent interest in sustainable development has prompted some authors to argue that a "long-run" time frame is a key element in the relevant definition of *sustainability* (Ikerd 1990). Although the ordinary English grammar of the word *sustainable* permits uses that are equivalent to "capable of enduring over the long-run," there are at least two problems with this suggestion (Thompson 1995, 153–54). One is that the long run is rather indefinite. The problem here is that nobody has advanced compelling reasons for adopting geologic time scales as the ideal paradigm for modeling development. Further, the earth's history, as interpreted by both biological and physical science, suggests it is naive to think that any human activity will continue indefinitely. A second problem is that endurance is only accidentally related to the notions of harmony, balance, and integrity which underlie the connection sustainable development advocates posit between ecological and social sustainability. It is quite possible for perfectly sustainable systems to perpetuate gross inequities. An equally plausible approach to sustainability could define it as the "ability to support, relieve, or nourish." Whereas the first definition masks normative aspects of development decisions, the second focuses attention on them.

Because the concept of sustainable development does not specify the norms used to connect sustainability with development, we unwittingly may champion morally objectionable development simply because it is sustainable. The strategy used to specify sustainability as a norm can either encourage or discourage this tendency. One strategy is to argue that there is added value in ensuring the sustainability of already just and valuable societies. A second strategy is to argue that sustainability can correct a development system, regardless of other traits. In the first case sustainability is a further goal to be prescribed after more fundamental goals have been met, while in the second it is intrinsically valuable (Thompson 1995, 158–67).

The first strategy encourages us to advocate a system's sustainability only after it has been judged to be valuable on other normative grounds that are rated independently of their sustainability. Although the criteria needed to make such judgments would be complex and susceptible to continual debate, adding sustainability does not create any additional complexity. A development scheme for the region encompassing the border between the United States and Mexico might, for example, be evaluated according to criteria of justice, fairness, or interests. Any combination of these (or other criteria) could be chosen to evaluate the desirability of a given development scheme. Having determined basic evaluative criteria, we would then add that the system should be sustainable as well. In this example the sustainability of the system gains significance as the means for preserving culturally validated qualities.

Alternately, we could identify sustainability as a norm that bestows value upon a system without regard to the system's ability to advance other goals. Thus, the slave agricultures of the ancient world deserve praise for their sustainability, if nothing else. An agriculture development scheme along the Mexico–United States border region which perpetuates gross inequities between humans who suffer and those who benefit from practices that demonstrate robust ability to withstand disturbances would be preferable to one that distributed suffering and benefit more fairly but resulted in less robust agricultural practices. In this case sustainability becomes analogous to the criterion of elegance applied to theoretical constructs, though there is no exploration of the reasons why it should be specified as a goal for human development. Such an explanation is unlikely to be forthcoming, for, as Burke (1984a) points out, goals that are intrinsically valuable require no further justification. He argues that "we ethicize something when we act toward it as though it were an intrinsic good, [and] . . . such ethical structures tend to become self-perpetuating" (238–39). Although sustainable systems have a kind of elegance or aesthetic admirability, the ethical implications of their value to human development may be negligible.

Further, although at first glance one might assume that this second approach would lead to improved environmental protection, past experience belies this expectation. For example, when called upon to justify the construction of an incinerator that will pollute the air of a community, traditional developers use the existence of an underclass, whose members' basic needs remain unfulfilled, to explain why the short-term economic benefits accrued by the community outweigh the additional air pollution that will result from the incinerator. Ignoring issues such as fairness also delays constructive change within community patterns of consumption. Managing such change requires far more resources (examples include time, information, and money) from the community than are required to send the garbage "someplace else," where people are accustomed to bearing a disproportionately large share of the consequences of environmental damage.

Despite the appeal of sustainability, there are at least two reasons to avoid advocating it as the primary goal of development (Thompson 1995, 162–64). First, no amount of sustainability should be allowed to outweigh an improvement in securing an overriding value such as justice. Conceiving of sustainability as an end in itself suggests that there ought to be some cases in which a robustly sustainable system would be preferred to an unsustainable society that temporarily secured ecosystem health, human flourishing, or justice (all of which are genuine possibilities). For example, consider a robustly sustainable slave agriculture in which minimal food supplies are produced under conditions of unbearable human misery and servitude. The sustainability of such a development system offers little social value to recommend itself over a reform that breaks up power and landholdings, produces food supplies that meet minimal caloric requirements of all current inhabitants, yet encourages land use that will deplete soil fertility over a century. With the possible exception of claims made by some deep ecologists, it is difficult to justify forgoing a few generations of relative freedom and contentment to achieve centuries of human misery.

A second reason for resisting the impulse to regard sustainability as an end in itself is that the ambiguities in drawing system boundaries are displayed by maintaining sustainability as a means, whereas they are masked by maintaining sustainability as an intrinsically valuable goal. It is possible to revise our definition of any system so that the system in question possesses the trait of sustainability. As such, however, sustainability becomes little more than juggling between arbitrarily determined system boundaries. We can alter the level of analysis in search of ecological sustainability or resilience, almost as if the criteria suggested by sustainability encourage us to condone human suffering and misery as necessary components of a larger natural order. We can use war, pestilence, and starvation, for example, to regulate any human development system we devise. Yet, as Robert Solow (1991) argues, "there is something faintly phony about deep concern for the future combined with callousness about the state of the world today." The point should not be to design some well-regulated development system but, rather, to describe development systems that meet key social values then to determine how we might fortify their ability to withstand disturbances and stresses, while maintaining as much of their productive abilities as possible. To achieve sustainable development we must understand and respect natural ecological processes, cultural values, and the interaction between the two. When paired with development, sustainability is a goal that should be sought only in conjunction with our judgment that the associated development system is independently valuable in terms of its ability to promote fundamental cultural values.

Sustainable Development and Modernity

The discourse surrounding sustainable development is difficult to analyze, for it has become a metadiscourse in which the claims to provide insights can only be evaluated in terms of the discourse itself. This should come as no surprise, given sustainable development's emphasis on modernistic goals such as consensus, control, prediction, and management. A distinguishing feature of any modernistic discourse is that it legitimates its own discursive practices (T. R. Peterson 1990). Within the revised discourse of environmentalism sustainability provides a point of reference apparently outside the confines of human experience, which also can guide human choices. The natural world is used both as a model for systems based on human intervention and a constraint on human development. As Burke (1984a) notes, "social relations were first ascribed to nature, and then 'derived' from it" (274). Sustainable development advocates have naturalized social behavior then legitimized that behavior by reference to the "natural" laws they have constructed.

Glacken (1973) argues that "the association of the idea of progress with the environmental limitations of the earth" was a post-Enlightenment development (654). Although the thinkers of the European Enlightenment developed a primitive concept of carrying capacity, they did not explore the human dimensions of environmental change. Rather than considering that the environment could deteriorate as a result of long-term human settlement, they assumed a stable physical environment as the backdrop for human progress. He adds that by the dawn of the nineteenth century Western civilization had replaced its traditional belief regarding the human relationship to nature with a modernistic perception that was "influenced by the theory of evolution, specialization in the attainment of knowledge, [and] acceleration in the transformation of nature" (705). Evolutionary theory, scientific specialization, and an unprecedented scale of economic development, then, provided the context for modernity, the context in which sustainability would develop social currency.

At the risk of oversimplification, I describe modernism as a belief that ideas grounded in Enlightenment philosophy and science can provide an appropriate basis for all social criticism and understanding (for a more comprehensive description of modernism as a communication context, see Pearce 1989). The now familiar critique of modernity is that it tends toward totalization in its recourse to "the grand narratives of legitimization," which are no longer credible (Lyotard 1984, 23). In terms of the history of sustainability modernism represents an attempt to use natural laws discovered through scientific inquiry to manage nature. In a sense modernism pits human ingenuity against external limits posed by nature. Managing nature does not necessarily entail understanding it, however, and the modernist position places humans both outside of and above the environment from which they have sprung.

Two key elements of the modernistic perspective toward the environment are significant to our understanding of the ambiguity entailed in the term *sustainable development*. First is association of the ideals of reason and freedom with the magic of progress. The evolutionary theory, technical specialization, and economic development mentioned earlier provide the context for this optimistic approach. Thus, the progress of science leads to an ever improving human condition. The increasing visibility of science in our society, however, has made it almost impossible to consider the idea of progress without thinking of its critique, which is not confined to postmodernist writing. Richard Weaver (1953, 214), for example, lamented that progress was the only value for which Americans felt committed to sacrifice. In 1958 Lévi-Strauss pointed out that "progress . . . is neither continuous nor inevitable; its course consists of leaps and bounds. . . . These . . . are not always in the same direction" (21). Despite the hold of scientific progress over the popular imagination, a diverse group of critiques has continued to warn against ethicizing it. The second element of modernity found in the concept of sustainable development refers to science as providing both the basis for legitimizing its own discourse and the basis for criticism of past development policy. Science, therefore, simultaneously provides the means to define and transform nature then to critique the resulting relationship between humans and nature.

Notwithstanding the material improvements to which science has helped give rise, "development" still has to confront a deep-rooted difficulty. If human progress only can be achieved by destroying the environment, and ultimately the resources on which development depends, then the theory of development lacks legitimacy. Since no idea can long retain power without some degree of public legitimacy, developers have sought to legitimize their acts by coupling them with the concept of sustainability. Sustainable development, then, is an idea that seeks to legitimize its own propositions by recourse to what are assumed to be natural laws. By incorporating the ecological concept of sustainability within the economic account of development, the discourse of the environmental sciences is used to strengthen, rather than weaken, traditional suppositions about progress. *Development* becomes synonymous with *progress* and is linked with "natural" limits, expressed in the concept of sustainability. Thus, the discourse surrounding nature, and what are assumed to be natural laws, is viewed not as part of a socially constructed view of progress but, instead, as part of an essentially nonhuman logic, located in biological systems. Like other models derived from nature, sustainability acquires legitimacy from its biological origins. Sustainable development then becomes a methodology, as well as a normative goal, a model for planning, a strategy involving purposeful management of the environment.

In sum, the use of a concept drawn from the natural sciences (ecology) to justify decisions made in the social realm conveys several ambiguities. First, sustainable systems occurring in nature are used as a model for environmental management, without reference to the differences introduced by human choices. Second, incorporating the ecological idea of sustainability represents a way of dampening the contradictions of development. These contradictions then can be viewed as minor malfunctions of the system which can be corrected by small-scale human interventions. If sustainable development is to meet the problems presented by global environmental degradation, however, we need to embrace a realistic position that includes (but is not limited to) the realization that our values and policy instruments are culturally constructed. We need to develop a foundation for environmental policy that includes the concept of "motive" in its calculation.

Summary

Philosophers and scientists have debated the need to achieve sustainable use of environmental resources for centuries. Questions of the appropriate relationship between humans and nature did not draw broad popular attention in the Western world, however, until the 1960s, when publications such as Rachel Carson's ([1962] 1966) *Silent Spring* galvanized a generation, and permanently politicized ecology. Even after this, the environmental movement remained marginalized for some 20 years. During the 1980s many environmentalists began working with, rather than against, developers. While some environmentalists worry that this will lead (or has led) to coaptation by conservative economic forces, the partnership has slipped environmentalism into the political mainstream. The term *sustainable development* vaulted into public view with the 1987 publication of the Brundtland report, *Our Common Future.* This groundbreaking report revised the international environmental debate by postulating that environmentally sound development was in the best interests of all nations. The report defines sustainable development as "development that meets the needs of the present without compromising the ability of future generations to meet their own needs" and offers it as a realistic means for integrating development and environmental policy (43). While such a concept is difficult to oppose, it is equally difficult to implement, for the ambiguity that attracts diverse groups opens it to a multitude of interpretations.

The confusion surrounding our inability to behave according to biological injunctions is central to the appeal of sustainable development. It eases the passage from scientific uncertainty to political prescription, providing the moral force that is so essential to modernist discourse. Much of the writing on sustainable development takes its message from the natural sciences. This has been a message of hope, as people have lived longer and consumed more goods during their lifetimes, especially in the North. Sustainable development, in this tradition, is about seeking consensus and agreement, in the belief that, by more carefully managing nature, we can eliminate the contradictions of development. This approach to sustainability, then, represents a renewal of modernism. A more critical perspective regards science as part of the problem as well as the solution. It takes issue with the inevitability of economic growth and its consequences for human society. This perspective suggests that environmental management, as a strategy to cope with the externalities of the development model, is found wanting. Redclift (1993) argues, for example, that modern economics has played a major role in the unsustainable development of the planet. He claims that "the pursuit of growth, while neglecting its ecological consequences, has its roots in the classical paradigm which informs both market economies and state socialist ones" (19). Yet sustainability's basis in "natural" law induces both policy makers and the public to use it as a model, rather than as a critique, of the relations between humans and their environment.

Where we once hoped that scientific progress would convert individual misery and folly into comprehensive contentment for all humanity, we now hope for sustainable development to accomplish these goals. Advocates ranging from World Bank officials to leaders of the National Association for the Advancement of Colored People (NAACP) tout sustainability as a comprehensive historical notion that works because it contextualizes social planning within the objective truths of natural science. We cannot, however, see the full contribution of our practices to the sustainability or nonsustainability of humanity's transect across time. As postmodern women and men, we abandon the notion of progress, but, as humans, we need something to take its place. Sustainability may provide an appropriate substitute because it is less boastful and confident, but it remains equally ephemeral and contested.

Sustainable development offers the hope that we can make sense of the noisy cacophony of voices that influence particular occurrences within infinite intersections of time and space. The notion of sustainability encourages construction of development models that do not use clock time but nonetheless have the criteria for their own death built in as explicit components. Although such a system might endure indefinitely, the notion of performance criteria posits a condition at which it has failed and beyond which the temporality of the system has no meaning. Seen in this light, the move toward sustainability is a move toward a bounded (though potentially indefinite) temporality for which system failure and death are genuine possibilities. Although the concept of sustainable development remains a product of modernism, this bounded temporality provides some protection from the modernistic tendency to revert to totalizing narratives.

The challenge faced (or ignored) by those who offer sustainable development as a substitute for progress is to assume responsibility for human action as we explore the need to alter our underlying social commitments. The global project must be expanded to include an examination of the symbolic interactions that contribute to our current environmental problems yet fail to equip us to deal with them. The next chapter will discuss how rhetorical criticism enables us to use the creative tension within the term *sustainable development* to meet this challenge.

Chapter 3

The Power of Ambiguity
Rhetorical Critique as a Means of Highlighting and Maintaining Internal Contradictions

There is no information outside of communication, no utterance outside of communication, no understanding outside of communication.

Niklas Luhmann 1992, 254

Rhetoric . . . is rooted in . . . the use of language as a symbolic means of inducing cooperation in beings that by nature respond to symbols.

Kenneth Burke [1950] 1969, 43

Debates among social theorists reflect an ongoing controversy over the relative significance of symbolic action (or communication) and material existence in constructing social situations. There is growing agreement, however, that symbolic and material dimensions of reality influence and are influenced by each other (Beck 1992; Giddens 1979, 1984). Social theorists who emphasize the processes whereby communication constructs reality, rather than the accuracy with which it portrays reality, increasingly challenge the traditional view of communication as representation. The challenge accepted by those who take communication's constitutive force seriously is to understand how people mutually create the multiple social realities within which they live. Kenneth Burke and Niklas Luhmann are two twentieth-century theorists who focus on communication as a center for the study of human society. Complementary aspects of their theoretical perspectives can be synthesized to provide a guide for exploring how the term *sustainable development* has evolved as well as for influencing its future developmental directions. Burke is a rhetorical theorist who is most interested in the symbolic processes that enable or disable the building of community. Luhmann, a systems theorist, examines society as a self-organizing system that is distinguished from its environment by communication.

Burke ([1950] 1969) asserts that, while the human experience is grounded in material existence, materiality is insufficient to explain social motivation. Rather, a more complete explanation of social reality can be achieved by exploring rhetoric, or language used to provoke identification and cooperation among human beings. He explains that "once you have a word-using animal, you can properly look for the linguistic motive as a possible strand of motivation in all its behavior." He argues further that the chief end of rhetoric is *identification*, or a sense of unity with our fellow humans. Luhmann (1989, 1992) claims that all social systems operate on the basis of communication. Further, he argues that society is defined by its communication and that whatever is not communication is more appropriately viewed as an aspect of a society's environment than as part of the society itself. According to his theory of function systems, contemporary society is best conceptualized as a loosely coupled set of subsystems that recognize each other's existence only through reliance on intra- and intersystem communication. Thus, when political leaders discuss sustainability, they draw upon the language developed within various function systems, and they have in mind a rhetorical purpose of persuading members of their various audiences that sustainability is a goal that should be shared by all.

The analyses presented in this book are grounded in Burke's notion of rhetorical selectivity and bounded by Luhmann's theory of function systems. Burke claims that the vocabulary, or terms, that make up our rhetoric serve as "terministic screens," emphasizing some aspects of reality while downplaying others. Luhmann's theory of modern function systems provides a conceptual pattern for analyzing the limitations of sustainable development models within the context of contemporary Western culture. A rhetorical analysis informed by his social theory indicates that, by emphasizing or deemphasizing certain social spheres, the language of sustainable development has produced terministic screens that unnecessarily constrain visions of appropriate environmental policy. The existence of these constraints, however, is not the problematic issue, for any model of reality imposes constraints. Rather, the problem is that the concept of sustainable development has considerable unrealized potential for expanding the scope of environmental advocacy. The realization of this potential hinges largely on enhancing our understanding of the interaction between the terministic screens provided by the terms *sustainable* and *development*.

Despite the complications discussed in the previous chapter, *sustainable development*'s rhetorical strength lies in its philosophical ambiguity and range. As an oxymoron, the term both draws attention to the obstacles intrinsic to resisting exploitation (which brings temporary profits but future losses) and encourages the invention of alternative forms of resistance. Yet the phrase is not constructed of two coequal terms. Both ethical concerns with the human condition and the grammatical structure of *sustainable development* indicate that development, rather than sustainability, should remain the key trope. Our desire to avoid advocating the sustenance of inhumane patterns of development combined with this linguistic pattern magnifies the threat that environmentalist agendas will capitulate to the agendas of traditional economic development. If *sustainable development* is to become more than another meaningless bit of jargon, the productive tension within the term must be maintained. In this chapter I summarize those aspects of Burke's and Luhmann's theories which are most relevant to my discussion of the rhetoric of sustainable development. Following this chapter, I develop three case studies of sustainable development that illustrate both the need for greater reflexivity on the part of those involved in that discussion and the danger that advocates of conventional development patterns will co-opt the term if allowed to do so.

Rhetoric as Symbolic Action

Research on the technical possibilities for sustainable development provides little guidance for understanding what it means to society, what values it emphasizes, or what motives it affirms. A rhetorical analysis of the discourse surrounding this issue offers a means of exploring those questions. Burke's theory of rhetoric focuses on humans acting through language to form common bonds. He posits that to be human is to feel estranged from, yet desire identification and socialization with, others of our species. To overcome our state of estrangement or separation we use language to create elaborate social hierarchies that simultaneously enable and constrain our interaction. The social hierarchies we construct to achieve unity, however, simultaneously result in more estrangement and divisiveness, for members of the hierarchy differ, both symbolically and materially, from one another. We use rhetoric as a symbolic means of expressing the common interests needed to achieve the social unity we desire (Burke 1966, 15–16, 88–89, 301–2; [1950] 1969, 19–27, 45–46, 55, 138–41). Since rhetoric's function is to proclaim unity, the rhetorical critic's function is to discover and analyze the symbols used to achieve that unity. Thus, rhetorical criticism of sustainable development functions to discover and analyze aspects of that discourse which encourage diverse groups of people to identify with one another's beliefs regarding the appropriate relations between human society and the natural environment.

Despite Burke's primary interest in the use of symbols by the human animal, he repeatedly reminds us that symbol use is grounded in materiality. He writes that although "symbolic action is *not* reducible to terms of sheer motion . . . there can be no action without motion" (1978, 814). He suggests that the material and the symbolic realms are linked by the intermediate realm of experience but does not provide a blueprint of how the transformation from one realm to the other occurs. Burke devotes relatively little attention to the processes through which humans transform motion (materiality) into action (symbolicity), because his primary theoretical concern is to understand the symbolic practices involved in influence attempts once that transformation has occurred. He does, however, designate the presence of choice as essential for moving humans from the realm of mere motion into the realm of action.

Burke describes humans as "choice-making animals," which means that to him the human experience entails a degree of both autonomy and constraint. Whereas a wholly constrained body may respond to stimuli and a wholly unconstrained body may move freely, neither chooses between alternatives (Conrad and Macom 1995). The communication practices implicated in conceptualizing and implementing sustainable development place their practitioners in that structured yet not wholly predetermined situation wherein meaningful choice occurs. Whereas some analytical frameworks focus attention on the social structures that simultaneously constrain and enable symbolic (and material) action in concrete situations, Burke directs our attention to those symbolic acts that are constrained by social structures but still voluntary. His repeated claim that those symbolic acts that define us as human beings are grounded in materiality indicates his awareness that symbol use remains constrained by structures that extend beyond us, both in time and space. In other words, the human proclivity toward symbolic action is grounded in material existence, which is entailed in symbolic action.

It is not unreasonable to extend Burke's claims about the mutual constraints humans exert within their own species to the mutual constraints between the natural and humanly constructed environment. In fact, Blankenship (1993), Thompson and Palmeri (1993), Rueckert (1994), and others have examined the ecological implications of Burke's analytical framework. Perhaps our propensity to use language to "persuade" nature is even more basic than our propensity to use it to persuade other humans. Armed with language, human societies have imagined, discussed, and implemented technologies for controlling, manipulating, and transforming nature. As Rueckert (1994) points out, Burke describes the human capacity for rhetorical action as grounded "in the pre- and nonverbal realm of nature" (173). An ironic aspect of this conceptualization of the relationship between rhetorical and natural systems is that, despite their interconnectedness, rhetoric and ecology conflict with each other, because humans' rhetorical capacity "makes it possible for them to study, master, manipulate, transform, and destroy ecosystems" (174). More significantly, because an ecosystem is fundamentally material, rather than symbolic (as are rhetorical systems), careful attention to an internally consistent set of terms cannot rehabilitate a battered ecological system. Conversely, rhetorical systems demonstrate incredible resiliency and adaptability in the face of competing material realities. Rhetoric can serve the Sierra Club, the Wise Use Movement, Edward Abbey, Dave Forman, and James Watt equally well. The rhetorical systems employed by these material entities survive changing political winds, fluctuating membership roles, and physical death while remaining available for use in the next campaign. They cannot, however, emerge without embodiment within some material entity. Despite its symbolicity, rhetoric remains grounded in the human body, which depends for its continued life on the materiality of the biosphere.

Burke repeatedly notes that humans cannot live by symbols alone. His writing suggests that, because it is folly to assume that we have the same freedom with, and power over, ecosystems as we do over language, rhetoric must give way to ecology at certain points. These two logically oppositional systems "must learn to live together or perish together" (Rueckert 1994, 178). Although the sheer volume and breadth of Burke's writings ensures that he will vacillate regarding the likelihood of such cooperation, in his more hopeful moments he argues that the same symbol-using capacity that has enabled humans to design and promote self-destructive technologies can enable them to invent a more healthy relationship between themselves and their natural environment. He writes of his hope that, through careful criticism of symbolic logics, "a worldwide political system adequate to control its [technology's] uses and misuses *can somehow be contrived*" ([1937] 1984b, 340). The sort of criticism Burke recommends for this purpose must serve an admonitory function, without becoming negativistic. It would include a commitment to continued criticism, because it would recognize that any attempts to achieve such a political system must be imperfect and therefore temporary. Rather than lamenting the inevitability of imperfection, however, that recognition would include respect for the continued struggle and encourage a constructive criticism that is tolerant of human foibles.

Burke's concept of dramatic frames has particular utility for understanding how one can apply these principles of criticism to broad cultural notions such as sustainable development. He argues that the symbols we choose to achieve social unity reflect our attitudes toward society in general. To choose a symbol, therefore, is to have an attitude toward the material object or experience that symbol represents. An analysis of the dramatic frames used in discussing sustainable development, therefore, provides a general guide to the attitudes of those involved in the discussion. In *Attitudes toward History* ([1937] 1984b) Burke explains dramatic frames as the symbolic means of dealing with the dilemmas in which we become entangled. These frames guide us through difficulties by shaping our dilemmas into manageable situations. He writes that "out of such frames we derive our vocabularies for the charting of human motives. And implicit in our theory of motives is a program of action, since we form ourselves and judge others (collaborating with them or against them) in accordance with our attitudes" ([1937] 1984b, 92). Dramatic frames provide a structure of meaning which enables people to accept a situation at the same time they seek means for correcting disagreeable aspects of that situation. In the second case they also serve as guides for correcting the situation.

Burke labels the dramatic frames that enable people to feel "at home in" their material conditions as either tragic or comic. He distinguishes these frames according to their attitudes toward social interaction, rather than their literary force. While both treat the topic of human struggle, warning against hubris, Burke insists that the comic frame offers the more humane corrective to troubling situations. It encourages acceptance of material conditions by acknowledging that all aspects of reality are somehow related to all others, whereas the tragic frame emphasizes separation and division, which encourages oppositional interpretations of situations. Burke does not intend the concept of acceptance to equal passive acquiescence. Rather, "it provides the charitable attitude towards people that is required for purposes of persuasion and cooperation, but at the same time maintains our shrewdness" ([1937] 1984b, 166). The comic frame, therefore, "should enable people *to be observers of themselves while acting*. Its ultimate would not be *passiveness*, but *maximum consciousness*" (171). Comic criticism, then, encourages greater understanding of one's situation in order to achieve more productive, community-based means of improving it.

Tragic and comic criticism both provide a means for exposing oppressive aspects of social hierarchies. Critical discourse constructed within the tragic frame demystifies the social hierarchy by literally or ritually sacrificing the protagonist, whereas comically framed criticism achieves demystification by exposing this person as a fool. The fool's role wards off serious threats to the social hierarchy by exposing stupidity or incongruities between ideals and practices which constitute specific elements of that hierarchy while enabling the underlying principles of organization to continue. While the tragic frame envisions life as a drama wherein heroes battle villains to thwart the ascendence of evil, the comic frame envisions a game of poet-scholars disputing with fools to impede the expansion of stupidity ([1937] 1984b, 4, 35–41). Rachel Carson's ([1962] 1966) fable of mass destruction at the beginning of *Silent Spring*, for example, offers a tragic interpretation of the quest to improve humanity's quality of life and standard of living. The crusaders are destroyed by their own hubris. Alternately, Leopold's ([1949] 1968) land ethic, while providing an equally incisive critique of our hypertechnologized society, merely derides the presumption of those who aspire to improve human life by dominating nature. Essentially, criticism from within the comic frame focuses attention on humanity in society, whereas tragedy's subject is humanity in the cosmos.

Burke claims that the comic frame enables more productive criticism of the social condition because it discourages tragedy's tendencies toward euphemism, cynical debunking, and absolutism. He argues that these approaches disable productive criticism because they equate acceptance with acquiescence and encourage combative, rather than cooperative, notions of change. The first approach is exemplified by the Evangelical Christian's promise of a better life in the next world, which encourages passivity by offering euphemistic transcendence from material conditions. Critics who use the second approach are equally offensive because their consistent attacks on political and social structures, for the sole purpose of discrediting or destroying them, encourage combative approaches to problems. Finally, Burke opposes any criticism that closes the door to alternative points of view. Polemical criticism threatens humanity's very existence because it attempts to eliminate freedom of thought, which would eliminate discussion of alternatives. Burke's insistence that criticism should open possibilities for reconstructing an alternative social structure (which is then subjected to further criticism) date to his earliest writing and contributed to his disaffection from Marxism in the 1930s. He cautions that any criticism rooted in tragedy can unwittingly promote absolutism and prevent transformation by rejecting new ideas because they are less than perfect. Comic criticism, on the other hand, encourages awareness that situations are ambivalent, related to others, and constantly in process. Rather than rejecting sustainable development out of hand, a comic perspective recognizes that it is an inadequate attempt to conceptualize an appropriate relationship between humanity and the larger world because all such formulations will be inadequate and suggests alternative formulations that will, in turn, be subjected to criticism.

Burke does not leave the critic without tools for exploring the expansive social dramas formed around terms such as *sustainable development*. He suggests three interrelated concepts that facilitate the exploration of how dramatic frames function within and between social hierarchies: an *occupational psychosis*, which is constituted through a *terministic screen*, results in *trained incapacity*. A fourth term, *perspective by incongruity*, clarifies the role of criticism in discovering damage then fostering appropriate repairs to the social fabric. These concepts provide the rhetorical critic with a guide for scrutinizing the texts various individuals and groups have constructed for interpreting *sustainable development*.

An occupational psychosis is a way of thinking which develops out of a certain pattern of living then reinforces continued reliance on traditional cultural patterns in nontraditional conditions (Burke [1935] 1984a, 37–50). When Burke uses the term *occupation* he refers to more than a professional vocation such as being a professor or a steelworker. Rather, an *occupation* is a descriptive term that runs throughout all aspects of life. An individual's occupation, for example, might be to have arthritis, to be beautiful, or to be an environmentalist. Further, Burke's concern with a generalized occupational psychosis that absorbs society relates more directly to this analysis than do the variants to which individuals might fall prey. Burke borrows the term from John Dewey, who suggests that a society's primary means for sustaining itself provides the pattern for all additional activities. This psychosis has a "creative character which, when turned into other channels of action or imagery, will shape them analogously" ([1935] 1984a, 37–49, 39). For example, if a tribe's means for obtaining food and fiber is the hunt, it will reveal a corresponding "hunting" pattern in other social activities and rituals ranging from children's games to marriage. In other words, a society's historical environment corresponds with its most basic methods of production. Burke recognizes that, while no society is homogeneous in its occupational psychosis, certain occupations are more characteristic of certain societies than are others. He argues that contemporary Western society suffers from a "technological psychosis," which he describes as an expectation that, if humans continue their technological progress, they can transcend their own mortality by achieving absolute control over nature. Although Burke endorses neither the desirability nor the practicality of this goal, he claims it provides the patterns we use to measure the appropriateness of all social activity.

Individuals, and the societies within which they live, develop a vocabulary, or a *terministic screen*, to make sense of their occupational psychoses. This working vocabulary involves much more than a set of isolated symbols. Over a period of generations people weave individual terms together, forming a screen that enables its users to consider and discuss which aspects of raw experience are important, what that experience means, and what sort of action it calls for. Terministic screens provide the tools for naming and confronting the social hierarchies within which we find ourselves. As such, they influence our observations at two levels. First, they direct attention, emphasizing some aspects of reality and relegating others to the background. Second, this direction of attention results in our "observations" of reality becoming nothing more or less than *"implications of the particular terminology in terms of which the observations are made. . . .* [They] may be but the spinning out of possibilities implicit in our particular choice of terms" (Burke 1966, 44–55, 46). Thus, a terministic screen provides a meaning system that constrains our ability to turn reality into information, provides tools for evaluating and naming situations, and encourages us to adopt appropriate roles within those situations.

As an occupational psychosis diffuses throughout a culture, society selects certain vocations as more central than others, and this choice is reflected in the dominant terministic screens. The centrality of these vocations then leads to increased legitimization of their significance to the material scene, which in turn reinforces interests associated with them. For example, the technological psychosis has encouraged centralization of numerical measurement as a means for determining empirical reality. The vocabulary of numerical measurement works well for determining income and standard of living. It works less well for determining happiness and quality of life. Within a terministic screen that encourages its users to consider numerical measurement as the most legitimate means of determining empirical reality, happiness becomes a less significant indicator of a society's achievement than does income. Although when the implications of this terministic screen are drawn out to their logical conclusions people perceive their absurdity; in the normal course of events they have little cause to do so. The critical project is not to do away with terministic screens altogether, for neither society nor individuals could function without them. Burke points out that "to explain one's conduct by the vocabulary of motives current among one's group is about as self-deceptive as giving the area of a field in the accepted terms of measurement. One is simply interpreting with the only vocabulary he knows" ([1935] 1984a, 21). The difficulty arises when, rather than reflecting on the terministic screens they have used thus far, when faced with a new problem, people state *the problem in such a way that [their] particular aptitude becomes the 'solution' for it"* (242–43).

Occupational psychosis combined with nonreflective use of its accompanying terministic screen leads to *trained incapacity*, or a condition in which our abilities "function as blindness" ([1935] 1984a, 7–11, 49). Because our terministic screens constrain our observational possibilities to those in keeping with our occupational psychoses, we see new experiences in the terms provided by our past training. Of course, if the conditions of living have undergone radical changes since our terministic screen was developed, its serviceability may be impaired. Thus, our training becomes an incapacity. In this sense our occupational psychosis works as a "deskilling" process that encourages us to cling to tested methods of dealing with our vocation as an arthritic, a beauty, or an environmentalist while disabling us from seeing new possibilities that might work better. The technological psychosis, with its accompanying terministic screen, may have been relatively functional during the early days of the industrial revolution. The new world in which we find ourselves (produced largely by the success of that terministic screen), however, calls for a different consciousness. Burke argues that a rigid motivational hierarchy can interfere with the very social processes that it was intended to facilitate ([1950] 1969, 141). Trained incapacity promotes rigidity at the very time flexibility is most needed.

One strategy for correcting such rigidity is to adopt *perspective by incongruity* within the comic frame. Constructing a new and incongruous name for our material circumstances enables us to "remoralize" situations that have been "demoralized" by our trained incapacities. It turns our social hierarchies inside out to expose their foolishness. It is "impious. . . . It 'puns' categories of symbols established by custom" ([1937] 1984b, 308–9). Simply revising elements of our original perspective is insufficient to achieve incongruity; instead, the fundamental point of view must be changed. Burke calls this practice "verbal atomic-cracking," wherein a symbol is wrenched from its usual meaning, enabling us to reinterpret our material circumstances by removing words from their traditional patterns. A comic criticism of environmental advocacy would enable us to shift fundamentally the relationships we have considered possible between the technologized and natural worlds.

The ideal comic criticism serves as an amplifying device, rather than a reductive one. It acknowledges that life is always in process and that the most productive ways of dealing with it will account for its complexity, resisting the compulsion to reduce this complexity to an oversimplified, orderly description. In order to avoid oversimplification it encourages people to broaden their terminology, enables awareness of ambiguity and irony, and promotes metaphorical vision. It should enable people to recognize and use rhetorical resources such as metaphor and irony to transcend the categorical and logical barriers constructed by society's terministic screens and rigidified by its trained incapacities. Comic criticism promotes integrative, social knowledge wherein people are corrected rather than punished, because it is charitable without being gullible. It offers neither an absolute criterion for truth nor any kind of rigidified orthodoxy. Because the major emphasis is always reconciliatory and constructive, it cannot advocate terrorism of any sort. Instead, it promotes the knowledge that any social structure develops self-defeating emphases and unintended by-products over time. Comic criticism offers an analytical frame for discovering aspects of our social constructs which need revising and encourages us toward that project. It offers the hope that we can move toward a better life through improving the quality of public dialogue.

The genius of comic criticism is that it allows for the kind of cultural stretching which enables rhetorical criticism of extended texts, such as the discussion surrounding sustainable development, while retaining a focus on the language out of which that concept develops. Comic criticism of sustainable development offers an opportunity to pun the tragic drama of development's conventional form impiously by changing the point of view to a perspective that celebrates sustaining things, a concept traditionally antithetical to developing them. Sustainable development enables us to reject the values of the traditional development creed through a synthetic possibility that does not require the tragic destruction of developers. Burke would caution, however, that possibilities rarely translate completely into actualities. The critic must turn the principles of comic criticism on themselves, remembering that perfection remains something to strive toward, never to be reached. Because any critic will be bounded by particular terministic screens and the material world will continue to change, each instance of criticism should be seen as an invitation to further criticism. This should not, however, discourage the search for a genuine synthesis between *sustainability* and *development* but should direct attention, instead, to discovering means for preventing one aspect of the term from dissolving into the other.

Modernity and Social Fragmentation

Luhmann's (1989) functionalist social theory differs in fundamental ways from Burke's rhetorical project. It does, however, help explain how any model of sustainable development manages to produce a terministic screen that constrains the vision of appropriate environmental policy. It both clarifies the extent to which the fundamental assumptions underlying certain models for sustainable development provide a narrowly deterministic basis for public policy decisions and presents a framework within which we can use the comic frame to critique potential repercussions of basing natural resource management decisions on these perspectives. Luhmann proposes a radicalized functionalism as a theoretical perspective toward society and its environment. Rather than viewing functional relations as causal, he characterizes "cause" as a special, and singularly opaque, case of function. Functional relations exist between a problem and a *range* of possible responses, and problems that do not acquiesce to such a range are not social problems (T. R. Peterson and M. J. Peterson, 1996; M. J. Peterson and T. R. Peterson 1993).

Luhmann (1989) uses the concept of autopoesis to model society as simultaneously closed (organizationally) and open (structurally). The theory of autopoesis relies on the powerful notion that all systems examine themselves and regulate their own functioning through a process analogous to cognition. Autopoesis suggests that the most basic communicative operation is that of categorization (Ulrich and Probst 1984). Any unity, including human society, can be differentiated into its constituent parts by drawing further distinctions. One can differentiate commonly accepted elements of sustainable development such as the discussion of forest harvesting techniques, the introduction of "appropriate" agricultural technologies into developing nations, and the implementation of water purification systems in rapidly growing cities. Alternately, one can distinguish between the social system within which these examples occur and their environment, thus emphasizing differentiations within the environment. For example, the social system includes neither the moisture level in the forest, the soil types in the developing nation, nor the contour of the bay where the city is located. The whole process of differentiating entities from their background is based upon this simple cognitive process, which specifies the organization of a system.

While Luhmann's interpretation recognizes that society has an environment, it presumes that social relations with it are internally driven *responses to*, rather than *interactions with*, the environment. In other words, the environmental disaster detailed in the "Fable for Tomorrow," which begins Carson's ([1962] 1966) *Silent Spring*, was not the result of interactions between society and its environment so much as the result of *internally* driven responses to environmental conditions. Society's rush to control nature, its headlong pursuit of technologically defined progress, and the public's naive trust in scientific interpretations of the natural world combined to produce the disappearance of songbirds, withered vegetation, and puzzling illnesses that gripped farm families. The desolate community she describes is the culmination of elements internal to the social world which constrained both awareness of and responses to environmental conditions. Instead of asserting that the system adapts to its environment or that the environment selects the system that survives, autopoesis emphasizes the way the social system shapes its own future according to its internal structures.

The organizational closure assumed by autopoesis means that society can react to its environment only according to its own mode of operation, which is communication. Luhmann (1992) claims that, when studying society, "one must not begin with the concept of action but with the concept of communication. For it is not action but rather communication that is an unavoidably social operation" (252). He defines society as an "all encompassing social system of mutually referring communications . . . [that] originates through communicative acts alone and differentiates itself from an environment of other kinds of systems through the continual reproduction of communication by communication" (1989, 7). Society is seen as an autonomous, closed system because it strives to maintain an identity by subordinating all change to the maintenance of its own organization as a given set of relations. It does so by engaging in circular patterns of interaction (within itself) whereby change in one element of the system is coupled with changes elsewhere, setting up continuous patterns of interaction which are always self-referential. The inability to incorporate Aldo Leopold's ([1949] 1968) land ethic into U.S. conservation legislation illustrates system closure at the institutional level. Although Leopold's holistic view of the environment is both familiar to and respected by politicians, environmental lobbyists, theoretical ecologists, and natural resource managers, environmental legislation takes an atomistic approach. The Endangered Species Act, for example, directs attention toward individual species and away from the ecosystems within which they exist. The political system's self-referential nature prevents it from acting in ways that are not specified in the pattern of relations that define its organization. As an autonomous system, society's supposed interaction with its environment is both a reflection and a part of its internal organization: it responds to the environment in ways that facilitate its own self-production.

Further, that response comes only in the form of communication. Luhmann (1992) postulates that communication occurs "through a selection . . . of *information*, selection of the *utterance* of this information, and a selective *understanding or misunderstanding* of this utterance and its information" (252). No communication exists unless all three of these components are present, for without their presence we remain in the realm of perception. Although other social theorists, including Austin (1962), Habermas (1979), and Searle (1969), focus on these components of communication, their concern is with communication's success or failure in transmitting messages or understanding. Alternately, Luhmann

(1992) emphasizes the emergence of communication. Instead of interpreting information, utterance, and understanding as communication functions or speech acts, he argues that "there is no information outside of communication, no utterance outside of communication, no understanding outside of communication—and not simply in the causal sense for which information is the cause of the utterance and the utterance the cause of the understanding, but rather in the circular sense of reciprocal presupposition" (254). Thus, communication is a closed system that creates the components out of which it arises through practices of communication.

In describing society as closed and autonomous, Luhmann is not characterizing it as completely isolated. The closure and autonomy to which he refers are merely organizational. Society closes in on itself to maintain stable patterns of relations, and this process ultimately enables it to maintain itself as a system. Because it functions as a closed loop of interaction, society has no clear beginning or end point. Luhmann's rejection of the input-output model distinguishes his approach to social theory from that used by many systems theorists. Because the system envisioned by Luhmann cannot escape the closed loop, it makes no sense to say that society directly interacts with its external environment. Rather, apparent transactions between society and its environment are really transactions within the social system which have been prompted by resonance among society's function systems.

Although society is organizationally closed, it remains structurally open. Systems maintain stability by sustaining processes of negative feedback which allow them to detect and correct deviations from operating norms and can evolve by developing capacities for modifying these norms to account for new circumstances. The source of change, then, is located in random variations occurring within the system. This structural openness allows seemingly unrelated aspects of a system to interact with one another. The structural openness specified by the theory of autopoesis encourages us to understand transformations of society as the result of internally generated change, rather than as adaptation to external forces.

Chaos theory, which began developing in the 1960s, suggests that random changes in a system can lead to new patterns of order and stability (Crutchfield et al. 1986). Random variation within society, then, generates possibilities for emergence and evolution of new system identities. Of course, possibilities do not necessarily translate into practices, and the attendant potential for importing negative entropy does not always result in its importation. Erratic changes can trigger interactions that reverberate through the system. The final consequences of these changes, however, are determined by whether the current identity of the system dampens the effects of the disturbance through compensatory changes elsewhere or whether it encourages a new configuration of relations to emerge. For example, the Right-to-Know Computer Network (RTK Net) discussed in the previous chapter dampens the potential for fundamental changes in the increasingly privatized control of publicly owned information. Because the RTK Net provides noncorporate individuals and groups with access to the U.S. government's Toxics Release Inventory, these individuals and groups may be less likely to demand fundamental reform of an information system that privileges corporate information users over grassroots community organizations and private individuals.

Luhmann interprets the aspects of social systems which enable these transactions to occur as communicative interactions rather than as individual elements. Society thus is structured by self-referential operations (communication) which are produced within society's subsystems. Luhmann (1989) characterizes these operations as communicative acts, which are the sole means for differentiating society from its environment. Communication, which refers to "the common actualization of meaning," rather than to information transfer, provides society's "*mode of operation,* and the *environment* includes everything that does not operate communicatively" (x, 7). The society wherein these communicative transactions take place is a centerless set of "function systems" that constrain both what can be communicated and how it is communicated. Luhmann argues that, because each subsystem fulfills only one primary function (hence, the name "function system"), it cannot substitute for another, as was the case within traditional societies that were differentiated through stratification. In medieval Europe, for example, the authority of the pope, who occupied the pinnacle of the social hierarchy, could be brought to bear on any sort of problem. Whether the issue was religion, economics, or education, the same ultimate authority ruled. Because modern society recognizes no single authority figure that can cut across all questions and social issues, however, individual functions assume primary authority for resolving problems.

Luhmann labels economy, law, science, politics, religion, and education as the most important function systems in contemporary society.

These systems constrain both what experience becomes information and what kind of information it becomes. He writes that because "self-reference (or reflexiveness) is not a property peculiar to thought or consciousness but instead a general principle of system formation . . . there are many different possibilities for observing the world, depending on the reference system that is taken as basic" (1992, 251–52). Function systems act as terministic screens by sorting all experience that is allowed to become information according to a binary code, wherein negation secures system closure by ensuring that every value refers exclusively to its countervalue. Luhmann (1989) labels the codes for society's most basic function systems as: ability/inability to pay (economy), legality/illegality (law), truth/falsity (science), in/out of office (politics), immanence/transcendence (religion), and better/worse (education). These codes reproduce system closure by resolving tautologies and paradoxes and by limiting further possibilities. Within the function system of science, for example, a claim that is not true is false, and a claim that is not false is true. Members of society are spared both the tautology that "truth is truth" and the paradox that "one cannot truthfully maintain that one is truthful." The principle of negation imputes binary codes with universal validity because something that is not identified by one term must be identified by the other. Thus, the binary code of truth/falsity precludes the consideration of alternative criteria when evaluating a scientific event. Binary codes operate similarly in each function system. While the principle of negation (as materialized in the binary code) ensures organizational closure, it also guarantees structural openness by inducing society to examine the possibility of that which does not exist (T. R. Peterson and M. J. Peterson, 1996).

Each system's programs, which *refer to* its binary code yet are not terms of the code, further retain the system's openness. At the same time they operationalize the system's binary code, they must remain variable, because determining the relative suitability of one or the other binary value when appraising an experience requires information from outside the system. Programs, then, refer to the conditions necessary to determine the selection of one binary term over the other (Luhmann 1989). For example, decisions about whether to conduct studies designed to determine the truth or falsity of scientific claims made in the Brundtland report depend on codes from the systems of politics (who is in/out of office), law (what is legal/illegal) and the economy (who has the ability / inability to pay). Structural openness, then, allows social systems to utilize terms from within other function systems, without losing their previously determined identities.

Luhmann (1989) argues that functional differentiation limits society's potential responses to environmental disturbances, for responses can be formulated only in terms of existing function systems. Whenever society is unable to ignore environmental disturbances, the resulting "resonance" between society and its environment is channeled into a function system and treated in accordance with that system's binary code. Experience that cannot be translated into the binary code of a function system never becomes information. Yet, even though function systems screen society from its environment by sharply reducing what counts as information, they make up for this by producing resonance at the internal boundaries of society—where communication across function systems *defines* society.

Function systems form one another's environments, for the world is not constituted so that events fit neatly within the framework of one function alone. This interdependence is illustrated when a pharmaceutical company forms a legal partnership with the government of a developing nation which allows the company to study then extract potential pharmaceuticals from that nation's biological resources. In this case *scientific* analysis of the biological resources found in developing nations has become *economically* feasible through *political* decisions about *legal* liability limitations. Despite overlap among function systems, however, they lack integration to the degree that a positive valuation in one system does not automatically entail a positive valuation in the other systems. For example, *scientifically* validated information used in the Brundtland report indicates that the strain of exponential population growth in developing nations portends an *environmental* disaster. Rather than mitigating that disaster, however, *political* decisions amplify it by providing legal justification for an *economically* and *religiously* based decision to postpone *educational* family planning initiatives. Even in cases such as this in which function systems do not produce coordinated responses, their communicative interdependency ensures that operations can switch quickly from the code of one function system to the code of another.

Luhmann (1989) cautions against defining other function systems solely in terms of their relationship with a single sphere. He claims that the attempt to derive the near totality of other sociological phenomenon from any one sphere is hopelessly reductionistic. As previously illustrated, the terministic screen provided by each function system's binary code differs markedly from that provided by another function system's code. This variation occurs because each function system's binary code provides specific constraints. Each function system experiences the environment through its own programs and codes. Terministic screens that privilege one mode of experiencing over all others threaten to distort the social experience. For example, when observation of the natural environment is interpreted in light of ability / inability to pay the costs for preserving a landscape, the social system only can observe interpretations of that landscape after arbitrarily decontextualizing it from its noneconomic milieu. Additionally, it can communicate about the relationship between society and that landscape only through economic theories already in existence, thereby choosing which experience will become information, with no external (noneconomic) means of rationalizing the selection (M. J. Peterson and T. R. Peterson 1993).

In sum, when the criteria and programming of any function system are privileged over all others, the number and variety of experiences that count as information in a society are sharply reduced. Because society's ability to find resonance with its environment is almost completely dependent on the secondary resonance that develops among its function systems, this boundary activity is essential to the perception of environmental disturbances. Secondary resonance enables society to compensate for its inability to interact directly with its environment. Only through recognizing the limitations of each function system can society benefit from the internal complexity of the integrated system into which it has evolved.

Rhetorical Selectivity in Modern Society

Luhmann and Burke together provide a basis for exploring means whereby sustainable development discourse produces, reproduces, and transforms environments at the same time that those environments constrain the discourse. Burke suggests that social dilemmas such as environmental conflict arise from the failure to form adequate bonds of identification among those most interested in environmental advocacy as well as between that group and the larger public. Sustainable development has become so popular because it allows people to select a point of identification between themselves and others from whom they must otherwise remain alienated. Luhmann's concept of a fragmented modern culture, wherein stimuli become information only after being "re-formulated" in terms relevant to one of society's major functions, helps explain the difficulty entailed in achieving a communal sense of sustainable development without sacrificing diversity of perspectives.

The Burkean critic recognizes that comic criticism cannot, in and of itself, solve our environmental conflicts. Rather, it positions us to view them from a different perspective. That new perspective offers the possibility of transcending conflicts. Yet, "since the transcendence of conflicts is here contrived by purely *symbolic* mergers, the actual conflicts may remain" (Burke [1937] 1984b, 180). The fact that material conflicts that are not reducible to symbolic resolution do exist does not minimize the potential of rhetorical criticism. Instead, it suggests the utility of complementing such criticism with a functionalist approach such as that offered by Luhmann. Burke offers critical tools for exploring the symbolic practices whereby humans create meaning, and Luhmann offers a systematic explanation of the products that result from those practices.

Sustainable development offers a representation of environmental policy decisions as comic, rather than tragic, drama. In the tragic drama of radical ecologists or counterenvironmentalists winning the battle, often accompanied by destruction of an adversary, assumes central importance. Sustainable development offers a comic alternative, but its critical potential relies on retaining the tension within this internally incongruent perspective. An analysis of the rhetorical processes that drive society's function systems to prefer some relationships between human society and nature over others can call into question the cultural values that the current technologized worldview emphasizes and create fresh possibilities for environmental policy.

In the following three case studies I analyze ways in which terministic screens that have developed out of various rhetorical frames and function systems have constrained the discourse of sustainable development. Participants' concerns with sustainability and development move from the global and generalized, in the first episode, to the local and particular, in the third. Conversely, my interpretation of what counts as rhetorical text grows more expansive as I move through the three episodes.

Chapter 4

Sustainable Development Goes to Rio

Implications for Global Environmental Governance

> Human beings are at the centre of concerns for sustainable development. They are entitled to a healthy and productive life in harmony with nature.
>
> UNCED 1992 *Rio Declaration on Environment and Development*

The 1992 United Nations Conference on Environment and Development (UNCED, or Earth Summit), which was held from 3 through 14 June in Rio de Janeiro, is the principal international event relating to sustainable development in recent years. Although the delegates signed several accords, conflicts between North and South as well as conflicts within traditionally allied blocks limited both the quantity and quality of agreements reached. Both participants and observers expressed disappointment in the accomplishments of the conference and in U.S. performance there. Two texts that focus attention on problematic aspects of the conference are the *Rio Declaration on Environment and Development* and the speech given by President George Bush (UNCED 1992 *Rio Declaration;* Bush 12 June 1992). Numerous delegates claimed that the Bush Administration had abdicated the United States' historical leadership in the area of environmental policy. They argued that, rather than building from its base as an international leader, the U.S. comedy of errors at Rio merely offered a distraction from the real work of the conference. The *Rio Declaration,* on the other hand, provided a basis for much of the discussion at UNCED. Its first principle explicitly indicates sustainable development as the conference's central tenet. The declaration's internal contradictions, however, display the political difficulties involved in an attempt to derive policy from principles of sustainable development without reaching consensus about what those principles are.

The difficulties encountered by conference delegates who spent long months in preparation for UNCED then long days at Rio indicate that, although there is broad acceptance of the normative value of sustainable development, acceptance does not constitute agreement regarding the meaning of sustainability or its appropriate implementation. Instead, divergent interests led participants to mutually contradictory claims about sustainable development which were contingent upon factors specific to particular geopolitical regions. Delegates failed to form significant bonds of identification which could have fostered a move to transcend traditional political rivalries. They brought incompatible terministic screens to the conference and were discouraged from exploring the potential richness that could result from resonance among their diverse perspectives. Further, because nongovernmental organizations (NGOs) were marginalized by UNCED organizers, many perspectives that were incongruous with the traditional development paradigm were excluded from deliberations.

A summary of the Earth Summit's accomplishments and media accounts highlighting U.S. participation provide a context for analyzing some of its discourse. Perceptions of the Earth Summit contrast sharply with those of the 1987 Montreal Protocol (a UN-sponsored agreement designed to protect the ozone layer). This contrast illustrates how the Earth Summit differs from other recent UN conferences, both in terms of conference scope and of the roles played by the U.S. (which traditionally has been a leader in questions of international environmental governance) delegation. In comparison to the Montreal Protocol, the Earth Summit encompassed an incredibly broad set of related yet distinct issues. Key areas of contrast in U.S. involvement center around strong U.S. interconnectedness in the Montreal negotiations versus U.S. isolation at Rio. Analysis of the speech President George Bush delivered at Rio and responses to it indicates that Bush destroyed the U.S. bid for leadership at Rio by emphasizing a second, divisive motive of promoting a local economic agenda over global concerns. Most important, the text of the *Rio Declaration* reveals significant ambivalence and contradictions within the alluring phrase *sustainable development*.

Agreements Reached at the Earth Summit

Five concrete accords came out of the Earth Summit. Two conventions, the first to limit emissions of greenhouse gases and the second to protect the diversity of the planet's plant and animal life, were signed by most nations attending the conference (UN 1992 "United Nations Framework Convention on Climate Change," "Convention on Biological Diversity"). Only the United States refused to sign the second convention. A third document that delegates accepted was the *Rio Declaration on Environment and Development*, a statement of the philosophy upon which all summit accords are based (UNCED 1992). As the excerpt from the *Rio Declaration* quoted at the beginning of this chapter suggests, human health and well-being are assumed to be complementary with environmental health. Delegates also accepted a fourth document, which was a statement of principles to guide forest conservation (UNCED 1992 *Forest Principles*). Finally, *Agenda 21*, a comprehensive blueprint for international environmental policy was finalized and accepted (UNCED 1992). Both conventions as well as the *Rio Declaration* were negotiated in separate committees and concluded shortly before Rio. Although no vote was taken on them, conference attendees had to work out details of the *Forest Principles* and *Agenda 21* at Rio (*Agenda 21 and the UNCED Proceedings* [Robinson 1992] and *Environmental Policy and Law* [August 1992] cover the conference as well as preparatory sessions).

Conventions

One of the most controversial aspects of U.S. participation was the Bush Administration's behavior regarding the conventions (Frye 1992). The United States alienated both traditional friends and foes during presummit negotiations of the climate convention. The *United Nations Framework Convention on Climate Change* took 15 months to prepare and was adopted on 9 May. It focuses largely on reducing energy demand and stabilizing carbon dioxide emissions. The major difficulty during negotiations for the climate convention was reaching an agreement between the United States and the European Community on how to limit carbon dioxide and other heat-trapping gases emitted as a result of human activity. The Europeans insisted that carbon dioxide emissions be stabilized at 1990 levels by the year 2000, while the United States rejected the notion of targets and timetables. Bush, who had maintained considerable distance from specific environmental issues during his entire presidency, insisted that it was unrealistic and counterproductive to include timetables in the climate convention. To persuade the United States to sign the convention, disgruntled European nations agreed to delete all timetables and deadlines. In contrast to the European response, some U.S. industries publicly expressed their delight at the removal of target dates and timetables. For example, when Donald Pearlman, who represented U.S. coal and utility interests, learned of the decision, he told the press that, "notwithstanding attempts by certain European countries to rewrite these paragraphs so as to create at least an impression of a requirement to return to 1990 levels by the year 2000, those efforts failed. . . . Obviously we're pleased" ("Compromise" 9 May 1992). Statements such as this further alienated both developed and developing nations from the U.S. negotiating team.

Conflict followed the convention to Rio, where the oil-producing states of Kuwait, Saudi Arabia, United Arab Emirates, Iran, and Iraq refused to sign because of its emphasis on carbon dioxide emissions. Delegates from the Netherlands, Austria, and Switzerland, who had argued to retain deadlines, introduced a separate agreement that included the timetables and deadlines suggested in the original draft of the climate convention. Although this did not become an official UNCED document, Germany led several other European nations in announcing that it would support the agreement. Washington, on the other hand, advised the three sponsoring nations that to persist with such an initiative would damage their relations with the United States. For example, the Swiss environment minister received a memorandum from the U.S. State Department, telling him that the resolution was "potentially embarrassing, unnecessary in light of the treaty, and detrimental to Swiss-American relations." The three nations expressed hostility toward U.S. pressure to drop the initiative, with the Austrian minister complaining that the U.S. State Department "treated us like we are some kind of colony" (Robinson and Weisskopf 9 June 1992).

The second convention focused on protecting biodiversity. The *Convention on Biological Diversity* took nearly four years to prepare and was adopted by its negotiating committee on 22 May. The convention is intended to ensure both national and international action to curb the destruction of biological species and ecosystems. Contracting parties are required to adopt regulations that conserve their biological resources, to assume legal responsibility for environmental impacts of their private companies operating in other countries, to transfer technology on a preferential basis to fellow signatories, and to compensate developing countries for extraction of genetic materials from their environments. Industrialized countries agree to provide developing countries with financial assistance that will facilitate species conservation.

Bush refused to sign the convention, claiming that it was flawed because language included in it could harm the U.S. biotechnology industry and require the United States to provide unconditional financial aid to developing countries. Bush feared that vague aspects of the convention directing how patent rights can be granted and how living organisms can be exploited commercially would retard the U.S. biotechnology industry, fail to protect U.S. intellectual property, and reduce royalties. The White House Council on Competitiveness, headed by Vice President Dan Quayle, explicitly opposed the convention. The U.S. biotechnology industry also lobbied extensively against it. Richard Godown, director of the Industrial Biotechnology Association, told Bush on 14 May that the convention would "hurt an industry that the United States dominates so that other countries may impede the U.S. industry's growth while developing their own industries using our technology" (Devroy 10 June 1992). In a nationally televised news conference in the United States, Bush said that he would "not sign a treaty [the Convention on Biodiversity] that in my view throws too many Americans out of work" (Schneider 6 June 1992). Unlike his response to the climate convention, Bush did not suggest alterations in the biodiversity convention.

In fact, when William Reilly, administrator for the U.S. Environmental Protection Agency (EPA), sent a confidential memorandum asking the White House to consider an amended version of the biodiversity convention, a White House official leaked a copy to the *New York Times*. The memo indicated the Brazilian delegation's willingness to alter aspects of the convention which were most bothersome to the Bush Administration:

> As I indicated last night, Brazil has offered to try to "fix" the Biodiversity Convention so that the United States could sign it. . . . As I indicated last night, the U.S. refusal to sign the Biodiversity Convention is the major subject of press and delegate concern here. . . . The changes proposed, while not making everyone in the U.S. Government totally happy, would address the critical issues that have been identified. (Reilly 5 June 1992)

Reilly, who learned of the leak from a reporter, spent the next few days defending U.S. policy to both the press and fellow delegates. Following the leak, negative characterizations of the United States became more vocal. Jamsheed Marker, Pakistan's ambassador, explained that "the perception of the U.S. is not one of leadership, but that of block-ing." Ros Kelly, Australia's environment minister, suggested that, based on conferees' perceptions of U.S. policy, Bush "will not receive an en-thusiastic reception . . . [when he] arrives" (1992, 226). A senior European negotiator said that the leaked memo "confirms what many people have suspected—that Bill Reilly is a fig leaf for a not very committed govern-ment" (Weisskopf 8 June 1992). German environment minister Klaus Topher said sadly, "I am afraid that conservatives in the United States are picking 'ecologism' as their new enemy" (Brooke 12 June 1992a). An unnamed staff member within the Bush Administration bolstered Topher's concerns by referring to the Earth Summit as "a circus" (Brooke 12 June 1992b). In the end the United States was the only industrialized nation that did not sign the biodiversity convention.

Statements of Principle

In addition to the two conventions three statements of principle were adopted by UNCED. These statements, which did not entail a vote and do not require separate ratification by states, provide the basis for fu-ture international agreements. When Bush arrived in Rio, he attempted to lead a drive to include a formal statement on forest principles in the agreements signed at the Earth Summit. Developing countries, how-ever, traditionally have opposed international forest initiatives, which they see as an abridgment of their national sovereignty. At a 1991 UN-sponsored meeting regarding forest conservation, developing countries had walked out after developed nations refused to apply the same in-ternational restrictions to their own forests which they wanted to apply to forests of developing nations. Given the current gulf between the stan-dard of living experienced in the United States and in most developing nations, Bush's refusal to consider the biodiversity convention because it might handicap the U.S. biotechnology industry may have com-pounded existing suspicions toward his motives. Ting Wen Lian, a Malaysian diplomat, declared, "we are certainly not holding our forests in custody for those who have destroyed their own forests and now try to claim ours as part of the heritage of mankind" (Stevens 7 June 1992). This statement represents the perception of many developing nations that, since Bush was not willing to share economic and technological resources with developing countries, they were not interested in shar-ing local forest resources with the United States.

Klaus Topher, leader of the German delegation, finally brokered a compromise statement between the United States and developing countries on the forest issue (Frye 1992). The resulting statement of principles calls for "global consensus on the management, conservation and sustainable development of all types of forests" (UNCED 1992 *Forest Principles*). The statement designates forests as natural resources and recognizes that in developing countries people depend on forest products for food, fiber, fuel, and shelter. It also acknowledges the global value of forests as sources of medicine, wildlife habitats, and carbon fixation. The statement further suggests that the principles outlined therein should serve as a guide when constructing binding international policies for forest conservation.

The summit also produced *Agenda 21*, a detailed blueprint for future environmental action which covers all the major environmental issues discussed at the summit (UNCED 1992). This voluminous document elaborates strategies and programs to reverse environmental degradation and to promote sustainable development in all societies. It is made up of four sections, which are further divided into approximately 10 chapters each, resulting in a total of 40 chapters. The sections are titled "Social and Economic Dimensions," "Conservation and Management of Resources for Development," "Strengthening the Role of Major Groups," and "Means of Implementation." The UNCED Preparatory Committee, which completed the draft of *Agenda 21* used in Rio, grouped programs around seven organizing themes:

1. Revitalizing growth with sustainability (The Prospering World);
2. Sustainable Living (The Just World);
3. Human Settlements (The Habitable World);
4. Efficient Resource Use (The Fertile World);
5. Global and Regional Resources (The Shared World);
6. Managing Chemicals and Waste (The Clean World);
7. Participation and Responsibility (The People's World).

The section titled "Social and Economic Dimensions" addresses the first two themes. "Conservation and Management of Resources for Development" addresses the third, fourth, fifth, and sixth themes. The section titled "Strengthening the Role of Major Groups" addresses the seventh theme. The final section details "Means of Implementation," such as science, technology, and legal mechanisms.

Finally, the conference produced a statement of philosophy "recognizing the integral and interdependent nature of the Earth, our home" (UNCED 1992 *Rio Declaration*, preamble). The *Rio Declaration* encourages international cooperation in achieving "a higher quality of life for all people," because "eradicating poverty [is] an indispensable requirement for sustainable development," and offers guidelines for negotiating binding international agreements regarding conservation and development in the future (UNCED 1992 *Rio Declaration*, principles 5, 8). Yet even the broad, humanistic sentiments articulated in the declaration sparked conflict between the United States and developing countries. When meeting with Kenya's negotiators in his office, for example, India's minister of environment, Kamal Nath, said: "the United States told us they want to remove the phrase 'right to social and economic development.' . . . We must not budge from 'the right to social and economic development'" (Brooke 12 June 1992a).

Contrasts between Montreal Protocol and Rio Earth Summit

The contrast between U.S. participation at the 1992 Rio Summit and at the 1987 Montreal Protocol provides a partial explanation for the disappointments of Rio by clarifying varying U.S. levels of commitment to the two conferences. In 1986 Richard Benedick, U.S. deputy assistant secretary of state for environment, health, and natural resource issues, was assigned by Secretary of State George Schultz to lead the U.S. delegation charged with negotiating a protocol on protecting the ozone layer (Benedick 1991). On 16 September 1987 the *Montreal Protocol on Substances That Deplete the Ozone Layer* was unveiled. Benedick recalls that the signing was marked by uncharacteristic excitement. For example, "the head of the Japanese delegation exultantly waved a last-minute cable that contained his authorization to sign the protocol, [and] the Venezuelan delegation, which all morning had been suffering through the lengthy roll call of nations while anxiously awaiting word from Caracas, broke into cheers when a breathless messenger finally arrived with the authorizing cable" (Benedict 1991, 75–76). Mostafa Tolba, executive director of United Nations Environmental Program (UNEP), closed the meeting: "As a scientist, I salute you: for with this agreement the worlds of science and public affairs have taken a step closer together" (Benedick 1991, 76).

The general enthusiasm surrounding the Montreal Protocol, however, was not universal. Among the developing nations both India and Malaysia opposed the treaty. Although Malaysia did eventually ratify the protocol, a Malaysian negotiator at Montreal characterized the treaty as "trade war by environmental decree." Indian officials did not contribute to negotiations and characterized the issue as a "rich man's problem." India has never ratified the Montreal Protocol (Benedick 1991, 100–101).

Despite its shortcomings, the Montreal Protocol generally is considered to have been successful in producing an international agreement that set specific regulatory guidelines limiting production and use of ozone depleting gases such as chlorofluorocarbons (CFCs). Benedick claims that seven crucial elements facilitated the accomplishments of the Montreal Protocol. The most basic was that science and scientists were drawn into the negotiations from beginning to end: "The U.S. government provided major funding for research on the ozone layer and then heeded the results" (Benedick 1991, 30). The culture of science postulates that uncertainty will always exist, and, therefore, the idea of delaying policy decisions until potential environmental damage levels were certain seemed ludicrous. Along with the centrality of scientists came an acceptance of the need to formulate policy in the face of uncertainty. Because they were not pressed to produce certainty, scientists were able to provide continual information updates to the nonscientists who participated.

In sharp contrast, scientists played more peripheral roles at the 1992 UNCED. Although extensive preliminary scientific research was available to negotiators involved in preliminary meetings, scientists themselves were less involved. Instead of emphasizing a need to proceed based on the best available scientific evidence, Bush repeatedly emphasized the potential harm decisions made in a climate of uncertainty posed to the fragile U.S. economy. Rather than working from the assumption that science is inherently uncertain, the existence of differing estimates of the potential environmental damage caused by human activities was used to justify avoiding decisive action.

A second crucial ingredient in Montreal's relative success was the existence of a well-informed and involved public that mobilized governments to act, even in the face of uncertainty. Both the UNEP and the U.S. government participated in massive public education campaigns aimed at both governments and citizens. The U.S. publicity campaign enabled U.S. negotiators to weather a brief antiregulatory backlash in the United States, epitomized by Secretary of the Interior Donald Hodel's "personal protection" program. In an interview with the *Wall Street Journal* Hodel was quoted as saying that "people who don't stand out in the sun—it [ozone depletion] doesn't affect them" (Benedick 1991, 60). He suggested that, rather than increase regulations, that small group of individuals should wear broad-brimmed hats and sunglasses. Hodel's aides mistakenly supposed that "the ozone layer" was an unfamiliar abstraction for most people and that, therefore, the public would support Hodel's "plan." The information blitz coordinated by UNEP had been reflected and amplified by the U.S. media to such an extent, however, that many of Hodel's potential supporters found his flippant statement embarrassing. The statement backfired, and Congress, environmentalists, the press, and the public all lampooned Hodel. There was no parallel public education campaign associated with either of the conventions (limiting greenhouse gases and protecting biodiversity) negotiated for the Rio Summit.

Benedick claims that U.S. commitment and leadership were vital to the ozone negotiations. Despite the persistence of conflicting estimates regarding exact damages, the U.S. government took regulatory action against CFCs. Although it was the largest single producer and consumer of suspect chemicals, the United States adopted progressive domestic policies on ozone-depleting chemicals, thus legitimizing its central role in the drive for an international agreement. In 1985, for example, the United States introduced a separate resolution authorizing UNEP to reopen negotiations with a 1987 target for achieving a legally binding protocol for suspect chemicals. Although the European Community opposed the resolution, it passed with the collaboration of Denmark, the Federal Republic of Germany, the Netherlands, and several developing nations (Benedick 1991, 45–46). The U.S. negotiating team sometimes numbered over 30 and included prestigious representatives of at least a dozen government agencies. "As the next-largest delegation had only four members, the Americans were a conspicuous presence" (Benedick 1991, 57). Because European stratospheric scientists did not enjoy the same access to government policy makers as did their U.S. counterparts, they shared information more promptly with U.S. negotiators than with European Community negotiators. U.S. officials, who gave them an attentive hearing, profited by firsthand knowledge of global stratospheric research. This knowledge provided a solid foundation for their leadership in the ozone negotiations.

The only characterization of U.S. behavior at the Rio Summit which even approaches leadership is the "Lone Ranger" role in which Bush was cast. The United States was seen by other nations at UNCED as "dragging its feet" (Stevens 7 June 1992), as a "villain," (Brooke 2 June 1992), as "blocking the summit's progress," (Weisskopf 8 June 1992), and as "having abandoned its role as the world's most environmentally concerned country" (Schneider 5 June 1992). Environmentalists at the summit put the United States at the top of their list of "worst" nations (Brooke 10 June 1992). Another article notes that "the United States, a pioneer of environmental protection, has emerged as a principle obstacle to key agreements on global warming and financial assistance, ceding leadership to less cautious governments in Europe and Japan" (Weisskopf and Preston 3 June 1992). The U.S. leadership that was so significant in negotiating the Montreal Protocol was noticeably absent from Rio.

Another essential element in the Montreal Protocol's success was the cooperation of the private sector and NGOs. Environmental organizations, industrial associations, and private corporations cooperated in the ozone deliberations over several years. Leading producers of CFCs in the United States, such as Dupont, both reinforced and took advantage of the public concern about the ozone layer by publicizing research and development that was directed toward producing safer alternatives. Here, again, the contrast between Montreal and Rio is pronounced. Although environmental organizations participated to some degree in preparations for the Rio Summit, they were marginalized at the conference. Faced with exclusion from UNCED, they participated in an "alternative summit." Rather than cooperation, the private sector presented a hostile front. For example, representatives of both the U.S. biotechnology and energy industries were widely quoted as opposing the proposed treaties.

There were, however, certain elements that remained similar across the two conferences. Both were coordinated by a respected international institution (the United Nations) over a period of several years. Mostafa Tolba, an Egyptian scientist who directed the Montreal Protocol, used his role as a scientist and director of an international forum to encourage multiple nationalities and professional affiliations to participate. Maurice Strong, a Canadian businessman who made his fortune in the oil industry and now is involved in ecotourism, attempted to do the same in his position as director of the Rio Summit. Tolba's professional affiliation and nationality may have contributed to the previously discussed centrality of science as well as encouraged developing countries to cooperate with other nations at the Montreal meeting. Strong's professional affiliation, however, failed to secure the support of the energy industry.

Benedick describes the process and protocol design as the final elements contributing to the success of the ozone negotiations. Both were similar to those used in Rio. In each case the problem was subdivided into smaller components to create more manageable units. Both conferences were preceded by an extensive prenegotiation phase. Although scientific participation was less direct at Rio, both conferences relied on extensive preliminary scientific groundwork to produce their initial drafts of conventions and other formal statements. Finally, the protocol resulting from the conferences was designed to be dynamic. All treaties were written so they could be adapted to new scientific information with minimum changes to the basic structure.

George Bush as the "Lone Ranger"

Given that the United States played a leading role in the Montreal Protocol then gave up that role at UNCED, an examination of U.S. president George Bush's brief appearance at UNCED is instructive. On 12 June 1992 Bush spoke before the delegates assembled at UNCED. In his speech he expressed the U.S. desire to lead the world toward more environmentally sound development policies (Bush 12 June 1992). The speech was delivered within a rhetorical situation created by his own statements regarding environmental regulation in general and the Earth Summit in particular; related statements made by White House staffers and other insiders; and his increasingly urgent campaign for reelection. Responses to his speech, as well as public opinion polls taken after its delivery, indicate that Bush neither presented the United States as an appropriate leader for global environmental governance nor improved his standing in the U.S. presidential race.

The United States bore the brunt of criticism regarding the degree to which the Earth Summit failed. Criticism prior to UNCED focused on U.S. efforts to delete enforceable timetables and deadlines from the climate convention and its refusal to sign the biodiversity convention. Bush's belated decision to attend the summit also provoked negative perceptions of the United States. Environmental Protection Agency administrator Reilly said that during UNCED he felt like he was "bungee jumping where someone else might cut the cord" (Frye 1992, 342). Biotechnology interest groups including the Association of Biotechnology Companies, the Industrial Biotechnology Association, the Pharmaceutical Manufacturers' Association, and the American Intellectual Property Law Association lobbied the Bush Administration to oppose the biodiversity convention. Bush refused to sign the convention, explaining that, as U.S. president, he was required to place U.S. interests first (Frye 1992).

Bush's Address at UNCED

George Bush faced an antagonistic audience when he stepped up to speak before the Earth Summit delegates. Although the brief address formed only a small part of the UNCED puzzle, it offered an opportunity to ameliorate hostility between the United States and other conference attendees. The speech gave Bush a chance to reframe his vision for the politics and ethics of development within the concept of sustainability. Rather than explaining U.S. environmental initiatives as contributory to international sustainable development, however, he labeled sustainability as a nonissue because warnings about the perils of unlimited growth were unwarranted. He immediately followed his perfunctory greeting to conference organizers and delegates with a claim that the "pessimism" of those who have warned of the potential disaster posed by nuclear war and unlimited growth "is unfounded." He then presented a list of misperceptions regarding environmental governance, providing the U.S. corrective for each inaccurate assumption. He followed this section with a list of U.S. plans for environment and development. He concluded by telling delegates that, although their attendance at Rio was commendable, actions taken after the conference concluded would be far more significant. Throughout the speech he emphasized the U.S. role as world leader.

The first major section of Bush's speech lists then corrects five misperceptions. Each begins with the phrase "there are those who say . . ." then proceeds to correct the error. This form undermines any potential for Bush's rhetoric to enable his audience of divided individuals to identify with one another or with him. Both intuitive sense and speech act theory suggest that, when talking with another party, agreements are preferred over disagreements. Additionally, direct disagreement,

especially when used unnecessarily, creates the appearance that the dis-
agreeing party holds authority over other participants (Peterson 1988b).
By repeatedly using this discursive form, Bush created a situation within
which his opponents would lose face if they replaced their current perspective with the corrective he offered. After correcting the rest of the
world's thinking, Bush listed six U.S. goals for Rio. Six times he repeated,
"We come to Rio . . . ," then pointed out how the United States had
outdone (and would continue to outdo) other nations in environmental
conservation.

Bush began his first section by responding to "those who say that
cooperation between developed and developing countries is impossible."
They had only to "come to Latin America" to see how wrong they were.
Those who assumed that environmental protection should be directed
by the state, rather than by the market, were directed to the pollution of
Eastern Europe. Those who feared that "the interests of the status quo"
would retard change were referred to Brazil's policy for managing its
rainforests. Those who questioned the compatibility of "economic growth
and environmental protection" were referred to the United States as an
exemplar of successful integration between economic growth and environmental protection measures. He told those who thought that world
leaders did "not care about the earth" to look at the attendance at the
Rio Conference. It did not help his credibility that, when asked (in May)
if he would attend the entire conference, Bush had replied: "Well, no, I
couldn't possibly do that. We have an election on in the United States
this year" (12 May 1992). Substantial public awareness of the hostility
between the United States and developing nations in the Americas and
the rate at which rainforest harvest continues weakened the validity of
his other correctives.

Bush led into his second section by "inviting [his] colleagues to join
in a prompt start on the [climate change] convention's implementation."
His colleagues, however, were still smarting from his insistence that they
delete all implementation timetables from the convention. Bush then
outlined a U.S. proposal for forest conservation, technology cooperation, increased aid to developing countries, and sharing scientific
knowledge with developing nations. He explained that he had "come
to Rio prepared to continue America's unparalleled efforts to preserve
species and habitat" and was "proud of what [the United States has]
accomplished." Both prior to and during the speech Bush indicated that
the United States was more committed to the issue of forest conserva-

tion than to any other issues dealt with at the conference. There were, however, problems with Bush's plan to conserve the world's forests. Developing countries that hold most of the world's forests were not eager to accept the direction of the man who had refused to sign the biodiversity convention. They saw this refusal as an attempt to block, rather than to facilitate, the spread of science and technology.

Throughout the speech Bush emphasized his role as the leader of the nation whose "record on environmental protection is second to none." He explained his refusal to sign the biodiversity convention as an exemplar of this leadership: "It is never easy; it is never easy to stand alone on principle, but sometimes leadership requires that you do. And now is such a time." He followed this explanation with references to the proud "record on American leadership" (which he intends to "extend") and his "continuing commitment to leadership" (12 June 1992). Yet at Rio Bush was a leader with no followers. Statements prior to the Earth Summit set the tone he would carry throughout his speech. On 12 May Bush announced his decision to attend Rio, declaring that the United States "has been a leader for environmental matters." When discussing his upcoming visit to Rio with reporters he proclaimed that, "when we go to Rio, the U.S. will go proudly as the world's leader, not just in environmental research, but in environmental action" (Bedard 2 June 1992). The day before he delivered his address Bush had announced: "I will stand up for American interests and the interests of a cleaner environment. And if the United States has to be the only nation to stand against the biodiversity treaty as now drawn so be it" (11 June 1992). Given statements such as these, perhaps the speech's emphasis on solitary leadership was inevitable, despite its clash with the emphasis on cooperative leadership stressed by conference organizers and other attendees. Rather than presenting a conciliatory message at Rio, Bush delivered a highly confrontational speech.

Responses to the Address

Conference responses to Bush's plea for a forest convention were positive, with the exception of several developing nations. Although William Reilly echoed the themes Bush had presented, he adopted a less confrontational tone. He began his formal statement to the conference by explaining that, because the delegates are "meeting in the nation that is home to the largest and richest forests on earth, it is fitting that we here give to conservation of forests our highest priority" (1992, 236).

He then explained the U.S. initiative that Bush had presented two days earlier and invited all countries "to join [the United States] in this initiative" (1992, 237). Formal statements made by representatives of developed countries responded positively to Bush's forest initiative and ignored the rest of his address. German chancellor Helmut Kohl said, for example, that, because forests were important to "[him] personally, [he welcomed] the initiative of President George Bush" (1992, 230). Ros Kelly, Australian minister for the arts, sports, and the environment, said that Australia would "support the development of a non-binding statement of forest principles" (1992, 226). Developing countries, however, were less enthusiastic. Malaysian prime minister Mahathir Mohamad tied the biodiversity convention to the forest conservation initiative in his conference address:

> The poor countries have been told to preserve their forests and other genetic resources on the off-chance that at some future date something is discovered which might prove useful to humanity. . . . But now we are told that the rich will not agree to compensate the poor for their sacrifices. The rich argue that the diversity of genes stored and safeguarded by the poor are of no value until the rich, through their superior intelligence, release the potential. . . . The North demands a forest convention. Obviously the North wants to have a direct say in the management of forests in the poor South at next to no cost to themselves. The pittance they offer is much less than the loss of earnings by the poor countries and yet it is made out as a generous concession (1992, 232).

His speech was a thinly veiled reaction to the U.S. refusal to sign the biodiversity convention while pressuring those nations holding most of the earth's forests into preserving, rather than utilizing, their natural resources.

Other responses rebuked Bush more politely. After explaining "why the European Community would have preferred the Convention on Climate Change to establish more precise commitments and objectives," the Commission of the European Community's statement pointed out that it "regards the Convention on Biodiversity as being too timid" (Extracts 1992, 238). It then highlighted the point at which Europe parted company with the United States, despite its belief that the climate change convention was too vague and that the biodiversity convention was inadequate: "the Community has decided nonetheless to sign them both, for there is no denying their importance. . . . I am very pleased . . . by the initiative of Chancellor Kohl in inviting all the signatory states of the convention on climate change to take part in the first follow-up conference to be organized in Germany" (1992, 238). A similar invitation extended by George Bush, the man who insisted on removing the "precise commitments and objectives" from the convention, was ignored. While UNCED secretary-general Maurice Strong mentioned the need for "continuing progress towards an effective regime for conservation and sustainable development of the world's forests," this recommendation was part of a long list of concerns including desertification, war, and trade barriers. He also called for "a new sense of real partnership," because "traditional notions of foreign aid and of the donor-recipient syndrome are no longer an appropriate basis for North-South relations" (1992, 244, 243). Austrian chancellor Franz Vranitzky elaborated on this point, explaining that "sustainable development is indivisible. It is a process based on partnership and sharing, in which we are all students and teachers at the same time. If taken seriously it offers the opportunity for a joint learning process" (1992, 226). If other delegates shared Vranitzky's interpretation of sustainable development as including "joint learning," Bush's offers to "spread green technology," "increase U.S. international environmental aid," and "share [U.S.] science and to lead the world" (Bush 12 June 1992), ranged from irrelevant to anathema. Given the centrality of sustainable development as indicated by its frequent usage in official conference documents, Bush attenuated any opportunities for identification between the United States and other nations by claiming that sustainability was not a principal concern of international development.

Informal responses to Bush's performance at Rio amplified the negative tone. James Brooke reported that, "in contrast to other Western leaders speaking here today, Mr. Bush did not make public any major financial initiatives. . . . Chancellor Helmut Kohl of Germany, a nation widely seen to have assumed a major leadership role here, promised to increase Germany's aid for development of poor countries to 0.7 percent of its gross national product" (Brook 13 June 1992). Later both Japan and France announced specific increases in aid, heightening "the isolation of President Bush from environmental policies advocated by the other six major industrialized nations" (Brook 14 June 1992). The day after Bush delivered his address Tommy Koh, chairman of the conference's main working session, muttered, "this will teach the United Nations not to hold a conference in an American election year"; Michael Oppenheimer, senior scientist for the Environmental Defense Fund, responded: "you can't be treated as a world leader on any issue without being a player on the environment" (Stevens 14 June 1992). Lewis wrote that "the Bush administration appeared divided and paralyzed" (Lewis 15 June 1992). When questioned about the adversarial relationship that had developed between the United States and most other nations, EPA director Reilly explained that the other nations participating in the summit had "misunderstood" the U.S. positions (Weisskopf and Devroy 13 June 1992).

Bush suggested that his position stemmed from his ethical responsibilities to U.S. citizens. Indeed, he was heavily lobbied by several industries that feared negative economic consequences would result from both the climate change and the biodiversity treaties. Even within those industries, however, reactions were mixed. For example, the president and chief executive of Genetech Inc. wrote a letter commending Bush for his refusal to sign the biodiversity convention. Yet a group of scientists employed by Genetech disagreed. They composed a letter of dissent, stating that the convention was important for scientific advancement and that, although it might raise difficulties for some biotechnology companies, its long-term business impact would be favorable. The letter of dissent was sent through electronic mail, reaching at least 2,000 additional employees before its circulation was halted (Lehrman 1992). An article in the *Wall Street Journal* argued that, "because of the stand taken by Bush by not signing the Biodiversity Convention, other countries are likely to retaliate by sharply restricting U.S. access to key raw materials: the genetic and biochemical resources used in agriculture, medicine, and industry" (Reid 8 October 1992). Frye (1992, 344) points out that, given the solitary position of the United States on this issue, the global market may pressure U.S. biotechnology firms to fall in line with the rest of the world. Developing nations probably will prefer to sell their genetic stock to firms that agree to pay royalties, rather than to U.S. firms. As French adds, developing countries will cooperate more willingly with those nations that provide them with needed economic resources (1992). Thus, even among those sources upon which Bush relied for support, criticism overwhelms praise.

A Failed Bid for Leadership

When Bush spoke before the delegates to the United Nations Conference on Environment and Development, he expressed the U.S. desire to lead the global efforts to achieve sustainable development. Yet he diminished any leadership potential by emphasizing the motive of promoting the U.S. economic agenda and his personal agenda of ensuring reelection. By explaining his refusal to sign the biodiversity convention as protection for the U.S. biotechnology industry, Bush contradicted the claim that he could fairly mediate interests in the era of global environmental governance. He promoted past U.S. leadership, and his own agendas, to such a degree that he dismissed or denigrated the concept of sustainable development.

Rio also was a domestic disaster for Bush. Faced with a challenger to his bid for reelection who was steadily gaining ground with labor, Bush was under severe pressure. The lagging U.S. economy contributed increased urgency to the fear that the timetables included in the climate change convention might produce environmental regulations that could eliminate U.S. jobs. He would have alienated important political supporters had he signed the biodiversity convention. U.S. responses to questions from Dunlap et al.'s *The Health of the Planet* public opinion poll, however, which Gallup Associates timed to coincide with UNCED, suggest that this may have been a tactical error. U.S. respondents demonstrated a high degree of concern about the environment. When asked to choose whether environmental concerns should be emphasized over economic concerns or whether economic concerns should be emphasized over environmental concerns, 58 percent chose to emphasize environmental concerns, 26 percent chose to emphasize economic concerns, and 8 percent said they should receive equal emphasis (Dunlap, Gallup, and Gallup 1993, 78). Sixty-five percent said they were willing to pay more for the environment, 24 percent said they were not, and 11 percent were undecided (Dunlap, Gallup, and Gallup 1993, 78). Conventional wisdom says that, although people may respond favorably to questions about the environment, that response does not translate into action. Within the past year, however, 57 percent of the respondents said they had purchased products that were less harmful to the environment even though they were more expensive than an equivalent product that inflicted greater damage on the environment (Dunlap, Gallup, and Gallup 1993, 86). This behavior gains additional significance when one considers that purchasing the "green product" required consumers to change a past purchasing habit. These responses suggest that environmental governance may not be the most propitious international issue for a U.S. president to ignore. It is an issue about which the public has an abundance of information (much of it conflicting) and one to which it is exposed regularly. The significance of human relationships with the natural environment has held a profound place in U.S. tradition, and products of environmental conservation efforts, such as the U.S. National Parks, enjoy high levels of public support and participation (Harrity 1995; Peterson 1986, 1988a). In short, environmental governance is one international issue that U.S. citizens embrace.

George Bush's abrupt dismissal of the belief that humanity urgently needs a new perspective toward development distinguished him from other UNCED delegates and indicated that the recognized leader of at least one industrialized nation felt that blanket support for the concept of sustainable development was not politically expedient. Those documents that attempt to define and explain, however, rather than reject, this increasingly popular term probably contribute more to our understanding of its function in the contemporary debate over the proper intersection of environmental protection and economic development. Most likely, the principles articulated in conference documents will provide a more comprehensive basis for exploring this issue than will speeches, position papers, and informal statements to the press. Therefore, I will close this chapter with a critique of the highly publicized *Rio Declaration.*

Defining Sustainable Development

The *Rio Declaration on Environment and Development* (UNCED 1992), which has come to symbolize the Earth Summit, is a deeply conflicted text that defines principles of sustainable development. This brief guide for future development attempts to provide a working definition for the term that can guide conference delegates representing a diverse array of interests into a new paradigm that integrates environmental protection with economic development. Rhetorical analysis of this text discloses many of the tensions and ambiguities within the idea of sustainable development.

In the preparatory stages of the UNCED three working groups were established to design both substantive and procedural elements of the conference (UNCED 1992 *Agenda 21*). Each working group met four times to prepare for the 1992 conference. These sessions, which were held in

Nairobi (August 1990), Geneva (March, August 1991), and New York (March 1992), were attended by governmental representatives, UN affiliates, and NGOs. During the second preparatory conference Working Group III was assigned the task of creating an "Earth Charter." To assist this process the UNCED secretariat compiled a set of previously adopted principles, to which numerous delegations contributed suggestions, corrections, and objections. During the final preparatory session a committee drafted a consolidated document, retitled the *Rio Declaration on Environment and Development,* which the working group accepted for submission to the conference at Rio. This draft, which was approved during the conference, includes a preamble and 27 principles.

The declaration begins with a preamble that provides UNCED with spatial, temporal, and nominal identity by stating, *"The United Nations Conference on Environment and Development,* Having met at Rio de Janeiro from 3 to 14 June 1992 . . ."* (UNCED 1992 *Rio Declaration,* preamble; Carmin 1994). It then positions UNCED as an attempt to build upon "the United Nations Conference on the Human Environment, adopted at Stockholm on 16 June 1972." Although the declaration is an attempt to conceptualize and suggest implementation strategies for sustainable development, there is no reference to *Our Common Future,* the 1987 UN report that created mass public awareness of the term. Nor does the document mention that the United Nations was acting on *Our Common Future's* recommendation to hold an international meeting to work out strategies for sustainable development when, in 1989, it resolved to hold UNCED (UN Activities 1992, 204).

After establishing an identity and explaining its relationship with the Stockholm conference, UNCED's conveners state their motivation to form "a new and equitable global partnership through the creation of new levels of cooperation among States, key sectors of societies and people" (UNCED 1992 *Rio Declaration,* preamble). Equity among humans emerges here as a key theme of the conference. The preamble also introduces the concept of cooperation, noting that effective international agreements must "respect the interests of all" and recognize that humans exist as part of the earth's interdependent system. Finally, the earth is defined as "our home." The preamble thus defines the conference then rhetorically frames the body of the declaration with the concepts of equity and cooperation. The remainder of the declaration expands on the themes of equity and cooperation as basic to the concept of sustainable development. The declaration fails to recognize, however, incongruities involved in integrating (1) individuality and independence with community and interdependence and (2) humans within the biosphere.

Equity

Principle 1 (UNCED 1992 *Rio Declaration*), which emphasizes the theme of equity, illustrates the dilemma. It states: "Human beings are at the centre of concerns for sustainable development. They are entitled to a healthy and productive life in harmony with nature." To begin with, the emphasis on individual rights, or "entitlements," creates a terministic screen that undermines the theme of cooperation, privileging individuality and independence over community and interdependence. Second, it offers a disproportionate view of the relationship between humans and nature. On the one hand, humans "are at the centre" of things, while, on the other, they live "in harmony with nature." This construct suggests that the environment, or "nature," exists wholly for the purpose of satisfying human concerns. It places humans "at the centre" of sustainable development, despite generally accepted scientific principles indicating a dynamic ecosystem wherein humans interact with numerous other subsystems. Principle 1 implicitly denies any significance to nonhuman nature by limiting concerns for equity and cooperation to the human species. Further, cooperation among humans has been subsumed in a sense of competition over individual rights. Individualized development already has eclipsed ecological sustainability.

Principle 2 reinforces both the emphasis on independence and the environment's subordinate position when it asserts that "States have . . . the sovereign right to exploit their own resources pursuant to their own environmental and developmental policies." This principle responds to southern nations' anger at inequities between their standard of living and that enjoyed by most societies in the Northern Hemisphere by promising the "right" to "exploit" natural resources in the same manner as northern states. Although principle 2 claims that these nations should develop both "environmental and developmental policies," environmental policy designed to "exploit resources" does not suggest an emphasis on environmental protection. As the title suggests, the *Rio Declaration on Environment and Development* was formulated to promote a healthy relationship between environmental protection and economic development. Sustainable development is advanced as the concept that will enable appropriate establishment of that relationship. Yet in its first

two principles the declaration subordinates the environment to development, both at the level of individual rights and that of national
sovereignty. The preamble offers equity and cooperation as guiding concepts in the struggle to design and implement appropriate models of
sustainable development. Because the discussion of equity is couched
in the individualistic language of rights, however, it threatens to devour
any possibility of cooperation.

   Principle 3 continues the trend of valuing economic development
over environmental protection by stating that "the right to development
must be fulfilled to equitably meet developmental and environmental
needs of present and future generations [of humans]." Here development becomes a need as well as a right. This curious construct, however,
induces the reader to see the individualized *right* to development as a
means for securing a more community oriented *need* for development.
Thus, realization of the individual right to development enables us to
perform the ethical act required by our interdependence with future
generations. Principle 3 illustrates the (perhaps serendipitous) creative
potential of juxtaposing incongruous terminologies. The juxtaposition
enriches both constructs: equity infused with community values combined with cooperation infused with respect for diversity create new
possibilities for sustainable development which might allow us to return the natural environment to the playing field.

   Principle 4 follows up on this opportunity by suggesting that "environmental protection shall constitute an integral part of the development
process and cannot be considered in isolation from it." Significantly,
however, although environmental protection is recognized as a positive
act, it remains subordinate to development. Given the strong emphasis
on development up to this point, the power balance between
sustainability and development could have been partially rectified by
reversing the statement in principle 4 to read, "development cannot be
considered in isolation from environmental protection." Instead, this opportunity to revitalize the internal tension within *sustainable development*
slips away. Principle 5 intensifies the emphasis on development, stating
that "eradicating poverty" is "an indispensable requirement for sustainable development." By this point the declaration has construed
sustainability as a weak modifier of *development*, minimizing the possibility that either can provide a sufficiently incongruous perspective on
the other to enliven our conceptual base. Thus, hypotheses and ideolo-
gies drawn from the economic system are allowed to guide our

understanding of what sustainable development is as well as how it should be implemented. In sum, sustainable development is recognizable primarily by its ability to foster economic equality across cultures. The declaration's framers fall into the trap against which Luhmann (1989) cautions, when they limit society to a single function system, in this case the economic system. Sustainable development is thus reduced to the means for extending the numbers of people able to pay for the fulfillment of their own needs and desires, which are defined by the consumptive standards of advanced capitalism.

The theme of equity continues throughout the declaration. Principle 6 states that "the needs of developing countries . . . shall be given special priority." Lest readers assume that the UNCED advocates are giving unfair advantage to these nations, however, it retreats from this statement immediately with the claim that "international actions . . . should also address the interests and needs of all countries." Principle 6 illustrates a familiar double bind. The commission advocates extending equal rights and privileges (regarding the environment within which they live) to all humanity yet does not advocate treating individuals or cultures differently from one another. Yet it is difficult (if not impossible) to ameliorate the existing inequities without directing more resources (time, information, money, access, and so forth) to those who, for whatever reason, survive in disadvantaged positions. This leads to an inequitable situation wherein those who currently retain advantageous positions will receive less of those resources than the previous group. Although the declaration brushes the edge of this issue, it is never resolved.

The political emphasis on individualism comports comfortably with capitalist economic precepts. If sustainable development is economic development that focuses on individual human rights or entitlements, then the free flow of information and goods is essential for its success. Principle 12 promotes free trade, advocating an "open international economic system that would lead to economic growth and sustainable development." Apparently, the environmental degradation that continues to occur when more wealthy nations "help" less wealthy nations develop their natural resources has been forgotten. Despite the high value placed on competition as a leveling force, it is assumed that nations will not engage in competition when environmental protection is involved. For example, southern nations will no longer outbid one another to offer exotic wood at a lower price than their neighbors. Perhaps the free flow of information suggested in principle 10 will counteract any potential problems. Principle 10 states that "each individual shall have appropriate access to information concerning the environment that is held by public authorities. . . . States shall facilitate and encourage public awareness and participation by making information widely available." The assumption here is that access to information provides the conditions necessary for equitable participation in policy formation. Thus, if people have enough information, they will participate in decision-making activities. Second, this participation will provide the guidance necessary for appropriate development to occur. By minimizing the significance of the term *sustainable* and maximizing the significance of *development* the framers of the *Rio Declaration* have relegitimized the practice of considering economic development separately from environmental protection, creating a discursive context within which current patterns of degradation are reinscribed.

Cooperation

The *Rio Declaration* (UNCED 1992) also advocates cooperation among nations in their attempts to attain sustainable development. While equity is described as an ultimate goal toward which sustainable development will lead, however, cooperation refers to the human practices and performances that lead to achievement of the goal. Principles 5, 7, 9, 12, 14, and 27 all begin with the claim that "States shall [or should] cooperate." The statement is embedded in principle 13 and strongly implied in principles 18 and 19. The imperative *shall* communicates a considerably stronger message than does the suggestive *should* and indicates which cooperative actions are most essential. Principles 5 and 27 add increased emphasis by claiming that, in addition to states, all "people" shall cooperate in a set of targeted activities.

Principle 5's mandate that "all States and all people shall cooperate in . . . eradicating poverty as an indispensable requirement for sustainable development" is consistent with the belief that humans form the center of the biosphere and that sustainable development is simply the means whereby human enjoyment and comfort can be maximized while human suffering is minimized. On the other hand, principle 27, which is the final statement, uses the same device to marshal support for all accords accepted at the Earth Summit. It closes the declaration with the directive that "States and people shall cooperate in good faith and in a spirit of partnership in the fulfillment of the principles embodied in this Declaration and in the further development of international law in the field of sustainable development." Rather than mandating action on a specific issue such as human poverty, the final principle provides a summary of the principles in which UNCED was grounded as well as a call to action.

The declaration mandates cooperative action regarding environmental protection as well. Principle 7 directs that "States shall cooperate . . . to conserve, protect and restore the health and integrity of the Earth's ecosystem." This is the only principle in the entire document to make direct reference to the "integrity of the earth." It stands in sharp contrast to statements that "the polluter should, in principle, bear the cost of pollution . . . [if this can be accomplished] without distorting international trade and investment (Principle Sixteen)," "environmental standards . . . applied by some countries may be inappropriate and of unwarranted economic and social cost to other countries (Principle Eleven)," and "States have . . . the sovereign right to exploit their own resources (Principle Two)." Principle 7, which also asks industrialized nations to acknowledge primary responsibility for environmental protection "in view of the pressures their societies place on the global environment," was among the few principles challenged prior to acceptance of the declaration (UN Activities 1992, 224). By mandating collaborative restoration of environmental health, the declaration alludes to an awareness that environmental protection is contingent on shared responsibility and cannot succeed in the competitive arena framed by capitalistic economic precepts.

The final area in which the *Rio Declaration* (UNCED 1992) mandates states to cooperate returns us to the realm of human health. Principle 18 commands that "States shall immediately notify other States of natural disasters or other emergencies [that may harm those other States]." Further, it proclaims that "every effort shall be made by the international community to help States so afflicted." Principle 19 adds that states shall share information "on activities that may have a significant adverse transboundary environmental effect . . . at an early stage." Although the declaration does not shrink from labeling some disasters as "natural," it has no language for labeling those disasters caused by human activity. Instead, natural phenomenon such as hurricanes are termed "disasters," while events such as the Chernobyl explosion (and its aftermath) become more excusable "emergencies." Further, hurricanes are natural, whereas emergencies arising from human manipulation are "other." Perhaps principle 19's "activities" refers to these humanly induced disasters. States also are encouraged to "cooperate to discourage or prevent the relocation . . . of any activities and substances that . . . are found to be harmful to human health" in principle 14.

The declaration limits itself to recommending (as opposed to commanding) cooperation in other arenas in which a mandate might appear to infringe on national sovereignty. States are encouraged to cooperate in facilitating the open exchange of information and products discussed earlier as a means of increasing equity. Principle 9 suggests that "States should cooperate to strengthen endogenous capacity-building . . . through exchanges of scientific and technological knowledge, and by enhancing the development, adaptation, diffusion and transfer of technologies." This cooperative venture is urged as a means of achieving more sustainable economic development. Principle 12 moves directly into the economic realm in urging states to cooperate in promoting an "open international economic system."

Principle 27 closes the document with the promise that, if nations and people cooperate with one another, "good faith" and a "spirit of partnership" will lead to the fulfillment of the principles contained in the *Rio Declaration*. The theme of cooperation suggests that environmental protection is contingent upon and that economic development is enhanced by collaboration and trust among nations.

Cooperative Achievement of Equity

Principles 20 through 23 (UNCED 1992 *Rio Declaration*) acknowledge the existence of inequality among humans and offer the possibility that resonance among function systems could stimulate the emergence of a new identity for sustainable development. Although most of the 27 principles rely on the economic code to characterize both the relationship among humans and that between humans and the larger biosphere, these principles introduce codes from other function systems into the calculation for sustainable development. Women, youth, indigenous peoples, and oppressed people provide the subjects for these principles. It is encouraging to read that women's full participation in decision making is "essential to achieve sustainable development," with no caveat limiting the claim to situations in which it is "cost-effective." Rather than invoking the economic code of ability/inability to pay, this principle focuses on the political code of being in/out of decision-making roles. Principle 21 claims that by mobilizing the "creativity, ideals and courage of the youth . . . [we can] achieve sustainable development and ensure a better future for all." Here the code of better/worse, which represents the education function system, delineates sustainable development. Principle 22 directs nations to "recognize and duly support their [indigenous people's] identity, culture and interests and enable their effective participation in the achievement of sustainable development." The focus on cultural identity suggests the possibility of introducing questions of immanence and transcendence (drawn from the realm of religion) into the discussion, and the emphasis on participation maintains a space for political questions relating to involvement in decision-making roles. Principle 23 introduces the code of legality/illegality in advocating that "natural resources of people under oppression, domination and occupation shall be protected." Israel opposed the reference to "people under oppression" in principle 23. The United States, acting in Israel's behalf, led an agreement that this reference be removed from *Agenda 21* but remain in the declaration (UN Activities 1992, 224). Although science emerges in a few instances throughout the declaration, its consistent domination by economics dampens its ability to provide an opposing perspective. In contrast, these four principles temporarily break the stranglehold of the economic function system by introducing and developing tenets drawn from law, politics, religion, and education. By linking sustainable development to these social systems, the declaration again alludes to the importance of interdependence. The overall form and content of the declaration, however, ensure that these interdependencies are confined to systems constructed by and for humans.

Even those principles (with the single exception of principle 7 [UNCED 1992 *Rio Declaration*]) which discuss environmental protection adopt a reactive mode. Principle 13, for example, recommends that states shall "develop national law regarding liability and compensation." Although the declaration encourages international cooperation to promote economic systems that allow more accurate assessment of the costs of environmental degradation, require polluters to bear the cost of pollution, and lead to sustainable development, the dominant terministic screen is drawn from economics. In the rare instances in which a terminology from science (ecology) is drawn upon, its power is minimized by caveats about cost-effectiveness. By reinforcing state autonomy without advocating unified standards for acceptable versus unacceptable action, the declaration fails to address the problem of a commonly shared earth and the environmental interdependencies among states.

Evaluations of the Summit

We are left wondering to what extent the Earth Summit was a success or a failure. To the extent that it failed, should the United States bear the brunt of the blame? Or perhaps systemic flaws inherent to a meeting of this type doomed the conference from the outset. Finally, examining the *Rio Declaration* enables an exploration of what happens when a contested term such as *sustainable development* becomes the guiding concept for an international political event.

Reviews of the 1992 UNCED and the role played by the United States are mixed. Maurice Strong, the conference organizer, stated that he was "disappointed we don't have targets and timetables" for the climate convention. Without them "we have to push like hell to make sure implementation takes place" (Brooke 15 June 1992). He told wealthy nations that "no one place on the planet can remain an island of affluence in a sea of misery. . . . We're either going to save the whole world, or no one will be saved" (Weisskopf and Preston 3 June 1992). Strong was disappointed that pledges for increased aid to developing countries (which primarily came from Germany, Japan, and France) did not bring the total close to the $125 billion a year he had asked for. Many delegates claimed that the conference would have been more productive had the United States adopted a more cooperative stance. Events such as the White House leakage of Reilly's confidential memo and a senior administrator's reference to the summit as "a circus" led to an impression that the U.S. delegation in Rio was paralyzed by cynical political maneuvering (Brooke 12 June 1992b).

By the time the summit concluded, the United States had alienated both developing and developed countries. Attempts to pressure Austria, the Netherlands, and Switzerland resulted in accusations that the United States was "shooting sparrows with a cannon" (Robinson and Weisskopf 9 June 1992). Britain, France, and Japan joined forces in an unsuccessful attempt to persuade Bush to sign the biodiversity convention (Stevens 9 June 1992). At one point Bush lashed out at Germany and Japan, accusing them of "Bush-bashing" and characterizing their pledge to increase aid to developing nations as a "guilt-induced effort to be politically correct" (Devroy 10 June 1992). The Japanese responded quietly that they "have never engaged in Bush-bashing." The German response was more heated: "Guilty about what? The war? The Nazis? The last 500 years? If it's wealth we should be guilty for, the Americans are the richest of all of us. But we are the ones who feel the responsibility to help others" (Weisskopf 11 June 1992). Exchanges such as these dismayed Australian minister of the environment Ros Kelly, who claimed that the United States was "abdicating their leadership role." She added that the United States is "the biggest economic power in the world; they should take a leadership role at this conference and they're not doing it. It seems a great shame" (Robinson and Weisskopf 6 June 1992).

On the other hand, Richard E. Benedick, the former State Department official who had led the U.S. negotiating team for the Montreal Protocol during 1986 and 1987, was more optimistic. He claimed that "the history books will refer back to this day as a landmark in a process that will save the planet from deterioration." He said that the summit "should not be judged by the immediate results, but by the process it sets in motion" (Stevens 14 June 1992). Michael Zammit-Cutajar, the executive secretary of the UNCED negotiating committee, was optimistic about the future of the climate convention. Although individual signatories still needed to ratify the conventions in appropriate national forums, Zammit-Cutajar was confident that, despite the U.S. refusal to set target dates, "the treaty [would] be in force within two years" ("With Climate" 13 June 1992). Greg Easterbrook (1992), in the *New Republic*, claims that negative evaluations of U.S. behavior at the Rio Summit are inaccurate and overblown. He writes that the press was so busy covering Bush's blunders at the summit that it ignored significant ecological progress that is occurring in the United States. Easterbrook suggests that Reilly wielded more power than indicated in press accounts describing him as a mere pawn before the White House Council on Competitiveness. After all, Reilly persuaded Bush to attend the Earth Summit over the objections of administration figures, including, but not limited to, members of the council.

A third perspective, represented by Baruch Boxer (1992–93), who has served as a consultant to the UNEP and the White House Council on Environmental Quality, is that conferences such as the Rio Summit "are not the way to preserve the environment" (42). Boxer claims that those who blame the Bush Administration for the conference's frustrating conclusion are mistaken. He argues that we cannot tackle the fundamental conflicts between developed and developing nations in public forums such as the UNCED because the publicity created by an international summit encourages self-serving grandstanding. While Boxer does not claim that these fundamental conflicts will dissolve by themselves, he claims that resources are better spent "finding workable, short-run technical and policy solutions" (43). Boxer argues that, since comprehensive global agreements are doomed to failure, extravaganzas such as the Rio Summit do more harm than good, for they raise unwarranted expectations and encourage antagonism between conferees.

Indeed, conferences such as the Earth Summit do not provide forums for crafting specific techniques and methodologies. Rather, they prepare the way for the development of global environmental governance. French (1992) claims that, to achieve sustainable development, the international governing process must be opened to public participation, including those nations and individuals who traditionally have been excluded. A key question for determining the success of UNCED will be how active a role the United Nations Commission on Sustainable Development (CSD), which was created at Rio, plays in global environmental governance, for the *Rio Declaration*'s goal of sustainable development is meaningful only if it is achieved at a global level. On 14 June 1993 the CSD met for its first substantive session. Meetings continued through 25 June, with broad participation from developing nations, nations "in transition" (former members of the Soviet bloc), and industrialized nations (UN Activities 1993). The second session, which was held 25–27 May 1994, began an overview of implementation issues for *Agenda 21*. Several members expressed the view that, although sustainable development continues to evolve conceptually, it maintains a close connection with the concept of "equity." When discussion of implementation difficulties led to the question of compliance control, the Montreal Protocol was suggested as a model. Participants engaged in a polarized debate over the role of NGOs in implementing sustainable development. One group advocated expanding current "right to know or . . . right to be heard" privileges, while the other side pressed for additional rules and criteria to which NGOs would be held responsible before receiving access to information (UN Activities 1994). The commission continues struggling with thorny issues of implementation which could not be resolved at Rio.

Work on the conventions also has continued. The Convention on Climate Change, for example, had received 166 signatures by its 19 June 1993 deadline. It entered into force on 21 March 1994, and the first Conference of Signatory Parties was scheduled for 1995 (UN Activities 1995b). The United States joined other industrialized nations in supporting the Convention on Biological Diversity when newly elected president Bill

Clinton signed the convention in 1993. An international group of scientists and diplomats presented signatory parties with a proposal for establishing an international network of ecological databases which would provide scientists from developing countries with broad access to ecological data (Stone 1994, 1155). One hundred and six nations attended the first Conference of the Parties, held in Nassau, Bahamas, from 28 November to 9 December 1994 (UN Activities 1995a, 38), yet the convention remained controversial in the United States. Although the Senate Foreign Relations Committee approved the convention, Senator Robert Dole led a move that postponed Senate action until the conclusion of the 103d Congress, and "prospects for passage in the 104th Congress are dim" (Robbins 1995, 4). The means of implementing sustainable development which emerged from the Rio Summit have yet to be universally embraced in the industrialized world, to say nothing of those nations in which economic equity (with more wealthy nations) remains the primary goal.

Examining the definition of *sustainable development* which emerged from the UNCED leads to profound reservations associated with the complexities implicit in designing and implementing environmental protection programs that require fundamental restructuring of perspectives. Despite attempts to work across political and disciplinary boundaries, the working definition of *sustainable development* that emerges in the *Rio Declaration on Environment and Development* fails to fundamentally alter the traditional perspective on development. Instead, as *development* increasingly overshadowed *sustainability*, the synthetic possibility offered by *sustainable development* receded into the distance.

Chapter 5

Subverting the
Culture of Expertise
Community Participation in Development Decisions

If you're going to kill all our buffalo, just as well shoot us off too.
Frank LaViolette, Cree elder,
Fort Smith Native Band, Northwest Territories

The Cree and Dene/Metis people share a managed wilderness in and around Canada's Wood Buffalo National Park (NP) with the world's largest free-roaming herd of bison. The world's single remaining free-living flock of whooping cranes nests in the park each summer. Wood Buffalo NP, which has been designated as a World Heritage Site by the United Nations Educational, Scientific, and Cultural Organization (UNESCO), also provides habitat for wolf, moose, and countless other significant (although perhaps less charismatic) species of animals and plants. Analysis of discourse generated as part of a decision-making process regarding the management of wildlife disease in the region illustrates how diverse the perspectives toward appropriate sustainable development patterns can be. During hearings conducted to allow local residents to explain their vision of appropriate development, government scientists' technological discourse combined with the hearing manager's mechanistic reliance on technique to muffle competing interpretations of appropriate sustainable development offered by human residents of the region. The communication forms favored by those who managed the hearings centralized aspects of inquiry that further validated the scientific establishment while pushing others that were equally (and sometimes more) important to local communities to the periphery.

This conflict differs fundamentally from the sustainable development discussion held at the United Nations Conference on Environment and Development (UNCED). Delegates to the Rio Conference focused on the challenges of sustaining human development, almost to the exclusion of other life forms, and devoted little attention to daily interactions between humans and other animals. Residents of the Wood Buffalo NP region, on the other hand, live in a world in which interaction between humans and wild animals is fundamental to their daily practices. Even in this World Heritage Site, however, development pressures brought on by rapid human population increases, globalization of markets, and political changes exist. As the earth's human population grows by 92 million people annually, humans and their technology increasingly dominate every part of the earth's landscape (Postel 1992). Unprecedented rates of technological change have eliminated the classical wilderness environment from the earth. Even landscapes across which humans only travel bear traces of human civilization in the air, in the water, and on the land. *Wilderness* traditionally has been described as an area untouched by human society, or the condition of nature prior to the influence of technological civilization. Although human society has demonstrated considerable reluctance to admit the passing of classical wilderness, Botkin argues that, "since there is no longer any part of the earth that is untouched by our actions in some way, . . . there are no wildernesses in the sense of places completely unaffected by people" (Botkin 1990, 194). Analogously, there are no wildlife completely unaffected by people. Human population growth and technology increasingly threaten wildlife populations because of habitat conversion, fragmentation, and loss. Most ecologists now consider it more realistic to consider even large tracts of wildlife habitat as "managed" wilderness. In a managed wilderness ecologists rely on scientific facts to systematically privilege the nonhuman, indigenous life of that region. The management task is far from straightforward, however, because differing human situations lead to contradictory interpretations of the facts. As people talk about wildlife with which they share a region, they concurrently redefine and solidify aspects of their relationship with their nonhuman neighbors. Exploring this discourse can help us better understand how sustainable development is negotiated in the public forum as well as how symbol systems influence and are influenced by that negotiation. It also suggests that sustainable development concerns can encompass a broad range of life forms, including, but not limited to, humans.

Conflicts over wildlife management are important in themselves because their resolution will help to determine the kind of world we choose to sustain. They also provide rich opportunities to explore the relationships between the material and symbolic environment. Because wildlife, by definition, are not domesticated, they provide a material exemplar for the recalcitrance that constantly buffets our symbolic hierarchies. Unlike our meticulously manicured pets, they wander in and out of our lives at will. They are not immune to human control, for people hunt deer for food or sport, domesticate elephants for work, drive numerous species to premature extinction, and preserve others in captivity. Our exercise of that control, however, is bounded by the fact that they cease to exist *as wildlife* when we kill, tame, exterminate, or preserve them in zoological gardens. It seems that, as quickly as we devise a symbolic logic that makes sense out of the human relationship with other species in a region, we stumble into new problems created by a web of competing function systems and material realities. In the case explored here, for example, economic incentives combined with a growing human population led to increased nonindigenous human settlement in the region. Government subsidies for beef made otherwise marginal grazing land near Wood Buffalo NP economically desirable to ranchers. International markets promised by new trade agreements encouraged ranchers to increase the size of their cattle herds and made even the proximity of a communicable disease an economic liability. The disease had been introduced into the wildlife population as part of an attempt to avoid public outrage over "inhumane" treatment of wildlife in another region.

The controversy surrounding management policy for Wood Buffalo NP and the surrounding region provides a case study of the difficulties intrinsic to forming a sustainable development policy that explicitly accounts for the relationships between humans and other species inhabiting the same area. Aboriginal Americans who live in the Wood Buffalo NP region accounted for claims about bison disease in much the same way they would have accounted for claims about human disease. Canadian government representatives and most scientists, however, treated the bison and their disease as disembodied abstractions. Not surprisingly, the two groups disagree about what sort of development should be sustained in the region. While I make no attempt to champion any of the management strategies produced by these contrasting accounts, rhetorical analysis of the public hearings exposes patterns of interaction which offer clues to why development policies that seem inappropriate to many area residents have been approved yet not implemented. My dominant theme is that the quality of this debate surrounding wildlife disease policy as well as other debates over sustainable development can be improved by cultivating opportunities to include multiple stakeholders in governance decisions (Peterson and Horton 1995). Only under these conditions can we transcend enough of the incongruities between the multiple perspectives in play when development decisions are made to achieve the sense of community needed for their successful implementation.

I first describe Environmental Impact Analysis (EIA), which is the process local residents were required to use if they desired to participate in the decision about what sort of development would be sustained in their home. I then review the story of the decimation and subsequent recovery of bison in North America. After briefly discussing the history of bison disease in the Wood Buffalo NP region, I explore rhetorical dimensions of this conflict over appropriate development patterns by analyzing discourse drawn from public hearings regarding the disposition of bison herds that roam sections of Alberta and the Northwest Territories. Transcripts of the hearings conducted by the panel charged with deciding how best to respond to diseases carried by some of the bison illuminate dimensions of *mechanistic* communication, *poetic* communication, and their relationship to the function systems within which scientific inquiry and policy formation typically occur. The chapter focuses on the interaction between members of the (1) Northern Diseased Bison Environmental Assessment Panel, (2) Agriculture Canada (an agency roughly analogous to the U.S. Department of Agriculture), and (3) aboriginal bands that live in the region.

Revitalizing the Public Sphere

In 1982 Goodnight wrote that "many forms of social persuasion are festooned with the trappings of deliberation, even while they are designed to succeed by means inimical to knowledgeable choice and active participation. . . . [I]f the public sphere is to be revitalized, then those practices which replace deliberative rhetoric by substituting alternative modes of invention and restricting subject matter need to be uncovered and critiqued" (215, 227). In this case the Cree and Dene/Metis bands, which rely on the bison for subsistence and the provisions of "Treaty Eight" to ensure their continued access to bison and other natural resources, constitute the most directly affected public. The public hearings analyzed here are mandated as a means of enabling them to participate in development decisions through the EIA process. Both the hearing structure and the communication forms privileged by those managing the policy-making process, however, nullified possibilities for public deliberation.

Environmental Impact Analysis represents an approach to development policy which emphasizes synthetic, rather than analytic, problem solving. It was initiated in a U.S. statute signed by President Richard Nixon in January 1970 and is now used in at least 30 other countries, including Canada. A 1982 study of the implementation of EIA in the United States reported that, although some personnel continued to resist the interdisciplinary, integrative approach to planning required to perform EIA, progress was occurring. The study also concluded, however, that "public input to the EIA document was not regarded by government officials as particularly useful. . . . [T]he public was generally perceived to be poorly informed on the issues and unsophisticated in considering risks and trade-offs. . . . Public participation was accepted as inevitable, but sometimes with reluctance" (Caldwell 1988, 80).

These skeptical government officials are joined by many scientists in their claim that public involvement in environmental assessment is at best irrelevant and at worst detrimental to development decisions. Public perceptions are assumed to be based on irrational, subjective, and ignorant fears, as opposed to rational, objective, and informed planning. When describing concerns the public has expressed regarding the potential health hazard presented by pesticide residues in food and drinking water in the United States, for example, Carpenter (1991) claims that "the future of the world's food supply is too valuable to be trusted to uninformed public opinion and perceptions whipped to a panic. . . . What we as a society must continue to do is regulate pesticides strictly and appropriately based on risk and benefit, not fear and prejudice" (39). The assumption underlying Carpenter's appeal for regulation based upon balancing risk and benefit is that risk is a stable entity that can be universally defined, measured, and evaluated. His perspective represents that of experts who presume that tools and criteria constructed within a narrowly defined technical context are not only appropriate but also sufficient for assessing risks that develop significance extending beyond the technical context wherein they are defined. Although tools necessarily reflect the values of their builders, these values are not specified as such. Instead, their existence is obfuscated by claims of rationality, objectivity, and informed expertise. The tools and criteria employed by the general public for assessing risk are, on the other hand, described as socially constructed instruments that reflect their users' individual and cultural biases.

Members of the lay public certainly construct perspectives based on their subjective experiences and motives. Yet scientists and technicians do not reach decisions in a void (Halloran 1984). Because one does not cease to be human upon becoming a scientist, cultural influences such as disciplinary training, personal experience, and funding sources influence both what questions are asked and what kind of answers are possible. Halloran (1984), Prelli (1989), and Waddell (1990), among others, have argued that science is socially constructed and, while not exclusively rhetorical, has rhetorical dimensions. By extension environmental assessments derived from public perceptions, environmental assessments derived from expert perceptions, and the dichotomies between the two are problematic social constructions.

Wood Bison History

Taxonomists traditionally have categorized the North American bison into two subspecies based on phenotype: wood bison and plains bison. Although they can be similar in appearance, wood bison typically are larger, have a higher and more square back hump, and have different pelage (hair coat) characteristics. For example, wood bison do not display the wooly chaps characteristic of plains bison and have a pointed, rather than rounded, beard (NDBEAP 1990 *Report;* Michiel 1990; Geist 1991). When relocated to habitats historically used by plains bison, however, wood bison develop hair coats similar to those of plains bison. For this and other reasons Geist (1991) argues that the wood bison is an ecotype, rather than a separate subspecies.

Approximately 3,400 bison roamed the region in and around Wood Buffalo NP in 1991 (Carbyn, Oosenbrug, and Anions 1993, xxv). They are descendants of an estimated 60 million bison that roamed the North American continent in 1800. During the late eighteenth and early nineteenth centuries plains bison ranged from Mexico and Florida in the south, Pennsylvania in the east, northern California in the west, and north into the grasslands of the four western Canadian provinces. During the same period somewhere between 50,000 and 165,000 wood bison inhabited the aspen park land and boreal forests of northern Alberta, Saskatchewan, British Columbia, and southern Northwest Territories. Yet, by 1889, roughly 800 animals—approximately 550 wood bison and 250 plains bison—remained (Michiel 1990; Carbyn, Oosenbrug, and

Anions 1993). Biologists are uncertain about the role of overhunting, disease, or other factors in the declining wood bison numbers, because the herds lived in remote areas that were sparsely populated by humans. Conversely, the plains bison were decimated by meat and hide hunters on a massive scale. Additional hunting was motivated by U.S. and Canadian policies for managing the movements of aboriginal people which reasoned that "Indians" could be more effectively discouraged from escaping the reservations designated for their settlement if nonreservation food sources were eliminated. Bison should, therefore, be eliminated, because they constituted the single most important source for aboriginal people's food and fiber (McCreight 1950; McHugh 1979, 283–90).

Ironically, it was a hunter who retrieved the plains bison from the brink of extinction (Michiel 1990). Six bison calves wandered into Samuel Walking Coyote's hunting camp near the Milk River in the spring of 1873. For some reason Walking Coyote, who had spent the winter with the area's Blackfoot Indians, was moved to spare the little band of strays. He took them with him when he returned home to the Flathead Reservation (in western Montana). Two of the calves died on the journey, but 4 survived. By 1884 Walking Coyote had a herd of 13 bison. When his neighbors began to complain because Walking Coyote did not provide adequate fencing for the bison, he sold all but one to Charles Allard and Michel Pablo. When Allard died, his family sold his share to ranches across the United States. Most of today's U.S. bison descended from Allard's stock (Michiel 1990).

Pablo's herd grew until, in 1904, his neighbors began complaining. The U.S. government offered him $25 a head for the bison. Since he had paid nearly $200 a head, he decided that, rather than selling, he would relocate to a more remote ranch in Alberta, Canada. When he approached the Canadian government with a request to be allowed to purchase land, Banff National Park personnel offered to buy the herd. Following brief negotiations, he sold his bison to the Canadian government for $245 a head. Over the next five years 700 animals from this herd were sent to various Canadian locations, where the population expanded rapidly. By 1925 the plains bison appeared to be safe from extinction (Michiel 1990).

The wood bisons' saga, perhaps because their range was smaller and more remote, is less carefully documented than that of their plains cousin. Their remote range contributes to vague estimates of how low their population dipped and in what year the low occurred. Because their location prevented the wholesale slaughter that the Canadian and U.S. governments pursued with plains bison, their population numbers never plummeted so low as those of the plains bison. The herds in the Wood Buffalo NP region began recovering sometime during the late 1890s, when the Canadian government assigned six rangers to protect the herd (Aniskowicz 1990). By the time Wood Buffalo NP was established, in 1922, there were approximately 1,500 wood bison in the area (Carbyn, Oosenbrug, and Anions 1993, 19). There is no evidence that bovine brucellosis or tuberculosis was present in the wood bison populations at this time (M. J. Peterson 1991; Carbyn, Oosenbrug, and Anions 1993, 19).

The wood bison's robust recovery was disrupted, however, by a response to public outcry which occurred miles to the south. A large herd of plains bison in Buffalo NP, near Wainwright, Alberta, had been exposed to brucellosis and tuberculosis by nearby domestic livestock. Despite the presence of these diseases, the plains bison population was growing faster than available habitat within the park could support, and bison increasingly wandered into the area grazed by growing herds of domestic cattle (the Buffalo NP was dissolved during World War II, partially because of continuing conflict with ranchers). Ranchers were under government direction to eradicate brucellosis and tuberculosis from their herds. They claimed that eradication efforts were stymied by the presence of bison that had contracted both diseases through previous contacts with livestock and could serve as reservoirs for reinfection of their cattle. Ranchers demanded that the number of bison be reduced, and park managers responded to their demands by slaughtering 1,847 bison during the winter of 1923–24 (Michiel 1990; Aniskowicz 1990; M. J. Peterson 1991). A vocal segment of the Canadian public was outraged at what they perceived to be an inhumane and wasteful massacre. Bovine tuberculosis was diagnosed in slaughtered bison, but none was tested for brucellosis, although gross lesions consistent with this disease were observed. Even after the unpopular slaughter was concluded, the bison population at the Buffalo NP remained too large to be contained within park boundaries. Beleaguered managers, who were seeking to satisfy area ranchers while avoiding the public outcry that the previous slaughter had precipitated, found an attractive receptacle for the "excess" bison in Wood Buffalo NP. Assuming (correctly) that they could avoid a public confrontation by relocating the bison to a remote region, wildlife managers sent 6,673 predominantly young plains bison from Buffalo NP to Wood Buffalo NP between 1925 and 1928 (M. J. Peterson 1991; Carbyn, Oosenbrug, and Anions, 1993).

Scientists, both within and outside the government, opposed this move because they objected to translocating bison carrying tuberculosis, and probably brucellosis, into an area where the diseases had never been identified. There is no evidence that bovine brucellosis or tuberculosis was present in the wood bison populations prior to this translocation (M. J. Peterson 1991; Carbyn, Oosenbrug, and Anions 1993, 19). Scientists also feared that the native wood bison phenotype would disappear because of interbreeding with plains bison (M. J. Peterson. 1991). Confirmation of their fears regarding both interbreeding and disease introduction came in 1940, when it was assumed that "pure" strains of wood bison had become extinct. Systematic brucellosis testing of bison in the region was not initiated until 1959. When Wood Buffalo NP bison were tested for brucellosis during herd reductions conducted between 1959 and 1974, approximately one-third tested positive (Choquette et al. 1978). Both bovine brucellosis and tuberculosis remain present in bison in Wood Buffalo NP (Tessaro, Forbes, and Turcotte 1990).

Brucellosis, which appears to be the more controversial disease, causes abortion in many mammals. This concerns natural resource managers both because of the potential for transmission of the disease to domestic livestock and the possible impact on bison and elk herds (M. J. Peterson 1991). The form of brucellosis found in bison (*Brucella abortus*) is transmitted in mammals primarily by oral contact with aborted fetuses, contaminated placentas, and discharges (Blood, Henderson, and Radostits 1979; Witter 1981). In 1989 U.S. Department of Agriculture epidemiologists attributed a brucellosis outbreak in cattle near Dubois, Wyoming, to contact with infected Greater Yellowstone Area bison and / or elk (Bridgewater 1989), confirming ranchers' fears that wildlife serve as an active reservoir for reinfecting domestic livestock. Because brucellosis is communicable to humans under natural conditions, its relationship to human health also forms a significant dimension in policy deliberations (M. J. Peterson 1991).

Female bison often have rates of abortion (or birth of nonviable calves) greater than 90 percent during the first pregnancy after they are infected with *Brucella abortis*. During the second pregnancy after infection bison abortion rates drop to about 20 percent, and by the third pregnancy they approach zero, owing to naturally acquired resistance to abortion (Davis et al. 1991). Although brucellosis affects the number of viable calves born in the lifetime of an individual bison cow, it does not appear to produce long-term declines in populations of these long-lived animals (M. J. Peterson 1991; Peterson, Grant, and Davis 1991a, b). In fact, after plains bison carrying brucellosis and tuberculosis were introduced, the number of bison in Wood Buffalo NP increased from approximately 7,500 to a peak between 10,000 and 15,000 in the mid-1930s (NDBEAP 1990 *Report*, 4–7; M. J. Peterson 1991; Carbyn, Oosenbrug, and Anions 1993, 27).

Disappearance of the native wood bison phenotype, however, is questionable. In 1957 an isolated herd of what appeared to be wood bison was discovered in the northwestern portion of Wood Buffalo NP. Park employees transferred 37 animals from this herd to the Mackenzie Bison Sanctuary and Elk Island NP, where they have prospered. Bison in these two herds are as close to "pure" wood bison as can be found. Their distinctiveness, however, is the subject of considerable debate among scientists. Those who support eradication of the Wood Buffalo NP herd argue that contact between animals from the Wood Buffalo NP and the Mackenzie Bison Sanctuary or Elk Island NP will endanger the genetic purity of the latter two herds. Conversely, Geist (1991) argues that there is no valid taxonomic distinction between wood and plains bison and that the interbreeding that has occurred in Wood Buffalo NP "need not be a tragedy for conservation" (283). Other opponents of eradication argue that, because the (relatively) pure wood bison herds descended from only 37 animals, they have undergone extensive inbreeding and contain little genetic diversity. The Wood Buffalo NP herd, on the other hand, they argue, contains a large and diverse genetic reservoir that should be preserved. They add that both air and ground activity of the eradication process would "damage habitat in the park and cause a great deal of disturbance to all wildlife in the area" (Aniskowicz 1990, 38). Thus, disagreements that begin at the taxonomical level carry through into the arena of policy making.

Although scientists can agree to operate according to the code of truth or falsity, they differ about the appropriate data for determining truth, and, when the scientific question emerges as a political or economic issue, they disagree further. When moving beyond questions of "what is" to "what should be," scientists move into the shadowy realm of interpretation, for which their function system provides no guidelines. For example, even if scientists were able to ascertain the exact level of disruption which would accompany an eradication program, the code of truth or falsity could not determine whether that disruption or the presence of brucellosis was the preferable condition. To answer that question adequately, science would require supplementation from political, economic, and other function system codes.

Policy Options Considered

When policies concerning wildlife disease management are formed, proponents generally justify their enactment by claiming that their policies are based on "objective" findings. Yet analysis of the justifications for wildlife management policies approved for Wood Buffalo NP discloses potentially controversial assumptions upon which the management strategies were based. In other words, information used to justify one policy could just as easily justify several alternative policies.

As its name implies, the Northern Diseased Bison Environmental Assessment Panel was mandated to determine how to manage the "bison disease problem" in and around Wood Buffalo NP, rather than to determine whether a disease problem existed (see M. J. Peterson 1991, for a more detailed discussion). The panel's final report claims that the number of bison had been decreasing for 20 years, "due in part to disease, drownings, predation, and habitat changes" (NDBEAP 1990 *Report*, 11). Upon contrasting this situation to that of the Mackenzie Bison Sanctuary, where a bison population that was free of bovine brucellosis and tuberculosis rapidly increased in numbers during the same period, the panel assumed that the decline seen in Wood Buffalo NP was caused primarily by disease.

The panel considered five major options for managing bovine brucellosis and tuberculosis in Wood Buffalo NP. The first (despite the panel's mandate) was to accept the risk currently posed by the disease and do nothing. Not too surprisingly, the panel concluded that "the current situation is unacceptable because brucellosis and tuberculosis are unlikely to disappear spontaneously from the bison population, and the risk will continue to exist" (NDBEAP 1990 *Report*, 11). This conclusion relies on the assumptions that, first, the presence of brucellosis and tuberculosis constituted an undesirable risk and, second, that effective management policy should eliminate the risk. Questions exist, however, regarding what that risk is and to whom. The second alternative involved containment of the risk by methods such as fencing or maintaining a buffer zone free of bison and cattle around the park. The panel rejected this alternative because it was not "infallible" (with respect to the goal of risk elimination) and was expensive (NDBEAP 1990 *Report*, 29). The panel also rejected both treatment and vaccination because "there [was] no suitable vaccine for either bovine brucellosis or tuberculosis and no method of mass immunization . . . practical to use . . . to eliminate the diseases" (NDBEAP 1990 *Report*, 31). The fourth alternative rejected by the panel was a testing and salvage operation in which all bison in the region would be tested for brucellosis and tuberculosis, those that tested positive would be slaughtered, and those that tested negative would be retained. Rather than pursuing any of these four alternatives, the panel recommended the slaughter of all bison in the area, concluding that "eradication of the existing bison population is the only method of eliminating the risk of transmission of bovine brucellosis and tuberculosis from bison in and around Wood Buffalo National Park to domestic cattle, wood bison, and humans" (NDBEA 1990, *Report* 32). The panel assumed that, upon replacement with noninfected bison, the region would again support a population similar in numbers to the 12,000-head herd recorded during the 1940s. Further, the only way to guarantee that bison would not expose cattle to bovine brucellosis was to slaughter all the bison.

Alternative Explanations for Population Decline

A comparison of the diseased bison populations in the Wood Buffalo NP area and the Greater Yellowstone Area (U.S.), however, raises several complications (Peterson M. J. 1991). Both the Yellowstone NP and Grand Teton NP bison herds are infected with brucellosis. In contrast to the situation in Wood Buffalo NP, where bison numbers are declining, the Greater Yellowstone Area "bison brucellosis problem" is characterized by increasing bison numbers (Meagher 1989). The livestock industry perceives the Greater Yellowstone Area bison herds as a threat because they have been rapidly increasing in size, thus increasing the area over which they range and the probability of their contact with domestic cattle. Further, Grand Teton NP bison were brucellosis free when they escaped from captivity in 1970 yet infected when first retested in 1989. The herd has grown exponentially since 1970, and computer simulations indicate that the herd would have grown at a similar rate with or without brucellosis (Peterson, Grant, and Davis 1991b).

Given that brucellosis does not appear to alter population size or growth substantially in the Greater Yellowstone Area, the assumption that eradication of the disease is essential to healthy bison populations in the Wood Buffalo NP region is questionable.

Additional factors cast doubt on whether disease is the primary cause of declining bison numbers in Wood Buffalo NP. Although tuberculosis and brucellosis probably were introduced with the plains bison from Wainwright during the 1920s, bison numbers rapidly increased initially and remained high into the 1960s. Other pertinent hypotheses concern the ability of the park to support bison. The construction of the W. A. C. Bennet Dam on the Peace River altered the hydrological regime of the Peace-Athabasca Delta by stopping spring flooding since 1974. Sedges, which dominated the large delta meadows and upon which bison relied for winter forage, are being replaced by less nutritious grasses and aspen because of decreased flooding (NDBEAP 1990 *Report*, 9; Carbyn, Oosenbrug, and Anions 1993). This change alone might significantly decrease the area's carrying capacity for bison. If the carrying capacity has declined, perhaps the peak population from the 1940s (approximately 12,000 head) is an unrealistic expectation. The decrease in bison numbers at Wood Buffalo NP is almost certainly due to multiple interacting factors, including, but not limited to, disease (M. J. Peterson 1991; Carbyn, Oosenbrug, and Anions 1993).

In the face of these uncertainties it follows that the roots of policy recommendations will be shrouded in cultural expectations. The determination that the bison disease "problem" poses a significant risk to bison populations and to humans living near the bison range relies upon such assumptions. If, for example, the problematic risk is that individual animals may suffer or die from disease, the preferred policy should minimize the suffering of individual bison. Whether mass eradication would accomplish this goal is open to question. If, on the other hand, the primary concern is the health of the bison population and disease is not a primary cause of population decline, no action is called for. Hunters, for instance, cause mortality of individuals in free-roaming populations, yet there is no consensus about whether hunters necessarily cause changes in population size (M. J. Peterson 1991). The alleged risks disease poses to bison populations are certainly open to challenge.

Whether or not brucellosis constitutes a threat to infected wildlife populations, it does constitute an economic threat to ranchers who run cattle on land bordering wildlife habitat. Because brucellosis causes cows to abort their calves, one outbreak can destroy a rancher's economic viability. In addition to direct loss of income in the form of calves, U.S. law penalizes all producers in a state that is unable to be certified as "brucellosis free." Beef ranchers in uncertified regions receive less money for their product than they would if they operated in a certified region. Thus, ranchers have an economic interest in freeing their locales of brucellosis, regardless of whether their animals contract the disease. Canadian beef producers spend approximately $2.5 million a year for brucellosis testing, under current trade rulings. The recently passed Canada-U.S. Trade Agreement includes a special codicil "to remove the requirement of testing for brucellosis, provided that the last focus of brucellosis infection has been removed" (NDBEAP 1990 *Hearings*, 194). Neither the direct economic threat posed by lost domestic calves nor the more generalized economic penalties accrued by meat producers, however, provides evidence that brucellosis affects population sizes of free-ranging wildlife.

What, then, justifies the Northern Diseased Bison Environmental Assessment Panel's assumption that disease threatens the existence of the Wood Buffalo NP bison herd while it causes no detrimental population-level effects in Greater Yellowstone Area bison? As Markus Peterson (1991), in his comparison of bison disease in Wood Buffalo NP and Greater Yellowstone Area, speculated, there are many possible explanations. Perhaps brucellosis in conjunction with tuberculosis is more devastating to host populations than brucellosis alone. Similarly, wolves preying on diseased bison in the Wood Buffalo NP region may account for observed differences. One also could hypothesize that harsh environmental conditions in Wood Buffalo NP, in conjunction with disease, cause the disparity. Additionally, various combinations of these hypotheses also could explain observed numbers. The final report of the Northern Diseased Bison Environmental Assessment Panel, however, offered no such hypotheses (NDBEAP 1990 *Report*; M. J. Peterson 1991).

In summary, bison in the Wood Buffalo NP region are hosts for bovine brucellosis and tuberculosis, and this concerns livestock health officials, livestock producers, and other groups of people. There is little evidence, however, implicating disease as the primary cause for decreased bison numbers in the region. Inconsistencies and unanswered questions within the Northern Diseased Bison Environmental Assessment Panel's final report illustrate that this assumption was uncritically accepted as the basis for public policy recommendations.

An Opportunity for Public Participation in Decision Making

The Northern Diseased Bison Environmental Assessment Panel held seven public hearings regarding the Canadian government's future policy in Wood Buffalo NP during January 1990 (NDBEAP 1990 *Report*). Panel members traveled to Fort Vermillion, Fort Chipewyan, and Edmonton, in Alberta; and to Fort Providence, Fort Resolution, Fort Smith, and Hay River, in the Northwest Territories. The hearings conducted at Fort Smith and Edmonton each took two days; the other hearings lasted one day each. All of the hearings followed a similar format, with the panel chairman conducting the proceedings. At the Fort Resolution hearing Chief Bernadette Unka welcomed the participants, asked an elder by the name of Adeline Mandeville to open with a prayer, then turned the meeting over to the chairman. At all other hearings the chairman performed these introductory functions as well as conducting the proceedings. At all hearings a representative of Agriculture Canada delivered the first formal presentation. Following this presentation various citizens spoke, representing groups ranging from local aboriginal bands to cattle ranchers' associations to the World Wildlife Fund. A question and answer period usually followed two or three formal presentations. The meetings lasted late into the night, and hostility tended to become more overt as the night wore on. Each hearing ended with an oral summary provided by the chairman.

Agriculture Canada's status in the hearings was somewhat problematic, because it had already submitted a formal plan for removal of all bison from the area and, as such, was a proponent of one of the alternatives being considered. The panel's final recommendation was to implement a slight revision of Agriculture Canada's proposal. While the final report superficially notes issues brought forward by participants opposed to Agriculture Canada's plan, it does not respond substantially to them (NDBEAP 1990, *Report*). Political concerns regarding hostility from both the aboriginal bands and some environmental advocacy organizations have been cited as standing in the way of implementation, however, and no move has been made to act on the recommendations (B. Theresa Aniskowicz, conservation coordinator, Canadian Nature Federation, telephone interview, August 1992).

Representatives of Agriculture Canada and panel members not only advocated a different solution than did representatives of aboriginal bands; they also talked about the problem and its solution differently. The contrasting discourse forms favored by these two groups of people illustrate distinctive communicative strategies used by those who prefer to limit participation in public policy decisions to an elite group who merit inclusion because of their technical expertise and those who prefer to expand participation in public policy decisions to include all parties whose lives will be influenced by those decisions. For purposes of discussion I label them as "technological" and "creative" discourse. Technological discourse is *"language used to structure human action according to rules of closed systems"* (T. R. Peterson 1990, 78). It proceeds through a series of steps in which either a prearranged goal determines the sequel to each step or the question of appropriateness does not arise. As such, it proceeds from, while further legitimizing, the technological psychosis from which contemporary society suffers. Its fundamental assumptions exclude evidence and arguments drawn from nonnumerically defined experience. It provides its users with a rationale for excluding those whose competencies fall beyond the predetermined, technologically defined realm of expertise from the decision-making process.

Creative discourse, on the other hand, is language that proceeds through a series of interactions, none of which is determined by a predetermined goal but all of which are seen to have been inexplicably appropriate after the fact (T. R. Peterson 1990; Burke 1966, 486). It encourages participants to pursue previously unforeseen alternatives. Further, rather than providing a rationale for excluding people from participation in decision making, it seeks to expand the circle of potential participants to accommodate a constantly changing set of definitions and experiential bases. Creative discourse's expansive quality enhances flexibility on the part of its users. Although the hearings' orientation and structure penalized the creative discourse favored by aboriginal representatives, this communicative form enabled its users to discuss ideas that exist outside the technological realm as well as technological topics wherein they had no formally recognized expertise. Conversely, although the NDBEAP hearings' technological orientation and bureaucratic structure privileged the technological discourse used by representatives of the Canadian government, this form of communication also narrowed the range of alternatives its users could consider as possibilities. Contrasting the fundamental assumptions of these two communication forms offers a critique of the dominant psychosis and suggests an alternative perspective that could enable a more participatory model for sustainable development policy. Aboriginal community and Canadian government representatives consistently differed in their perspectives toward the concept of objectivity, the role of knowledge and information, the relationship between means and ends, and the degree to which issues are interconnected.

Existence of Objective Standards

Canadian government representatives presumed the existence of an objective standard against which decisions regarding the wood bison could be measured. This expectation led them to assume that there was a single "correct" solution to the disease issue. Aboriginal community representatives, however, assumed that no objective standards existed but, rather, that standards were human constructs. An interchange regarding the composition of the environmental assessment panel illustrates the differing views toward objectivity. Chief Sewepagaham, who made the first formal presentation following that of Agriculture Canada's at the first community hearing, pointed out that "upon being notified of the formation of the Panel we requested that an aboriginal spokesperson be appointed to this Panel. This was rejected. . . . The failure to appoint an aboriginal spokesperson to this Panel shows a lack of disregard and respect for the importance of our interests in this matter" (NDBEAP 1990 *Hearings*, 5). Following the completion of the formal presentations, the chairman, Robert Connelley, responded to issues that had been raised, beginning with Chief Sewepagaham's presentation. "You're quite right . . . that there is no aboriginal spokesperson on this Panel," he began. "I would point out, however, that panels are intended to be neutral, knowledgeable. Members are to be free of conflict of interest, and a Minister of the Environment in appointing a panel does take that into consideration" (NDBEAP 1990 *Hearings*, 9).

The aboriginal attitude toward traditionally defined objectivity is illustrated by the reply to the chairman's claim of neutrality. A member of the Cree band explained:

> Your Panel consists of a number of people who have professional expertise. It is impossible for any person embedded in any profession to escape the biases and prejudices of that field of professional learning. So, your Panel is not unbiased and neutral. Your Panel brings to it all of the professional biases and opinions, and all that we asked for was someone who could represent that body of knowledge that

has to do with the relationship between Indians and the environment and bring yet another group of opinions or knowledge. (Webb, NDBEAP 1990 *Hearings*, 9)

This statement represents a straightforward rejection of the notion of human objectivity. The Cree representative rejected the notion that expertise frees people of their biases. Rather, he claimed that all assessments are subject to social construction. Since a completely objective event must be independent of its observer, even neutral experts' assessments contain inevitable elements of subjectivity. Given that *objective human observation* is an oxymoron, both lay and expert opinions include elements of subjectivity. The chairman's discourse, on the other hand, was based in the belief that appropriate knowledge could only develop from objective observation.

The Role of Knowledge and Information

The contrasting attitudes toward objectivity led to conflicting expectations regarding the role of knowledge and information. Government representatives relied on neutral information to justify their claims. For example, one government scientist attempted to validate his presentation by explaining to the audience that "the first premise that I want to make, you know, is I am not making a judgment on whether it is more appropriate to leave the animals" (Novakowski, NDBEAP 1990 *Hearings*, 239). The amount of information, its precision, and its correctness, rather than its implicit valuation of various alternatives, were the most basic concerns for this panelist.

Aboriginal participants, who did not assume the existence of objectivity, were more interested in the appropriateness of information. They repeatedly demonstrated their distrust for experts by explicitly devaluing information that had been provided through official channels. Examples of these statements include: "Agriculture Canada has told us that this is necessary . . . They would have us believe . . . We have been told today . . . These so-called experts would have us believe . . . " (Chief Sewepagaham, NDBEAP 1990 *Hearings*, 4). Aboriginal participants assumed that, since all information developed out of a knowledge base that was constructed from cultural perspectives, its existence was less important than the source from which it came. Because they distrusted the Canadian government, information obtained through government channels was suspect.

Further, aboriginal participants claimed that panel members had failed to tap appropriate, and readily available, sources when they attempted to solicit information. For example, one woman asked the panel chair, if he had "asked the question of any of the harvesters, of any of the people living on the land in this area, in the Park and around the Park, of these experts perhaps not M.A.'s or B.A.'s or Ph.D.'s, but people who have worked, lived and lived in harmony and eaten these animals all their lives, hunted. Have you asked these experts?" (Moldaver, NDBEAP 1990 *Hearings*, 62). Chief Bernadette Unka, of Fort Resolution, told the panel that their disease estimates were wrong and that they had obtained estimates from the wrong people; she explained that, "when you talk with the owners, the aboriginal hunters and the ones who have the closest relationship to the buffaloes and the ones with the greatest storehouse of knowledge about buffaloes, they have been insisting all along, for many years, that no more than 2 per cent of our buffaloes are known to be infected" (NDBEAP 1990 *Hearings*, 112). A representative of the Dene/Metis Negotiation Secretariat proudly proclaimed:

> Local expertise has been left out of the proposal development process. . . . There is a lot of expertise. This expertise is viable, it's credible, it's been developed because of years of relationship with the animals. Generations of relationship with the animals. Generations of relationship with the buffalo. This is based on fact, based on way of life, based on knowledge gathered from direct contact. Not knowledge read in some book written by another biologist that now biologists are reading and calling from as fact. (Kurszewski, NDBEAP 1990 *Hearings*, 220, 221)

Tom Unka, a local chief, put it more gently, explaining that, "in light of the interest of my Band and many Native bands in bison management, I find it puzzling and frustrating that our interests have not been represented on this Panel" (NDBEAP 1990 *Hearings*, 311).

These statements, as well as others made by aboriginal participants, suggest that, because the scientists had not turned to the appropriate sources for information, their presentations did not account for the fact that buffalo were sacred to many of the aboriginal groups. Further, they exhibited considerable discomfort when asked about the rights of this sacred animal to expect an appropriate ceremony to accompany its harvest (death). One Agriculture Canada employee responded that, "[he] would kind of hate to get in the animal rights and what they may have or may not have" (Broughton, NDBEAP 1990 *Hearings*, 61). The technological metaphor gave him no vocabulary for such a conversation.

When serious questions were asked, the technical experts were unable to speculate or analogize between the current situation and others. One of the tribal elders asked, "is there any information available that indicates that at any time in the recent past cattle have been infected as a result of contact with buffalo?" The response was, "if you're referring in Canada, no" (Webb and Broughton, NDBEAP 1990 *Hearings*, 19). Although information regarding the transmission of brucellosis from bison to cattle had been collected in the United States and was probably known to this scientist, his communication form truncated the possibility of including that information in his response.

The Relationship between Means and Ends

Reliance on either the poetic or mechanistic metaphor also led to a different relationship between means and ends. Aboriginal participants differentiated carefully between them, whereas government employees tended to conflate the two. The procedure whereby the hearings were conducted was sacrosanct to panel members. The chairman gave similar responses to criticism ranging from anger about information gathering techniques to descriptions of past government incompetence or dishonesty to opposition toward how, when, or where the hearings were conducted. He usually said something like, "I'd like to say that I think the process is unfolding as it should" (NDBEAP 1990 *Hearings*, 252). When people asked why things were done in a certain manner he explained that "it is normal practice with Panel Reviews for the Panel which reports to Ministers, to the Minister of the Environment and it will also report its findings to the Minister of Agriculture, it is normal practice. . . . So that basically is the process we will be following" (49). Normalcy provided his principle justification for any procedure.

Even when further explanation might have been an appropriate means for easing the tension, the chairman was unable to offer further explanation. Aboriginal participants were not pleased to learn that the recommendations had been drawn up before public hearings were scheduled (even though this is normal EIS procedure). In his formal presentation Chief Bernard Meneen expressed his bands' displeasure that "the process does not allow communities to review Panel recommendations or to critically examine them at the end of the hearing process and before they go to Environment Canada" (NDBEAP 1990 *Hearings,* 7). Following the presentation the chairman reviewed the chief's points, explaining how the panel was attempting to resolve each problem. He offered potential resolution to several issues that were much more substantial, such as conducting new studies to estimate more accurately the effects of bison destruction on other animals, but was able to explain only that "the point raised in here that the process does not allow communities to review Panel recommendations once they're made is indeed correct. The process does not permit that" (Chairman, NDBEAP 1990 *Hearings,* 10). Stella Martin, who spoke on behalf of the Cree Band of Fort Chipewyan, closed her remarks to the panel as follows:

> We also wish to file our objection to the manner in which the EARP panel has chosen to "Study the views of Native people on this matter" through the hiring of a consultant retained by the Panel. . . . This approach reminds us of the old Indian Affairs colonial paternalist mentality and does not recognize the current political, cultural or Native reality of northern Canada. (NDBEAP 1990 *Hearings,* 287)

The chairman could only respond that the approach was used "because we could do that within the restrictions and the rules that we have to work in" (NDBEAP 1990 *Hearings,* 287). He made no attempt to explain why that consultant had been selected, nor did he offer to discuss a different approach. For those trapped within a technological communication model, the process of conducting public hearings, which had originally been meant as a *means* for encouraging public participation in decisions regarding EIA, had become the *end.*

Aboriginal representatives, on the other hand, were free to criticize the process used to conduct the hearings. Some bluntly stated that they "did not believe that the process by which this Panel was proceeding was fair" (Webb, NDBEAP 1990 *Hearings,* 12). Others went further, accusing the chairman of running a hearing that "has been basically an effort that has been used by the proponents to do a sales job, a sales job for their objectives that they have predetermined a long time ago. . . . You come here with your whole entourage of experts, expecting to sell to the Dene/Metis and to sell to the communities your outlandish, foolish, in my opinion insane proposal of a buffalo holocaust. It's not going to fly" (Kurszewski, NDBEAP 1990 *Hearings,* 224). For the aboriginal participants the hearings were simply an imperfect means that had been constructed to accomplish a goal. Although they disagreed among themselves regarding the specifics of that goal, they agreed that the process was a means and not an end.

Aboriginal participants were also skeptical about categorization on the basis of official naming. One of Agriculture Canada's justifications for eradicating such a large number of bison was that they were not genetically pure. Because plains bison had bred with wood bison in the region, their offspring could be categorized differently than wood bison. The following explanation from a representative of the Canadian Fish and Wildlife Service exemplifies the explanation that was offered at least once at each hearing:

> We have a hybrid bison, or what we consider is a hybrid bison, and Fish and Wildlife does not consider a hybrid bison to be wildlife and therefore we don't provide protection under our *Wildlife Act*, or we don't provide management of a diseased—or of a hybrid bison. Right now the general idea in Fish and Wildlife is that they are not wildlife and we don't regulate them whatsoever. We consider them to be—a hybrid bison to be the same as a plains bison, which is a domestic animal. So in terms of the way we look at things, we've got a herd of domestic animals out there, so we don't manage them. (Sabiston, NDBEAP 1990 *Hearings*, 29)

Anticipating this definitional problem, Chief Sewepagaham, who made the first aboriginal presentation at the first public hearing, began his summary by requesting that the "Wabasca Herd 130," which was slated for slaughter in Agriculture Canada's proposal but on which the tribe relied for subsistence, be reclassified. "The Tribe," he explained, "has requested that this herd, Number 1, be recognized as a wood buffalo herd" (NDBEAP 1990 *Hearings*, 6). If hybrid bison were at risk, the tribe would safeguard the animals by officially naming them as wood bison (which is what they had commonly been known as all along). Although Agriculture Canada did not take Chief Sewepagaham's suggestion seriously, offering it did not damage his credibility. Instead, his outrageous request enabled a fresh perspective by demonstrating that categorization is a social practice, rather than a natural process.

Not all aboriginal participants were as civil as Chief Sewepagaham. One man blurted out: "Boy you guys cheez me off. In Wood Buffalo National Park they're hybrid animals. They're the same as cows or they're

the same as domestic animals in Alberta, but in the Northwest Territories they're game. How did you ever get around that? How did
Government ever manipulate the buffalo to the point that it's almost a non-entity?" (Burke, NDBEAP 1990 *Hearings,* 65). Names, too,
represented a means for achieving an end. Government representatives took names as seriously as they did the process whereby the
hearings were conducted. The mechanistic metaphor, with its emphasis on parts rather than wholes, promotes names as permanent
and complete descriptions. Aboriginal participants, on the other
hand, viewed names as tentative labels that should change as the
situation changed. The poetic metaphor's assumption that the
"other" never can be fully described facilitates such flexibility regarding names, because each description is viewed as a temporary
pause in the movement toward a more complete description.

A poignant exchange between a tribal elder and a government scientist illustrates how differently technological and creative
communication focus attention. These two communicative forms foster
contradictory understandings of how means and ends are related. Mr.
LaViolette, who was an elder with the Dene/Metis Band, traveled to
several of the hearings. Over the years he had worked on numerous
government projects and had been angered by the treatment afforded
the bison. Because he believed that this project would be no different, he
repeatedly questioned those men with whom he had worked previously:

> *Mr. LaViolette:* I'm sure you supervised this to go to Hay Camp, what
> was the reason for so much animals to be left suffering for—the long-
> est one was three months, almost three months?
> *Dr. Novakowski:* I was, you, I was given a treatment regime, and that—
> in other words, you know, I'm not a veterinarian myself, and I was
> told what to do and I did it.
> *Mr. LaViolette:* I can't hear you, Doctor.
> *Dr. Novakowski:* I say I was told what to do and I did it.
> (NDBEAP 1990 *Hearings,* 239)

Mr. LaViolette could find no appropriate reason for bison being left
to suffer for three months and thus believed that it should not have been
done. Dr. Novakowski was unable to answer a question that strayed
beyond technological rationality. Instead, he found adequate justification in the fact that he was obeying orders.

The Interconnectedness of Life

Although aboriginal participants meticulously distinguished between means and ends, they were not prone to make distinctions within their web of life. They refused to grant distinctions between themselves and the bison, between the past and the present, or between dimensions of the ecosystem. They insisted that slaughtering the bison signaled an end to their lives as well. Mr. Morin explained that "the buffalo in the north, they've been through a lot. They've been treated very—with no respect at all. . . . If you kill our buffalo off basically what you're doing is you're committing cultural genocide" (NDBEAP 1990 *Hearings*, 449). Chief Henry Beaver, of the Fort Smith Band, pleaded with his audience: "I cannot understand the government's position on one hand, they want to be able to sit down with us and negotiate, and yet on one hand they want to destroy us. . . . We're still alive, and the bison in and around this area are still alive. We are like brothers to the bison" (NDBEAP 1990 *Hearings*, 230). Whatever fate the bison suffered, these people would suffer alongside them.

They also insisted that bison were biologically connected with other animals of the bush. Several were incredulous that Agriculture Canada would propose slaughtering the bison without considering what would happen to the relationships among wolves, moose, and other life forms. Chief Sewepagaham explained patiently that, "if you're going to be doing a study on the buffalo, then they have to do a study on the wolf, you have to do a study of the whole national Park, in terms of the whole ecosystem, so that you know how all of these animals are related in terms of dependence. . . . Like every animal sort of has a stage, has a role in the whole development of the bush" (NDBEAP 1990 *Hearings*, 13). Chief Henry Beaver told his audience: "our elders who understand the importance of the environment of the region know that the removal of the species will seriously affect all—seriously affect other animals and the habitat that they use. Everyone knows that you cannot remove any part of the natural environment without affecting the rest of it. Even biologists should know that" (NDBEAP 1990 *Hearings*, 231). Clearly, the experts upon whom the Canadian government relied for information were not highly respected in aboriginal culture; the interconnectedness of life's web was deemed so obvious, however, that even technical experts should recognize it.

The aboriginal participants also shared bitter memories of past projects gone wrong. Mr. LaViolette compared one project conducted by Agriculture Canada to German atrocities committed during World War II: "They [Agriculture Canada] had sacrificed all that buffalo they put in the holding corral. As they go into the—through the squeeze they inject the anthrax into them, definite amount, and they put them in the stall and watch them how they die. That's even more than what Hitler had done to the Jews. I don't think the Germans stand there and watch them how they die" (NDBEAP 1990 *Hearings*, 120). "Speciesist" prejudices attributed to Western European culture by deep ecologists were largely absent from aboriginal discourse in these hearings (Booth and Jacobs 1990). Because bison were his brothers, LaViolette saw nothing worse in the Nazis' treatment of Jews than in Agriculture Canada's treatment of bison.

The aboriginal people's familial bond with bison extended through-out all aspects of life. A story told by Chief Roy Fabian, of the Hay River Dene Band, sums up how complex the interconnections were:

> I don't know why, you know, the white man—you know, like I hate to say this, but why the white man always has to introduce a welfare system to solve problems for Native people. You're say-ing you're going to give our people that are now using the buffalo, that are now eating the buffalo, and what you're going to do is you're going to set up a welfare system for them. . . . The eating of it is just a small part of it. . . . The whole idea of a Native person going out and hunting and doing what he knows best is what the man is proud of, is what the Indian is proud of and what the Dene is proud of. . . . You've taken everything away from us and then you handed us welfare cheques, you handed us meat, you did everything you can and you destroyed the Native people. And now here we are, we're just struggling and we're getting back on our feet and you're going to introduce welfare again. . . . You're going to take all their pride, you're going to take everything away from them and you're going to hand them meat." (NDBEAP 1990 *Hearings*, 62–63)

In destroying the bison, the Canadian government would destroy the aboriginal people whose existence depended on the bison's pres-ence. As another participant explained, "there is no compensation for buffalo. There is just no compensation" (Burke, NDBEAP 1990 *Hearings*, 125–26).

Government representatives, whether they were panel members or speakers for Agriculture Canada, harbored no such notions of interconnectedness. In fact, they expended great amounts of energy keeping everything in its place. When asked what appeared to be simple questions, they carefully deferred to the appropriate expert. Other than defending the process, the chairman's most common statement was "I'm not an expert in that area." This reliance on technical expertise led to some difficulty, when Chief Harry Chonkolay's interpreter told the chairman that "Chief Chonkolay would like to raise a question on what sort of data do you have per month of animals dying of the disease":

> *Chairman:* Perhaps I could [ask] Agriculture Canada or others if they have that type of information? Would you please respond to that, please, Mr. Coupland?
> *Dr. Coupland:* I can't really, because we don't have any regular jurisdiction in the Park. . . . The exact question he's asked there we can't answer.
> *Chairman:* . . . I believe Dr. Tessaro has done some analysis . . . . But I'm not an expert on his particular studies.
> *Dr. Coupland:* . . . I haven't got the figures right in front of me. Dr. Tessaro will have it I'm sure. . . .
> *Chairman:* . . . I wonder if you could comment on that?
> *Dr. Fuller:* I think that maybe there are two things at issue here, and either Dr. Broughton or Dr. Coupland could maybe comment on this.
> (NDBEAP 1990 *Hearings*, 18)

In Dr. Tessaro's absence no answer, not even an estimate, was forthcoming. The stock response to questions was "we are also concerned about this very question, and we have engaged a technical expert also to look into this issue" (Chairman, NDBEAP 1990 *Hearings*, 35).

In contrast to the aboriginal insistence on connecting everything, Agriculture Canada carefully separated the bison from the disease they carried. Dr. Coupland explained that, "as far as Agriculture Canada is concerned, their objective is to clean up the diseases. It is only coincidental that one of the animals threatened and the animal that originally was there is supposedly a wood bison. Now, that has nothing to do with

Agriculture Canada" (NDBEAP 1990 *Hearings*, 12). The agency's experts presented themselves as objective, disinterested seekers of knowledge whose only responsibilities were to report the results of that search. Any actions on their part were merely the results of their search for knowledge. Coupland's reference to Agriculture Canada, an organization to which he both belongs and is currently representing, as "they," further distances individual agents from responsibility for recommendations that are derived from the facts they discover.

This tendency to break the issue into its constituent parts frustrated the aboriginal participants' attempts to place responsibility for the proposed slaughter on any single person or agency. When asked how his agency could agree to Agriculture Canada's proposal, the representative of Fish and Wildlife said, "it's not Fish and Wildlife's concern, it's the farmers, it's the RCMP, it's whose ever, but it's not Fish and Wildlife's concern, because we don't regulate them as wildlife" (Sabiston, NDBEAP 1990 *Hearings*, 39). When asked to explain how the wood bison and plains bison could be differentiated, Dr. Coupland answered: "we're not geneticists, that's not our field. We're here on the disease aspect, but perhaps Dr. Gates could respond to that" (NDBEAP 1990 *Hearings*, 66). When asked to explain some conclusions that did not make sense to aboriginal representatives, the chairman answered, "we have their reports with their conclusions in them, and I think it would be unfair for me to try to represent their views here this evening" (NDBEAP 1990 *Hearings*, 61). When a report with his name on it was challenged, Mr. Van Camp answered: "all right. Well first of all, I didn't have anything to do with the preparation of this report except for the final few pages" (NDBEAP 1990 *Hearings*, 263). When aboriginal representatives asked about past Agriculture Canada projects in the region, such as the anthrax experiment described by LaViolette, they were told, "there's no connection at all" or "that's an issue that has nothing to do with this review" (McLeod and Chairman, NDBEAP 1990 *Hearings*, 173). Reliance on a mechanistic metaphor led government representatives to wrench the hearing from its historical context, thus devaluing the native communities' experiential basis for knowledge.

Although the chairman preferred to decide who would answer questions, LaViolette, who appeared at nearly every hearing, insisted in directing his own questions. This led to more than one altercation with the chairman:

Chairman: Mr. LaViolette, I'm not sure why you want this question answered.

Mr. LaViolette: You don't want me to talk, Mr. Chairman?

Chairman: No, I wonder what is the purpose of the question?

Mr. LaViolette: Because I'm going to get to something else.

Chairman: It's in the record, and Dr. Gates is looking it up.

Mr. LaViolette: Okay, I'll go on. . . . When you buried that buffalo with anthrax do you think you really solved the problem of anthrax?

Chairman: I think we're asking the questions to the wrong department here, that particular question.

Mr. LaViolette: No, I want to ask these people because they were there.

Chairman: Well, the point is that I—

Mr. LaViolette: My grandfather left things for me that I'm using now.

Chairman: The point is I'm not sure they can answer that question. It would be better directed to somebody else.

(NDBEAP 1990 *Hearings,* 161)

The technical experts chose not to address LaViolette's question regarding the preventive value of the anthrax experiment. The technological orientation would suggest that, unless the experiment had been designed to determine whether the vaccine would prevent infection, speculation regarding prevention was superfluous. Perhaps government representatives feared they could not provide enough information to justify a definitive answer. Such a fear, however, was illogical from the aboriginal standpoint, because final answers to such questions were not expected.

Failure to Communicate across Perspectives

The real tragedy of these hearings is that they failed to achieve their purpose. Hostility between aboriginal and government representatives became more overt as the hearings progressed. The two groups never even approached a level of understanding which would have facilitated public participation in deciding how best to manage the bison and related aspects of the Wood Buffalo NP region. An excerpt from a protracted attempt by Chief Henry Beaver and Mr. McLeod, of the Department of Renewable Resources, to understand each other illustrates the impasse:

Chief Beaver: So what you're telling me . . .
Mr. McLeod: I don't think that's what our position was. . . .
Chief Beaver: So in fact the Department right now . . .
Mr. McLeod: I didn't say that. . . .
Chief Beaver: . . . isn't the Government's intent at this point in time . . .
Mr. McLeod: I'm not sure I understand . . .
Chief Beaver: What I am saying . . .
Mr. McLeod: No, what we were referring to were . . . .
(NDBEAP 1990 *Hearings,* 167–68)

This exchange continued for several pages of transcript, until the chairman intervened, and required that another formal presentation be made before it became too late. Examination of these men's interactions with each other, as well as with other participants, indicates that they had both entered the hearing process with a sincere desire to develop cooperative agreements. Despite their desires, however, they were unable to create a mutually satisfactory meaning for the situation.

At one of the later hearings an aboriginal participant tried vainly to share her experiential knowledge with the experts:

This past three years . . . the Parks management . . . have always been using all kinds of money on finding ways to get aircrafts and in that way to chase the buffalos out of Mission Farm back into the Park area. . . . Now, if I chased you and you didn't know why I was chasing you, for over a hundred miles and you were pregnant and I chased you into this corral, your endocrine system is going to be quite high. . . . I've cut up a lot of buffalos, and I haven't come across one which was not sustainable to my family, and I have five children. I've cut every inch of a buffalo, and I can probably safely say I probably know more about that buffalo than you do, because most of your learning is on book learning. Now I don't have a certificate sticking out of my pocket saying that what I'm saying is facts, but I know what is facts. (Beaver, NDBEAP 1990 *Hearings,* 265)

The chairman, however, dealt with her comments in much the same manner that a tired professor deals with an enthusiastic yet unprepared student, silencing her with, "I appreciate your views on this issue" (NDBEAP 1990 *Hearings,* 265). Because Mrs. Beaver integrated her experience as a woman (having been pregnant, butchering buffalo, and feeding her children) with her knowledge of the endocrine system, her views were seen as irrelevant.

The final speaker was Mr. Morin, of the Little River Cree Band. He concluded his presentation by stating: "the reason the great herds were gone is because that was the Government's way of trying to kill off us as aboriginal people, but we're still here and we will not allow that to happen again. Thank you" (NDBEAP 1990 *Hearings*, 450). There were no questions following his presentation. The chairman made a few perfunctory closing remarks, and the hearings were concluded.

Oppositional Discourse as "Perspective by Incongruity"

Rhetorical critique suggests that Canadian government employees who participated in these EIA meetings grounded their technological discourse in a mechanistic metaphor, while aboriginal participants grounded their creative discourse in a poetic metaphor (Burke 1984a, 65–66). Although the technological orientation and structure of the hearings contributed to apparent domination by those who spoke mechanistically, the technological metaphor also constrained the models of sustainable development available to its users. On the other hand, although the structure of the hearings worked against the discourse form favored by aboriginal representatives, their reliance on a poetic metaphor enabled them to create a model of sustainable development which transcended the technological realm of the hearings. In addition to the constraints posed by each group's dominant metaphor, the dramatic distinction between the two contributed to a communicative impasse. Despite their articulation at seven public hearings, aboriginal concerns were dealt with only cursorily in the panel's final recommendation regarding how best to manage the region these people call home. The inability to achieve a sense of identification among panel members, representatives of Agriculture Canada, and those speaking for aboriginal bands indicates that, although the same information was available to all groups, their immersion in competing function systems prevented collaborative definitions of sustainable development from emerging out of the hearings. As an *organizationally closed* system, the hearings subordinated all change to their own reproduction: discourse that did not fit the organizational pattern was treated as though it had not occurred. Alternately, the hearings remained *structurally open*: fears that implementation of the officially designated "best" model for development would generate political upheaval led to an indefinite moratorium on activity.

The controversies surrounding wildlife disease management in the Wood Buffalo NP region illustrate the difficulties that occur when development policy is formed prior to adequate investigation from the perspectives of all involved parties. The technological psychosis that encourages people to assume that doing something that might be beneficial is better than doing nothing encourages the quick fix. Ellul (1980) argues that, within this mind-set, experience that cannot be appropriately "managed, manipulated, utilized, is rejected and discarded as worthless" (46). Prompt denigration of aboriginal experience as "inappropriate" stabilized the hearings yet prevented participants from pursuing creative alternatives. Technological discourse flourishes as techniques become more sophisticated, and technologies take on purposes of their own. Burke (1984a) argues, "social relations were first ascribed to nature, and then 'derived' from it" (274). Technological discourse, then, masks its own temporality while provoking participants to forget the role of invention in supplying the background against which all action must occur. As awareness of invention is suppressed, technological discourse comes to be judged by rules reflecting its own values and assumptions.

Botkin (1990) points out several instances in which society's myths and metaphors, rather than defects in scientific methodology, have limited the development of reliable ecological knowledge and policy based therein. He maintains that the potential for humans to make progress with environmental issues is limited by culturally based assumptions. Ferguson (1984) suggests that resistance to technological domination is facilitated "if a substantial number of people act collectively and in a nonbureaucratic fashion to challenge the discourse" (208). The technical terms used by expert advocates of exterminating the Wood Buffalo NP bison shrouded their political and economic reasoning in the neutral code of science. Aboriginal participants in these hearings, on the other hand, explicitly politicized the experts' technocratic language by demonstrating an alternative form of communication which encompassed more of their situation than was possible with the mechanistic metaphor.

Although these hearings did not result immediately in increased public participation in public policy decision making, the oppositional discourse in which aboriginal participants engaged decentered the dominant technological metaphor. Once destabilized, that metaphor's hold on decision makers may weaken sufficiently to allow greater legitimacy to discourse grounded in a wider set of values. Ultimately, that move can enrich the evaluation practices that undergird development decisions. Numerous social critics have elaborated on the argument that human orientation and motivation rely on symbolic filters through which people view the world. Luhmann (1989) specifies that, no matter how carefully researchers control their experiments, they are ultimately doing "observations of observations," for humans can experience the natural world only as mediated by their perceptions. By extension we can assume that ecologists, environmentalists, aboriginal peoples, livestock producers, and government animal health agency workers view wildlife disease (and its relationship to human development options) through different, yet equally powerful, lenses.

Domestic animal health officials' driving motivation regarding brucellosis management is the eradication of the disease from all domestic animals. A corollary perspective is that there must be no risk of re-exposure. In fact, Agriculture Canada is mandated to achieve this goal. Agriculture Canada and the U.S. Department of Agriculture have demonstrated that removing all infected livestock from a herd (or from a province or state) will eradicate brucellosis from *that herd* (or from that region), which helps to explain why animal health officials would like to implement such programs with wildlife brucellosis. Thus, viewed from the perspective of Agriculture Canada, removal of *all* bison from the Wood Buffalo NP area and later replacement with disease-free bison makes perfect sense. That is, however, only one of many equally valid perspectives. Local residents who are immersed in the same environment as the bison hold a different view. They claim the responsibility to protect the animals that have long "sustained" them from irresponsible predation by Agriculture Canada. They do not limit talk of the sustenance provided by bison to food and fiber obtained from the animal's body. Their whole pattern of existence, rather, is sustained by the complex relationship between people and bison. Agriculture Canada's plan to slaughter the bison embodies, from this perspective, both reckless waste and immoral evil.

The contradictory results of much development assistance suggest that, because local residents will participate in the resulting risks and benefits, their participation in determining sustainable development policy is essential to its success. Rhetorical analysis of these hearings indicates that, while the biologists, veterinarians, geneticists, and other specialists may have had a more sophisticated grasp of the technical components of bison-disease interactions than nonspecialists, their classification system may have unwittingly devalued, or even excluded, components of this issue which community residents consider crucial to making development decisions. After all, even experts become nonscientists when the conflict shifts to another scientific arena. Further, when decision making slips into the codes of different function systems, scientists are left with a vocabulary that no longer fits the situation. Because they are no more (and perhaps are less) capable of recognizing how the risks inherent in policies they recommend will influence relationships within a community than are local residents, their specialized knowledge does not qualify them to make critical development decisions about issues that involve the well-being of these communities.

If we assume that both lay and expert perspectives are socially constructed, the symbolic processes whereby this construction occurs becomes a potential window into both the rationality and the subjectivity of knowledge. Rhetorical critique provides one means of exploring the symbolic practices people engage in as they construct competing realities upon which to base sustainable development decisions. Debunking the notion that, while the lay public makes decisions based on subjective experience, technical experts make decisions based on objective observation is an essential step toward developing forums for broader participation in public deliberation. Analysis of communication interactions between lay and expert perspectives can destabilize technological dominance by encouraging public inquiry into expert definitions of reality. Further, by exploring local residents' discourse about nonhuman life with which they share a region, we gain new insights into options for sustaining the precarious relationship between the technologized world constructed by humans and the natural processes upon which that world is grounded.

Chapter 6

Voices from the
Bottom of the Rio Grande
*Negotiating Sustainable Development
in Cameron County, Texas*

The point is, you can't come down here and be condescending
because it doesn't affect you. You don't live here. You've never experienced a child without a brain. You've never experienced the
poverty. You've never experienced the mess of the environment.

Rosa Ramirez I2, R30

Public health workers are frustrated when their tuberculosis patients
disappear into thin air. School nurses keep sick children at school rather
than send them home to cardboard shacks in neighborhoods with no
sewage treatment systems. Teachers hesitate to report communicable
disease among their students because the resulting investigation might
lead to a family's deportation. Childhood leukemia and anencephaly
rates rival those of Mexico City. There are no public hearings at which
residents on the northern bank of the river can speak out when factories
on the southern bank of the river spew untreated industrial effluent and
sewage into the public water supply.

Brownsville, the seat of Cameron County, Texas, is located in the
United States, a country that boasts of its international leadership in
environmental protection measures, such as the Clean Water Act. Neither people nor toxic substances, however, respect national boundaries.
Instead, residents of Brownsville drink and bathe in water that contains
pollutants over which the U.S. government has no jurisdiction. Because
the pollutants entered the water from the southern bank, water users do
not even have the right to know what those pollutants are. Mexican citizens pay their toll to cross the bridge from Matamoros to Brownsville,
or they swim the river. Either way, those eager for U.S. dollars find work

around Brownsville, usually in the fields. When they are exposed to unsafe levels of pesticides and herbicides, they cannot complain to a government agency. Instead, some of them appear unaffected, others get sick, and still others die. In their case the national boundary simply enables systemic disregard for human suffering. Although few residents of Cameron County, which is the most southern county on the border between the United States and Mexico, attend international conferences on environment and development, many of them confront these issues on a daily basis.

Sustainable development has taken on new urgency here, as Cameron County's internally driven response to alarming environmental perturbations. Because social change is internally driven, external shocks administered by the environment can encourage, but not compel, erratic changes that reverberate throughout a system. The resulting confusion within Cameron County allows seemingly unrelated aspects of society to interact with one another, generating possibilities for new perspectives on relations between humans and their environment. This transformation, however, depends on whether communication dampens the effects of the disturbance through compensatory adjustment within familiar relations or whether it encourages a new configuration of relations to emerge. The communicative performances that shape this transformation are the focus of this chapter, which would not have been written if an informant who began by saying she was "too busy" to talk with us had not relented.[*] When this carefully selected informant accused us of being scientists who had brought our "big government grant" to study her community, we panicked. Her reversal of the typical interviewer/interviewee roles left us groping for the right answer to her perfectly reasonable question: "Why are you here?" We gambled with a garbled version of the last two questions from our interview guide: "We just want to know what you think a healthy Brownsville would look like. What are the most important problems to tackle?" Whether because that was the right answer or because our panic-stricken faces had amused

* Interviewing expenses for this project were funded as part of EPA assistance ID# MX822144-01-0, "Addressing Coastal Challenges through Environmental Ethics Education," Susan J. Gilbertz, Tarla Rai Peterson, and Gary E. Varner, co-principal investigators.

her, she consented to participate in the project and to introduce us to other informants.

Just as the conflict over what to do with the bison in Wood Buffalo National Park revolves around the fact that wild animals do not recognize national park boundaries, the conflict in Cameron County revolves around the difficulty (and morality) of requiring people to honor international boundaries. Living at the confluence of first and third world conditions has provoked Cameron County residents to seek models of sustainability which are simultaneously local and global. Material circumstances have pressed them to think systemically about development. As many explained, "It won't help to fix things only on this side of the border."

I begin the chapter with a brief overview of life in this region, including discussion of the primarily U.S.-owned and -managed, Mexican-staffed, industrial complex that has sprouted up along the border. Second, I describe the techniques I used to construct a text for analysis. The bulk of the chapter is devoted to discourse elicited from residents who have become involved in an anguished conflict over what sort of development is best for Cameron County. Examination of this discourse indicates several shared themes as well as how these themes are integrated within stories told by different informants. Finally, the stories of two grassroots organizations, in which approximately one-third of my informants participated, illustrate possible visions of sustainable development in Cameron County.

Life on the Lower Rio Grande

Environmental conflict in Cameron County swirls around issues such as environmental justice, endangered species management, agricultural production, manufacturing, and human health and migration. Although residents have widely divergent backgrounds, they share a sense of alienation from the rest of the United States which predates the anti–federal government fashion of the 1990s by several decades. As Arturo Lozano, the priest for Our Lady of Guadalupe Church in Brownsville, claims, "the people from this area, the south-most part of Texas, have been forgotten not only by the state, but by the nation" (Selby 1994).

Cameron County lies at the bottom of the Rio Grande, which scientists frequently rate as the dirtiest river in the United States. Because there is minimal ground water in the area, the Rio Grande provides nearly all the water used to support human and nonhuman activity. The river begins in virgin snow pack high on Stony Pass of the San Juan Mountains in Colorado. By the time it dumps into the Gulf of Mexico just east of Brownsville, Texas, the sparkling waters have become "a human cesspool." Along its 1,885-mile journey the river picks up toxic tailings from mining in Colorado; radioactive tailings from bomb building in Los Alamos, New Mexico; and raw human sewage, factory discharges, and agricultural chemicals along the border of Texas and Mexico. Finally, there are the human bodies. Hundreds of unidentified people are dragged lifeless from the lower Rio Grande each year. Brownsville funeral home owner Aly Besteiro donates considerable resources for their burial. "A lot of them are from the interior of Mexico," he explains. "They're just unknowns" (Althaus et al. 1993). This is the river that sustains life in Cameron County, Texas.

Despite its woes, the region retains a rare beauty. Western desert, northern, coastal, and tropical plants, are concentrated within the semi-arid and subtropical climate of this unique ecosystem (Jahrsdoerfer and Leslie Jr. 1988). Numerous neotropical mammals, snakes, lizards, and salamanders reach their northern limits in the Lower Rio Grande Valley. At least twenty-one bird species, including the least grebe, olivaceous cormorant, red-billed pigeon, and brown jay, reach the northern limits of their range here as well. The remaining stands of sabal palm, *tepeguaje*, *anacua*, and Texas ebony provide habitat for the endangered ocelot and jaguarundi as well as for the lesser yellow bat, hooded oriole, speckled racer, and northern cat-eyed snake. Orioles, *chachalacas*, and green jays nest in remnants of coastal woodland consisting primarily of cedar elm, Berlandier ash, and sugar hackberry. The Texas tortoise, long-billed curlews, and a hypersaline-tolerant oyster population inhabit the tidal flats just east of Brownsville. About 700 vertebrate species, 145 of which the U.S. Fish and Wildlife Service has targeted for immediate protection, have been identified in this region. The U.S. Fish and Wildlife Service maintains two traditionally bounded wildlife refuges (Santa Ana and Laguna Atascosa) and a refuge consisting of 50 small tracts (Lower Rio Grande Valley) in the region. Santa Ana provides habitat for more endangered species than any other wildlife refuge in the United States; Laguna Atascosa was the location of the most recent ocelot and jaguarundi sightings in the United States; and Lower Rio Grande provides the beginnings of a wildlife corridor. This diverse habitat has a precarious existence, however. Since the 1920s more than 95 percent of the Lower Rio Grande Valley's native brushland has been cleared, and along the river 99 percent of the land has been cleared for agriculture or urban development (Jahrsdoerfer and Leslie Jr. 1988).

Cameron County's official population in 1994 was 260,120. This number is somewhat suspect, however, because people move in and out so often, and many choose not to advertise their presence. The county's average weekly wage was $362.00. The Brownsville Independent School District, which is the county's largest employer, is overwhelmed with a steady flow of new immigrants (Selby 1994). Compared to the rest of the nation, Cameron County residents have larger-than-average families and smaller-than-average incomes. Education levels are lower, while chronic disease rates are higher. Brownsville, the county seat, lies directly across the border from Matamoros, Tamaulipas, Mexico. Brownsville is Cameron County's major population center, with at least 112,000 residents (TDH-CDC 1992).

Whenever I walked into a Brownsville business, I was greeted by the steady hum of conversation typical to that business in any part of the United States. The hum, however, was in Spanish. The grocery clerk, the public school secretary, and the physician's receptionist quickly switched to English to accommodate an obvious outsider, yet in some restaurants my waiter was as dependent on Spanish as I was on English. Live music, with Tex-Mex rhythms and vocals, accompanied most of the meals I ate in public. The Texas Department of Health (TDH) estimates that at least 82 percent of Cameron County's population is Hispanic (TDH-CDC 1992).

Living in Cameron County means living on the border between the First and Third Worlds. Whereas most of us experience immigration as a relatively abstract political and economic concept, Cameron County residents confront, on a daily basis, the practical and moral dilemmas of requiring people to honor an international boundary. The woman who coordinates the beleaguered school nurse program for the local school district told me, "You can't blame them. If I was pregnant, I'd get over here to have that baby somehow. Nobody could stop me. And if I had kids, I'd get them over here too." Without exception, my informants explained that the border between the United States and Mexico is a fiction existing only in the minds of distant bureaucrats. They consider projects designed to forcibly halt illegal immigration, such as the much hyped "Operation Hold the Line" in the El Paso region (Thorpe 1995), to be violent, shortsighted, and counterproductive. Despite enormous efforts on the part of U.S. law enforcement agencies, pollution, disease, people, and other creatures constantly move back and forth.

The authenticity of constant movement across the river was personalized during my visits to Brownsville. I spent several nights in an old mansion (turned museum and farm cooperative center) located just east of town, while conducting interviews for this project. At about two-thirty one morning the dogs began barking and howling. I pushed open my window and stuck out my head but could see nothing unusual in the fields that spread around three sides of the house. I did, however, hear the sounds of cattle lowing as they plodded down the dirt track that wound past the front of the house to the river and the low rumble of an engine idling along behind them. Although it seemed an odd time to be moving cattle, I told myself that everything in this border region was unusual and went back to sleep as soon as the dogs quit howling. The next morning I was in the side yard pounding Rio Grande mud off my shoes when a stern man on a tall horse rode up to me, looked down at my shoes, flashed a badge, and began firing questions about the previous night. Apparently, a small herd of registered cattle had been stolen, and their tracks led past the house into the river. I was consumed by an irrational fear that he would accuse me of the crime because of the mud on my shoes. After he had satisfied himself that I really was there to interview people about their views toward the environment and development, he confessed that, although there wasn't much hope of retrieving the cattle from Mexico, he had to investigate. He left his business card so I could telephone him if I discovered anything about the theft. Another day I hiked through the nearby Santa Ana Wildlife Refuge after interviewing a U.S. Fish and Wildlife Service employee. I saw an incredible variety of exotic birds and wildlife as well as freshly discarded clothing, still wet from a midnight swim across the river, stuck to the thorn bushes. Personnel in the refuge office told me this was a common night crossing site.

Farming is an old profession in the Lower Rio Grande Valley. Long before Europeans settled the region, human settlers planted corn along the river's edge. Despite recent expansion of the manufacturing sector and the accompanying rise in an already rapid rate of human immigration, agriculture remains a significant economic activity. As you drive into Cameron County, the slightly rolling hills flatten into a humid coastal plain dominated by citrus, vegetable, sugarcane, corn, and cotton farms. Visible signs of agriculture's importance to the county range from modern implement dealerships to homemade roadside produce stands. Despite its continuity, however, agriculture has changed dramatically over the years. Following national trends, farms are larger and more mechanized. Most of the small farms east of Brownsville went out of production during the 1960s, when salinity levels at the bottom of the Rio Grande became too high for irrigating their mostly vegetable crops. Cotton is the county's major cash crop. The region's citrus industry runs a close second, contributing almost $200 million annually to the Texas economy (Althaus et al. 1993). Cameron County has a 341-day growing season, the longest in Texas. Because the climate enables farmers to plant and harvest crops year round, annual pesticide and herbicide use levels sometimes surpass those of more northern regions. Texas Department of Agriculture studies indicate, however, that residual levels do not surpass U.S. Environmental Protection Agency (EPA) standards (Jahrsdoerfer and Leslie Jr. 1988, 6, 17–25). Although Cameron County still relies heavily on income generated from citrus and cotton production for its economic base, farming is being supplanted by other industries, generally not those reputed to be clean or high-tech.

The *Maquiladora* Miracle

Maquiladoras came to the county two decades ago. They promised to rescue it from the economic malaise that afflicts many rural communities in the United States and is fueled by Cameron County's location as the southernmost spot in Texas. Just what constituted a *maquiladora* (or *maquila*) was open to question. The original concept was that a U.S.-based company—such as Fisher-Price, General Motors, or Dupont—would set up "twin" plants along the border. Basic assembly work would be accomplished south of the Rio Grande, where both employees and the physical environment could be treated differently than in plants constructed north of the river. The partially assembled product then would be shipped across the border for completion. This process enabled companies to minimize their operating costs, at the same time avoiding paying the duty required to import finished products into the United States.

Maquiladora industries have clustered primarily in automotive, electrical, electronic, furniture, ceramics, textile, and chemical production. The chemical industry has been, and is predicted to continue as, the fastest-growing segment, with a 92 percent growth rate reported in 1990

(Texas Center 1990). Air and water emissions, as well as improper disposal of solid waste, from these facilities can pose serious threats to the environment and public health. Many *maquiladoras* fail to meet legal requirements for returning hazardous waste to the United States. For example, of over 400 *maquiladoras* along the river between Texas and Mexico, only 11 were registered with the Texas Water Commission to return wastes in 1988 (Juffer 1988). An EPA regulator explained, "we know that legally, it [waste] is not coming back into the United States" (Tomaso and Alm February 1989). Hector Villa, district manager for the Texas Water Commission, reported that an exit check in September 1988 showed only 60 percent of the hazardous substances taken into Mexico were being returned to Texas. He worried that the remaining 40 percent "may have been dumped in the landfill or into the city's sewer and drainage system" (Texas Center 1990). It is difficult to confirm or disconfirm Villa's suspicions, because neither the Texas Water Commission nor the International Boundary and Water Commission have the appropriate laboratory facilities and the necessary funding to conduct extensive testing for industrial contamination (Juffer 1988). A review of Texas Water Commission records from January 1987 through June 1989 disclosed only 33 of the approximately 600 companies operating during that time returning waste from Mexican *maquiladoras* (Texas Center 1990). John Hall, chair of the Texas Water Commission, stated that "tons and tons of toxic materials are being improperly disposed of along the border" (MacDonnell 1991).

The preference to retain toxic materials in Mexico, rather than to return them for disposal in the United States, is explained partially by differences between environmental protection practices in the two countries. Satchell (1991) points out that, although Mexican environmental protection laws compare favorably with those of the United States, Mexico does not have the resources to apply its laws. Problem areas include funding, disposal sites, waste removal technology, and personnel to ensure enforcement. Mexico has no legislation resembling either the U.S. Freedom of Information Act or community right-to-know laws that have been used to pressure U.S. officials into actions designed to reduce environmental degradation. Plants also are allowed to operate on "good faith," before obtaining their full complement of environmental permits. For example, of 1,600 *maquiladoras* operating on the border between the United States and Mexico, only one had all required environmental permits at the close of 1989 (Texas Center 1990). Additionally, *maquiladoras* have become Mexico's second-largest source of foreign currency, immediately behind oil, generating over four billion dollars annually (MacDonnell 1991). The U.S.-owned companies that have created this financial boom have established plants in Mexico for the lower operating costs, including fewer environmental restrictions (Hein and Von Zante 1991). Thus, even where inspectors are available, they are under heavy pressure not to alienate companies that bring dollars into Mexico's troubled economy (Guillermoprieto 1990). Given these conditions, the incentive to dump the waste in Mexico, rather than to transport it back to the United States—where disposal costs range from $200 to $2,000 a barrel—is high ("Texas Border" 1990).

These questionable operating practices are exacting a high price in terms of environmental degradation. Even those who support maintenance of current working conditions in *maquiladoras* recognize that environmental damage should be controlled. De Forest (1991) argues, for example, that, although *maquila* wages and working conditions may be considered exploitative by U.S. standards, they are nonproblematic because both are an improvement over typical conditions for Mexican workers. She agrees, however, that environmental pollution is "a problem" that must be addressed. Several surveys of the border region have demonstrated that indiscriminate dumping is poisoning the soil, raw sewage and waste are being pumped into canals and rivers, and toxic fumes are being discharged directly into the atmosphere (Satchell 1991). Each day millions of gallons of untreated waste flow into canals along the thousand-mile border between Texas and Mexico ("Texas Border" 1990). These canals connect directly to the Rio Grande, which is the region's primary water supply. Greider (1992) describes *maquiladora*-induced pollution in Brownsville and Matamoros as "toxic stew." He discusses high rates of mental retardation and physical deformities among children in the area, pointing out that the American Medical Association has called the area a "virtual cesspool and breeding ground for infectious disease."

Maquiladora operations have prompted considerable debate among border residents. Over the years questions arose regarding how close to the border *maquilas* had to be located, how much of the work had to be completed at a plant located in the United States, and what happened to a *maquila*'s legal status when the parent company closed down the U.S. half of a twin. Although passage of the North American Free Trade Agreement (NAFTA) has rendered these aspects of the *maquiladora* debate moot, environmental conflicts associated with the manufacturing industry continue to multiply. Throughout the final months of the national debate over NAFTA, Cameron County residents were as bitterly skeptical about President Clinton's enthusiastic predictions of economic salvation as they were about Ross Perot's dire warnings of economic devastation. "We already have NAFTA," they told me. "It won't change things for us." In 1995 (after NAFTA's passage) their perspective had not changed.

The Anencephaly Scare

Most residents of the United States remained blissfully unaware of environmental degradation in Cameron County, Texas, until anencephaly thrust Brownsville into the national media spotlight in 1991. Anencephaly is one of three neural tube defects that occurs infrequently among the U.S. population. In the anencephalic fetus the anterior end of the neural tube fails to close, resulting in either partial or complete absence of the brain. Anencephaly occurs during the first sixteen to twenty-six days of pregnancy, and babies who are born with this condition die within a few hours (TDH-CDC 1992).

Dr. Margaret Diaz, an occupational health physician in Brownsville, notified the Texas Department of Health in April 1991 that three anencephalic infants had been born in Brownsville within a 36-hour period. When TDH officials investigated, they discovered that 6 anencephalic infants had been born in the same hospital between 27 March and 21 May 1991. Nationally, anencephalic births occur in approximately 3 per 10,000 pregnancies. This cluster indicated a rate of 60 per 10,000 pregnancies. Because predictions based on national rates were far fewer than 2 cases per year in Cameron County, the TDH contacted the Centers for Disease Control (CDC) in Atlanta, Georgia. The two organizations launched a cooperative investigation of neural tube defects, including spina bifida and encephalocele as well as anencephaly, reported in Cameron County during the past three years. Their study had four components: surveillance to define the magnitude of the problem, case studies to define parental risk factors, laboratory testing to screen for nutritional factors, and evaluation of available data on environmental pollutants (TDH-CDC 1992).

The final report, which was released on 1 July 1992, reclassified the occurrence as merely "a long-term incidence," rather than an "epidemic" (TDH-CDC 1992). This conclusion was facilitated partially by the investigation's focus on the broader category of neural tube defects, rather than on anencephaly. When examined over the three-year period, the Cameron County rate of neural tube defects was slightly more than triple the nationally reported rate of 6 per 10,000 (TDH-CDC 1992). The report listed lack of necessary data as the investigation's primary limiting factor. Cameron County, for example, did not have complete records of birth defects occurring in hospitals, much less any information on nonhospitalized births. Data on air, water, and soil quality also was lacking. To correct these problems the report recommended that Texas implement a statewide birth defect registry and conduct targeted environmental studies. Based on conclusions from recent studies of neural tube disorders in China, it recommended that the TDH provide folic acid supplements to women of childbearing age. The only strong correlation found in the investigation was a previously established positive relationship between low socioeconomic status and the occurrence of neural tube defects (TDH-CDC 1992). Local residents who had waited eagerly for the report were enraged by its inconclusive findings as well as its apparent minimization of their plight.

Television news brought a somewhat different story into the homes of viewers across the nation. On 26 March 1992, for example, ABC's "PrimeTime Live" ran the story of anencephaly in Brownsville. Diane Sawyer began the narration by inviting viewers to "imagine that you're pregnant and an epidemic, a kind of terror, is striking your neighborhood." Viewers were then taken on a tour of Brownsville, where they visited with Paula Steiner, a nurse who had spent hours going through records in her search for answers. Steiner, rather than Diaz, was identified as the person who first contacted TDH. Finally, viewers met Domingo Gonzalez, an activist who gathered water and soil samples for testing then led a "toxic tour" of Matamoros. On 18 and 19 May CNN ran its story, which began with photographs of shacks surrounded by filthy water, industrial plants with smoke billowing from the chimneys, and a drainage pipe emptying into the Rio Grande. Reporter Mark Feldstein introduced viewers to "one of the foulest environments" on earth, where "a mysterious new plague is spreading." He then interviewed some of the mothers of anencephalic infants. Feldstein used these interviews, along with an interview segment with a local pediatrician named Theresa de la Cruz Gomez, to explain the "plague" to his viewers (for a more complete analysis of television coverage, see Groenendyk 1994).

The story also was carried in local, regional, and national print media (examples of non-Texas coverage include Adler 1992; McClintock 1992; and Suro 1992). Many stories emphasized community activists' anger toward the investigation conducted by the TDH and the CDC. For example, Terrell (1992) reported local residents' claims that, since the investigators did not collect environmental data, it was not surprising that they found no correlation between pollution and neural tube defects. Further, residents pointed out that the case study component relied on a culturally biased English-language survey to collect information from people whose first (and sometimes only) language was Spanish. Despite the media's attempt to explore what was happening in Cameron County, many residents were angered by their arrogance. Gomez shared two experiences to illustrate the media's offensive behavior. She was especially angry with CNN reporters, who "focused on sensationalism" and sought out mothers of anencephalic infants who did not want to speak with them. "They were even disruptive here in the center" [Brownsville Community Clinic], she declared. "One mom was in the middle of doing a nutritional interview with a nutritionist. And they just came in with their cameras." In another incident an "Italian news reporter literally took the door of a mother off the hinges so that they could get inside her house" (I2, R19).

Anencephaly focused national attention on Cameron County and its *maquiladora* industry. Scientists rushed to propose studies they previously had thought possible to conduct only in developing nations. Reporters mobbed medical practitioners whose names had been connected with early reporting of the incidents. Following her appearance on television broadcasts Gomez received a flood of offers to provide legal representation, requests for interviews, simple statements of sympathy and support, violently hostile diatribes, and love letters.

Some area residents were not pleased with the attention. Accusations of irrationality long have been leveled at those who focus attention on questionable aspects of *maquiladora* operation. For example, on 27 May 1990 a fire broke out at Deltronicos, the General Motors *maquila* in Matamoros. When firefighters and medics attempted to get in the plant, guards locked the doors, refusing them entry. The guards also prevented workers, many of whom eventually were overcome with smoke inhalation, from leaving. Only when an official from Mexico's Interior Ministry arrived and arrested one of the guards were firefighters and medics allowed to enter. More than 70 workers were hospitalized. Although the full incident was covered in Mexican newspapers, the Brownsville newspaper did not mention the guards' actions and reported that the workers were treated for "hysteria symptoms" (Coalition 1990). The president of the Matamoros *maquiladora* association repeatedly has denied the possibility that working conditions and industrial effluent may be linked to high rates of birth defects among *maquila* workers' children. He has asked the Matamoros city council to have Gonzalez, the "toxic tour" guide, investigated by Mexico's Interior Ministry, which human rights groups have linked to deaths of journalists, labor leaders, and political activists (Selcraig 1994). The mayor of Brownsville called Dr. Gomez and other persons who have worked to facilitate further study of anencephaly, as well as other birth defects that occur at an unusually high rate in the region, "a bunch of lunatics" who are damaging the community's economic potential (Terrell 1992).

By the time I first visited Cameron County, in November 1993, its residents had become accustomed to notoriety. After serving as "guinea pigs" in countless scientific investigations, they discovered that science is conducted by human beings and funded by organizations that are deeply implicated in maintaining the status quo. They also learned that economic development carries hidden costs. Company executives for the border's new industries move from the Midwest and other U.S. regions into homes in the new subdivisions that are displacing the county's farmland and wildlife habitat. The promise of jobs in these industries increases the already heavy flow of human migration from the south, which further overwhelms the county's planning and development efforts. One result is the miles of densely populated *colonias* that have sprouted up next to luxurious subdivisions. In the *colonias* people live in houses constructed of corrugated metal, plywood scraps, and whatever else they can scrounge. Extension cords thread from one house to another, enabling people who have electricity to share with those who do not. School buses do not drive through the *colonias* in wet weather because they get stuck in the mud. Heavy rains also cause the outhouses to fill up and overflow. County development funds are stretched beyond the breaking point, and there is no indication that the influx will sub-

side in the near future. Sustainable development at the bottom of
the Rio Grande literally is a life-and-death question.

Rhetorical Analysis of Informant-Directed Interviews

In trying to discover how Cameron County residents constructed
the concept of sustainable development, I sought to integrate conceptual foundations drawn from rhetoric with a growing segment of
communication literature which advocates qualitative research to investigate the meaning systems within communities (examples include
Lange 1990, 1993; Waitzkin 1993). The face-to-face interview provides
one of the most powerful methods for understanding how people order
and assess their everyday world. Lincoln and Guba (1985) stress that
when the research goal is to explore value systems, a methodology that
captures this social construction of situations must drive the interview
process. With this in mind I adapted to this situation McCracken's (1988)
"long interview" protocol, which he suggests as a means for stepping
"into the mind of another person, to see and experience the world as
they do themselves" (9).

I first developed an interview guide to direct conversation toward
those aspects of community members' meaning systems most directly
related to the relationship between development and the "natural" environment (app. C includes a copy of the interview guide as well as
sample pages of interview transcripts). Questions were designed to give
informants every opportunity to discuss their attitudes toward environmental issues. No question, however, *required* them to discuss specific
environmental conflicts. One purpose of the interviews was to determine whether these issues were important enough to my informants
that they would mention them when asked less targeted questions. In
other words, I attempted to discover whether my informants considered the natural environment to be an important dimension of their lives
as well as how they characterized it. My goal in conducting the interviews was to produce a text that would illuminate my informants'
orientation toward sustainable development and enable me to understand the motivational hierarchy out of which it developed.

Selection of Informants

I began by telephoning people who were featured in television
and newspaper coverage of the region. I also telephoned city offices

in Brownsville, the chamber of commerce, the school district, the Port of Brownsville, hospitals, public and private medical clinics, members of the *maquiladora* association, local officers of environmental organizations such as the Sierra Club and Audubon, managers of the local irrigation district, and media outlets. Finally, I contacted relevant offices of the U.S. Fish and Wildlife Service, EPA, Texas Agricultural Extension Service, Texas Department of Health, Texas Water Commission, and the International Boundary and Water Commission. To expand my pool of informants I asked everyone with whom I spoke for the names of others with whom they interacted (either cooperatively or oppositionally). Rakow (1986) labels this technique for obtaining informants as "snowball sampling."

Appointments for personal interviews were obtained by telephone contact. If the person was willing to participate, a convenient time and location for the interview was arranged. Based on a review of the news coverage of the region, as well as telephone conversations with area residents, I initially categorized participants as representing one of the following interest groups: (1) health care (including physicians, nurses, therapists); (2) state and federal regulatory agencies (including the U.S. Fish and Wildlife Service, Environmental Protection Agency, Texas Department of Health, and Texas Water Commission); (3) industry (ranging from manufacturing of automobile parts and ships to agricultural production); (4) nongovernmental organizations (ranging from Audubon Society and Sierra Club to Valley Interfaith); and (5) educators (ranging from extension agents, media representatives, and others involved in public construction of environmental issues to public school personnel). I interviewed thirty-two people, divided approximately equally across these interest groups. Those representing manufacturing industries were most reluctant to speak with me.

I traveled to Cameron County several times, where I conducted interviews in locations ranging from hospital waiting rooms to private offices to restaurants. Three graduate students (Kathi Groenendyk, Jay Todd, and Jill Webb) who participated in this project took turns assisting me with the interviews. Interview length depended on the informant's interest, communication style, and competing time commitments, with the shortest interviews taking thirty minutes and the longest over two hours. All interviews were tape-recorded then transcribed at a later date. We conducted a second interview with approximately half of our informants six months following the initial interview. Reasons for failure to obtain second interviews varied. One informant died, several moved out of the state, and still others were too busy to talk with us a second time. Some informants invited us to participate in additional activities with them. We visited homes in which we helped carve a Halloween jack-o'-lantern, looked at albums of vacation photos, and ate homemade chili. Later we joined some of our informants at an annual beach cleanup and an Audubon bird count. After all interviews were conducted, we provided the participants with copies of their interview transcripts and a summary report.

Interviews were transcribed by a professional typist. The resulting transcripts provided the primary text for an analysis of sustainable development options for Cameron County. To provide additional background for this chapter, I used field notes taken while visiting Cameron County, proceedings and notes from public meetings, reports prepared by government and nongovernment organizations, and newspaper and magazine articles.

Analysis of Interview Transcripts

Three concurrent goals drove my analysis. I wanted to determine how community members described their own perspectives toward development and environmental protection; how they described the perspectives of other community members with whom they would have to coordinate to establish viable development policy; and possibilities they saw for dialogue across interest groups. With these goals in mind, I worked with members of a research team to identify distinct themes found in the interview transcripts then to reformulate the text obtained from those transcripts into broad conceptual categories. Finally, I used those categories to guide a rhetorical analysis of sustainable development in Cameron County. The rationale for this analysis grows out of previous analyses of stories for the purpose of enhancing communicative exchanges between land users and conservation agencies (T. R. Peterson 1991; Peterson and Horton 1995).

Initial analysis of interview transcripts was performed by three members of a research team, including myself and two people who had not conducted interviews in Cameron County. We worked with transcripts from 12 informants who had participated in at least two interviews, ensuring that we included participants from each of the five interest groups identified earlier. We began by examining the interview transcripts in detail then moved gradually to more general observations, adapting the five steps of interpretive analysis suggested and demonstrated by Peterson et al. (1994). First, we searched for individual themes in each transcript. We then developed each of the themes identified in step 1. Third, we determined the relative significance of the themes. Fourth, we searched for oppositions and thematic hierarchies among the themes. Finally, we compared these relationships across transcripts. Each of us worked individually through these steps then produced a brief report. Finally, we discussed our individual reports and used them as the basis for constructing a composite thematic profile (Gilbertz, Peterson, and Varner 1994).

At this point the themes that were excavated from informants' talk provided me with a basis for reconstructing the terministic screens through which my informants viewed environmental and development issues. I used the thematic profile we had constructed from the 12 selected interviews as a starting point for analyzing the transcripts of interviews conducted with all 32 participants.

Sustainable Development in Cameron County

The 32 people I interviewed stressed the interrelated concepts of border culture, complexity, and growth. A concern with improving the quality of life in the Lower Rio Grande Valley permeated discussion of all three concepts. The unique culture of the border concerned all my informants. They were alternately proud of or shamed by their status as a borderland, with its accompanying poverty, growth, migration, and cultural diversity. Informants also stressed the complexity of development, some of them focusing on social systems, others on natural systems, and still others on the complex relationship between natural and social systems. They spoke frequently of the chaotic nature of life in Cameron County. Many claimed that environmental protection and economic development initiatives were stymied by policy makers' ignorance of life in a borderland. The border also exacerbated difficulties associated with human population growth. Many informants blamed uncontrolled growth for degradation of both human health and the environment.

The paradox of the border seeped into everyone's talk, whether they were longtime residents or recent move-ins. I was told that the border mattered only in the minds of distant bureaucrats by the same people who claimed that the border defined their very existence. I experienced that paradox each time I visited. The downtown streets of Brownsville teem with the same enticing looks, smells, and sounds as the downtown streets of Matamoros. A wrong turn lands you in the middle of poverty and deprivation in either place. The filthy waters at the bottom of the Rio Grande serve populations on both sides. Just outside of town the goats on either bank look the same. When I flew home, I always felt out of place, alien, for a day or two. But, when I was no longer enveloped in the border mystique, I knew it mattered which side you were on. The difference between mundane existence in Brownsville and Matamoros, however, is considerably less than that between Brownsville and nonborder communities in the United States. Rather than being nonexistent, the border has become a hyperreality that creates a unique culture, alienating its members from other citizens of their own nations and bonding them to one another. Anzaldúa (1987) writes: "The U.S.-Mexican border *es una herida abierta* [is an open wound] where the Third World grates against the first and bleeds. And before a scab forms it hemorrhages again, the lifeblood of two worlds merging to form a third country—a border culture" (3).

Although informants generally agreed that more knowledge was needed to cope with complex development problems, there was marked disagreement regarding what kind of knowledge was most needed. Informants saw knowledge as developing out of scientific education, personal experience, or some combination of the two. Those who talked about science viewed it as potentially helpful but often harmful as used. Everyone had suggestions for properly managing the region's development. Preferences for managing the region's complex natural systems ranged from aggressive micromanagement to a completely "hands-off" approach. The range of preferences for managing social systems was less broad, with no informant advocating the hands-off approach. Perceptions of government involvement generally were negative. People representing all interest groups talked about the value of cooperation and local input when making decisions. They stressed that coalitions and alliances were essential to resolving development conflicts.

The overall perception of growth was negative, although informants were split over the valuation of growth within the manufacturing sector. Many followed the conventional tendency to privilege economic thinking over other forms of rationality when they labeled new manufacturing industry as positive because it expanded the region's economy.

They were ambivalent, however, about whether industrial growth led to a net profit because it also increased the region's rate of human population growth, which meant that the recently expanded economy had to be shared among more people. They indicated that the number of people who did not have the ability to pay for needed infrastructure increased faster than those who did have that ability. None of my informants viewed the region's human population growth as a positive feature. Many had seen local and regional planning efforts overwhelmed by rampant increases in human population. Most said that planning provided possibilities for resolving growth-related problems. Much of this discussion was related to border issues. Many of the planning efforts they were involved in, for example, focused on binational health care efforts or binational environmental plans.

Themes in Context

Brief examples drawn from eight informants' interviews illustrate how these themes relate to one another.* Hal Ketchum works as a liaison between a federal conservation agency and land developers. Although he grew up in Texas and graduated from a state university, he is not native to the Lower Rio Grande Valley. He did, however, grow up in a border community with a Mexican-American mother. He believed his ethnicity and childhood home enhanced

---

* The names used in this chapter have been altered to protect participants' anonymity; some personal details have been scrambled as well. The following questions provided a general guide for the interviews:
  1. What is it like to live here?
  2. What changes have you noticed?
  3. What are the most important issues you deal with?
  4. Who do you work with, or against, when dealing with these issues?
  5. What do you think motivates these people?
  6. What would a healthy Cameron County look like?
  7. What are the most important problems to resolve?
Quotations from interview transcripts are identified with the letters I and R. The I (1 or 2) indicates whether the discourse comes from the speaker's first or second interview. The R identifies the utterance within that speaker's transcript. For example, a segment identified as (I1, R4) would be the fourth utterance in the speaker's first interview.

his credibility when negotiating with most Cameron County residents because "cultural things come into play—you know, the same ethnicity. . . . You can say, 'I've been in that circumstance,' even though it may have nothing to do with the issue" (I1, R221). He emphasized the complex interconnections between the United States and Mexico, and between humans and other animals, when talking about life in the region. The border's legal and economic implications dominated his discussion of social issues. The *maquiladora* industry was important because it "attract[ed] people and it create[d] additional . . . need for highway and roadway infrastructure" (I1, R19). He found it illogical that "the U.S. Fish and Wildlife Service cannot get involved in anything that happens in Mexico . . . because . . . the *maquiladoras* . . . [are] funded in lots of cases by American monies and companies" (I1, R160). Ketchum described multiple ways in which endangered species serve as indicators of the health of biotic systems and, therefore, as warnings about problems for humans. For example, "even for human health concerns, the first thing they sample is, umm, water quality; bacteria in the water. . . . Those lower organisms [are] the first ones that show signs of some kind of bad impact. . . . So it's a way to predetermine what kinds of impacts you can expect to humans" (I1, R106). In his second interview Ketchum repeatedly characterized this relationship as useful for persuading people to support environmental preservation. He said that endangered species serve "human needs. . . . Maybe that's something—uh—that would help people understand, y'know, what's involved. Maybe it will hit home a little bit better" (I2, R73). Ketchum took care to label his statement as "an argument we use," rather than as deriving from his own perspective, which he characterized as "holistic type of thinking in that, y'know, all this is interrelated" (I2, R72). "I don't have a problem with coming up with ways to help people understand why should they preserve or protect or whatever," he added (I2, R79). Ketchum went on to explain that "aesthetics or whatever [are important]": "Personally I believe we should do it [preserve nature] because I think we have that obligation as a human race" (I2, R83). Cameron County's border location, he believed, demanded long-term planning to account for the inevitable human migration across the river. "We're gonna continue to have train wrecks when it comes to development because they don't have a very good regional land planning effort at all," he charged. "A lot of the farm land is now being developed. So it's lost permanently. . . . Once you have a mall on it y'know, it's gone forever. And it's not only fish and wildlife resources that are lost but other important economic resources like 'ag.' [agricultural] land" (I2, R57).

Norman Jones, a wildlife biologist employed by a state agency, emphasized scientific management in his interviews. Jones argued that the more hands-off management policy espoused by federal conservation agencies was misguided. He explained that biologists "have to do stuff to help the critters," because "nothing's normal anymore. I mean man has had his finger in everything" (I1, R47–50). He told me that, although he shared the goals of the Sierra Club and other environmentally oriented groups, he found their approach overly emotional. "I just cannot stand to even be around them [Sierra Club members] when they're out beating their drums on a particular thing," he declared. "Sometimes they just really take it to the *n*th degree" (I1, R42). He stated several times that such groups' conservation efforts were counterproductive because they ignored "the human problem." Jones described a healthy Brownsville as having "enough native habitat preserved to ensure the wild critters that we have in perpetuity. And it wouldn't be that much more than what we have, but I think it would take some planning" (I1, R47). After interrupting himself with a discussion of appropriate management of habitat for wild "critters," Jones told us that he "had something else to add" to his description of a healthy Brownsville. "Dumping," he proclaimed, "is the number one problem down here" (I1, R51). He then related several discoveries of unlicensed dumping, ranging from the remains of an old sofa to toxic chemicals. He claimed that, because Cameron County was on an international border, it drew more illegal dumping than would otherwise occur. Jones's sudden shift from wildlife habitat to illegal dumping, when discussing how to produce a healthy community, offers one example of the jumbled relationships between social and natural systems which our informants perceived. He offered no apology for abruptly changing conversational topics because, in fact, he had not changed the topic.

Enrique Gonzalez, a Brownsville physician, began his second interview by telling the following story:

Last night I went to see my mom. And, uh, one of the things that I saw was umm—it was about two in the morning—well it was right after the thunderstorm. And, uh, I noticed a certain aroma, . . . and I

said, "Mom, what's that scent that I've been seeing—or I'm smell-
ing?" . . . So we went and I could smell the—um, the aroma. . . . She
showed me a plant . . . some type of plant that blooms at night. It only
comes out at night . . . but I saw in the background there was a little
hummingbird. And—uh—that to me was kind of strange because I
had never seen a hummingbird come out at night. And I started thinking—she said, er I said, "look, can you see it?" And she's over sixty
years [of] age and she has a hard—y'know, vision problems. And she
said, "no, I can't." Then she started looking at it and it was a very
small—small hummingbird. And she said, "can you catch it?" I said,
"no." I said, "I'm gonna leave it—leave it alone because you never—
y'know nowadays, y'know there's certain, uh, plants and things that
have the, um, same—y'know, people will leave things alone if they
can. . . ." Yeah. So I said, "no." I said I was going to leave it alone. But
y'know trying to leave it the same, the environment the same, and
not disturb it. It was one of the things that I thought about. (I2, R4–14)

Like Jones and Ketchum, Gonzalez expressed a deep appreciation for
wildlife, but his management approach contrasted directly with Jones's
orientation.

Gonzalez was one of those who telephoned me to discuss the summary report I sent to all participants. He was happy with the report in
general but was concerned that I had attributed his story to someone
else. I reminded him that I had promised anonymity and told him that
was my reason for using pseudonyms. Although he accepted my rationale, Gonzalez requested that I arrange for direct contact between him
and anyone who contacted me with comments about his statements. He
explained that increased dialogue between all interested parties was essential for improving the quality of development decisions in Cameron
County and that the primary reason he had participated in the project
was to promote that dialogue. He shared Ketchum's frustration with
legal obstacles to binational efforts because "we're all together in this. .
. . Disease knows no boundaries. It doesn't recognize the Rio Bravo, the
Rio Grande" (I1, R53–55). In addition to legal obstacles the border posed
additional challenges. He explained that poor people from Mexico are
"gonna make sacrifices to be along the border towns," because getting
into the United States offers hope for their children's future (I2, R89).
The migration is so extensive that, according to Gonzalez, it is difficult
to figure out "how you could keep numbers on the people that are com-

ing over" (I1, R37). In the U.S. *colonias,* in which many of these people live, Gonzalez has "made home visits to areas where there's four or five people with families living in a household of 20' X 20'. . . . Dirt floors, and I guess you could call them Third World conditions" (I1, R3). Despite his frustrations, however, Gonzalez continued to strive toward binational health initiatives. He hoped that NAFTA would remove some of the roadblocks he has encountered in the past.

Susan Ramirez, a nurse at a local hospital, had married a Mexican national, raised her children near Tampico, Mexico, then returned to Brownsville. She characterized the border culture as equally alien from Mexico as it was from the United States. Ramirez noted: "We're part of the United States that's true but we're kind of in a little line; a division line that's a little bit of Mexico, a little bit of the United States. This is kind of a no-man's-land. And . . . for a while it was a forgotten land where people just kind of ignored us" (I1, R17). She believed the greatest challenge for developing a sustainable community in Brownsville was planning for "the influx of people coming over from Mexico to live here" (I1, R6). She focused much of her conversation on living conditions among that population. "You walk outside . . . their little shack," she explained, "and from about here to where that door is they will have an outhouse. And any time we have a lot of rain, the water level rises and the whole property is polluted" (I1, R13). Local business people, she maintained, have ignored this segment of the county's population because "it's not convenient that they have to be talking about the health problems here" (I1, R22). Others have said, "don't let them in schools. Y'know you've gotta get strict. You've gotta . . . build a wall. If you have to, arm it." Ramirez characterized her own perspective as more compatible with those who have felt they had to "do something over there [in Mexico], . . . because that sort of thing [the wall] is not going to work" (I1, R228). Although she opposed NAFTA, Ramirez joined Gonzalez in hoping it would remove existing obstacles to binational health care initiatives.

Ramirez was one of many participants who discussed significant interconnections between human health and the broader environment. She claimed that, "if we get a cleaner environment, we'll probably have less health issue problems" (I2, R52). Later she elaborated on this claim: "It's all interconnected, any way you look at it. It affects environment. Environment affects health. . . . All these things are interconnected" (I2, R307). Because she saw social and natural systems as intertwined, she believed that "it has to be more of a holistic approach to this [health] problem. . . . We've got to talk to people from the agricultural department. We've got to talk to other people who are doing some great things that we're not even aware of—that we could probably help with in some way" (I2, R266). She labeled the growth of manufacturing around Brownsville "a double edged sword" (I1, R22), because of "the problems that they're having with [*maquiladoras*] dumping and so forth in the river" (I1, R10). Ramirez offered herself as "a living example" of the new health problems experienced by many residents. "When I come back here," she contended, "I immediately start with the sinus problems, the eyes, all of that. . . . Now I didn't have that when I was here 10 years ago. What has really caused the change? . . . I mean the ground and the trees are still the same. So if you say it's plants and vegetation, uh uh, I don't think so. It has to be something that's been added" (I1, R18). That something, she believes, is the *maquilidora* industry. To illustrate the attitude of local business people who refused to see this connection, she said: "I mean you put two and two together and it becomes four for us [health care professionals]. But other people [local boosters], it's not convenient, it becomes a five" (I1, R22). Despite her antipathy toward this group, however, Ramirez admitted that Cameron County could only resolve its development woes when conflicting interests groups got "together over one table speaking together in normal terms without any fighting. . . . Then you would have to come to consensus" (I1, R42).

Frank Johnson, who manages a design engineering and manufacturing firm in Brownsville, claimed to be on good terms with the Texas Water Commission and devoted much of his interview to describing and demonstrating his company's waste disposal methods. He found labor in Brownsville to be "more available and less expensive [than in the Midwest]." He also found workers to be "less productive and less educated and less experienced" (I1, R22). Many of his own workers had grown up in rural Mexico, and to them a factory is "a totally alien environment": "They've never heard any talk about it. They've never seen machines like this. They've never even seen the products that come out of machines like this" (I1, R23). His own experience in Brownsville has been just as disconcerting. He explained that "language is a big [difference], . . . and there are some customs that I have to deal with here that are a little bit different" (I1, R58). He elaborated on this perception by relating a story from his first trip to Brownsville. On the last day of his visit he decided to enjoy a Sunday brunch before driving back to the airport. "All the families were coming in for Mother's Day," he recounted. "I looked around and I was the only person in the restaurant who spoke English . . . including staff" (I1, R59). He decided to accept his company's invitation to relocate despite his uneasiness about the language barrier. Johnson explained that he is studying Spanish because he "had a problem with feeling undereducated. I spent a lot of time in college and I come down here and everybody speaks two languages and I don't" (I1, R60).

He commented at length on managing social systems, emphasizing environmental regulations as a legitimate inducement to care properly for natural systems. He lumped humans with other animals when explaining that "they pass [regulations] to keep from killing the fish and birds and kids and stuff" (I1, R70). "Every time I catch a 19-inch redfish and have to put it back," he pointed out, "[I know] why rules like this exist. If we hadn't poisoned something we could keep the 19-incher because there would be plenty of them, and there aren't" (I1, R73). He described compliance with environmental regulations as "a legitimate cost of doing business." Further, he believed "there is a moral obligation to take care of the planet" (I1, R73). Those who violated the regulations were motivated by "greed." "I don't think it's economic survival," he asserted. "We've survived quite nicely obeying the rules" (I1, R72). Environmental regulations also provided his solution to the pollution that accompanied growth. "All you've got to do," he asserted, "if you don't want people coming down here and dumping their crap [is] tell them they can't, period. . . . Regulate it out" (I1, R35). He admitted defeat regarding pollution generated "on the other side" but believed that NAFTA would improve enforcement of environmental regulations in Mexico. Further, although he did not think NAFTA would impact Cameron County directly, he expected it to improve Mexico's economy, which would slow migration into the United States. "There's no other way," he argued. "We could build a wall. We could shoot them. Okay? What else are you going to do? If you are on that side of the border and you're starving and your family is starving, and over here you can survive, you have no choice" (I1, R40).

Martin Gilbertz and Rick Stone, who farm near Brownsville, were willing to talk with me only if I would interview them together. Throughout our conversation they emphasized the permeability of the border. Gilbertz pointed out that regulating agricultural chemi-

cals used by U.S. farmers did not provide consumers with much protection, because "a lot of chemicals we can't use, they're using over
there in Mexico. The stuff comes right back across the border. . . .
They may test one truck out of a thousand. . . . If they turn one truck
back, big deal. All of the other ones get through" (I1, R13–14). They also
believed that people passed through too easily. "Whether it be dope or
illegals or whatever," Gilbertz maintained, "there's really no control over
them [border crossings]" (I1, R90). When asked to describe life in the
region, he explained that, although "it's not Mexico, in a lot of ways . . .
this place is kind of run like Mexico" (I1, R49). Stone added, "it's a
different world" (I1, R59). He illustrated the claim that Brownsville
was more closely attuned to Matamoros than to other communities
in the United States by relating the results of a recent attempt to
combine Brownsville's school district with that of Port Isabel, a neigh-
boring Texas community: "The superintendent of Port Isabel said it
would be much simpler if you just consolidated Brownsville and
Matamoros" (I1, R45). Unchecked human population growth in the
region angered both farmers. Stone identified "population growth
as the biggest" problem facing them (I1, R97). Gilbertz blamed the
rate of population growth on Mexican immigrants, who "just pop [a
baby] out about every 9 or 10 months" (I1, R85). He believed that
the availability of welfare, combined with public willingness to educate children from Mexican families, encouraged this behavior.
"People from Mexico come here and have got our welfare system
pegged," he asserted. "They get every last dollar they can" (I1, R27).
Later he castigated the school district because "they keep throwing
schools up. . . . They just keep building them, and building them, and
building them, and it's crazy" (I1, R42). Stone also contended that "the
public . . . supports big families . . . [by] sending them to school" (I1,
R98).

Both farmers saw themselves as veterans at balancing competing
interests but decried nonfarmers' failure to balance all the appropriate
dimensions of development. For example, they had to respond to a public
that castigated farmers for using agricultural chemicals at the same time
it refused to buy the products that could be produced without chemicals. Stone explained that "if the public wanted an ugly tomato, an ugly
head of lettuce, then they would be buying it, and growers wouldn't be
forced to use fungicides and as many pesticides" (I1, R38). Later he reflected, "I love the land and I love wildlife. . . . I would like to see some

balance between wildlife and agriculture" (I1, R124). Neither urban developers, government bureaucrats, nor environmentalists, however, have learned to balance multiple goals. Environmentalists, for example, "can't see the balance between agriculture, the people who live in the valley, and wildlife. They want to tilt the scale in favor of wildlife completely" (I1, R103). Further, Gilbertz and Stone represented farming as the ideal balance, providing the economic support that is missing from natural brushland while protecting wild habitats that urban development destroys. Stone claimed that most farmers can maintain productivity and "have a fairly good coexistence with wildlife" (I1, R100). Gilbertz pointed out that "there's nothing that will live under a block of cement or concrete, but there's plenty of things that live out in a field of cotton. . . . You see quail, you see everything out there. Not one-legged quail or three-legged quail, just normal quail" (I1, R34).

Bobbe Jo Beason has taught science in the Brownsville Independent School District for eight years. Because she grew up in Brownsville but lived away from "the valley" for 10 years, she felt comfortable contrasting today's Brownsville with nonborder communities in the United States as well as with yesterday's Brownsville. She explained that Brownsville has "a lot more population similarities to Mexico than we do to the general U.S. population" (I2, R230). For example, "85–plus percent of the population's primary language is Spanish" (I2, R228). Most people, she claimed, "don't consider us part of the United States. We're actually part of Mexico that is on the wrong side of the river" (I2, R227). The temporal differences stemmed from human population growth rates, which she found "kind of scary." "The progression in Brownsville," she continued, "has not been arithmetic. It's been geometric" (I1, R16). Beason claimed that Brownsville's border location has driven this growth rate and that industrial development further accelerates it. She said that most of the labor force for Matamoros' *maquilas* live in "cardboard shacks on dirt roads" (I1, R96). They have little recourse against toxic waste dumped next to their homes because few of them have legal right to the land on which they reside. "And when they move up from that situation," she explained, "they move over here" (I1, R97), creating the *colonias* described by Ramirez and Gonzalez.

Many of Beason's students come from Mexican families that have migrated in search of the prosperity promised by border industries. She told me of "a student last year who was having trouble completing his homework. . . . [She] tried [to call]—no phone. Half of the mail was returned. . . . He was very proud and he didn't want to bring his mother in. He finally brought his mother in and . . . when she sat down with me, the first thing she said is 'We just got hooked up to electricity. He should be able to get his homework done now. We've been doing it with candles and a lantern'" (I1, R34). Beason classified her students' home environments as constituting "a huge rural ghetto" (I1, R149). As a science teacher, she found it "very hard to get them to even think about cleaning up the river or stop burning trash when that's how they keep warm" (I1, R21). She explained that "their whole life is tied up in just surviving, just getting food on the table. . . . Then when you try to talk to them about pollution . . . they can't relate to it very concretely" (I1, R29). She was angered by a federal bureaucracy that provided little assistance for her students' basic needs yet expected her to teach "poor kids who . . . don't even get the paper at home . . . to perform as well on a test . . . as our kids who go home to their families who are doctors and lawyers and run businesses and live in nice houses" (I1, R110). She attempted to introduce her students to an environmental consciousness by recycling, "because there was some money for certain things, such as the aluminum and the cardboard. . . . [They] didn't even think of it as recycling. It was just making money. . . . But we're trying to extend it . . . to educate them" (I1, R22).

Because her students' health was directly impacted by the polluted environment in which they lived, she incorporated into her professional role the responsibility of teaching them that "there's going to be benefits to helping the environment and it's going to make it a better place to live" (I1, R42). She has, for example, encouraged students to test the local water supply "as part of their science projects," because, she explained, "we're at the bottom of the Rio Grande. Those of us that have been living here for a long time have wondered about it." The projects have been limited to "common household testing kits," however, because testing for toxic substances "costs money, so we haven't gone on" (I2, R38). Despite her concerns about the region's population growth, Beason remained optimistic. "If you can get a spirit of community started [among the new immigrants] . . . you can start tying in some with the environmental concerns" (I1, R31–32). She recalled that 10 years ago residents had united against a proposal to burn a barge of waste off Brownsville's coast. When "the EPA came in for their community meetings, they expected to find, y'know, a few well-off, concerned citizens; and we had packed the auditorium with six or seven hundred people. We just kept our ears onto them and were able . . . to get the numbers of people to turn out saying, 'we don't want this here'" (I1, R79–80). Like most of my informants, Beason emphasized collaboration as the best means for determining appropriate development patterns in Cameron County.

Organizing for Sustainable Development

Participants identified both opportunities and imperatives for collaboration across interest groups. Ketchum, for example, suggested possibilities for land management professionals to build bridges with the health care community and emphasized the importance of all parties cultivating empathy for incongruous perspectives. Successful development could not be achieved without all parties reaching "better understanding—overall understanding of why they [conflicting interest groups] . . . think the way that they think" (I2, R122). Stone lamented: "there's so much lack of understanding. A lot of people on the environmental side of the picture don't understand the farmers' viewpoint. . . . And maybe farmers don't understand their perspective either" (I1, R52). Gonzalez explained that "it is very important that we should all try to work and have more communication, more coalitions and more working together with other agencies. . . . There's not enough resources that one state agency or one entity can cover all the different things that are environmental factors and problems" (I2, R22–23).

Awareness of possibilities for collaboration, as well as a simultaneously reflective and activist orientation, probably was higher among my informants than among the general public. Several had initiated, then continued to participate in, community action groups designed to resolve development dilemmas. One woman had been a founder of Valley Proud, a traditional beautification club. Another had spearheaded the region's first beach cleanup. A third informant was organizing a binational team for monitoring tuberculosis patients. A high school administrator missed his second interview because he was in Washington, D.C., working out details of a district-wide science education grant he had obtained from the National Science Foundation. The farmers I interviewed were active in their growers' associations, and some had initiated their first outreach committees. Without planning to do so, I interviewed members of the Lower Rio Grande Economic Development Council, *Frontera* Audubon Society, Coalition for Justice in the *Maquiladoras*, and a local AIDS support group.

I now highlight two unusual organizations that deal explicitly with development conflicts. The first, the Agriculture Wildlife Coexistence Committee (AWCC), seeks "to address problems and conflicts related to implementing the Endangered Species Act in Cameron County and to develop and offer functional solutions to the regulatory agencies that will promote compliance with the law and allow the coexistence of endangered species and the agricultural interests in Cameron County to the greatest possible extent" (Lockamy, field notes). The second, One Border Foundation, seeks to "support research, services, outreach, and other activities that address health problems on both sides of the Mexico and USA border" ("One Border Foundation" n.d.). Both organizations exemplify possible responses to the challenges encountered when attempting to conceptualize and implement sustainable development.

Agriculture Wildlife Coexistence Committee

Background. Cameron County provides a habitat for an amazing variety of bird species, despite the pressures exerted by an exploding human population. The U.S. Fish and Wildlife Service determined in 1987 that the endangered aplomado falcon, which had nested throughout Cameron County well into the 1950s, should be reintroduced. Few Cameron County residents were aware of the bird's existence, much less of plans to introduce it into their landscape, until county agriculture officials received a notice from the EPA informing them that they would be restricted from using 17 pesticides that had been determined potentially harmful to the aplomado falcon or its habitat. A grower told me that suddenly "everybody knew what they were": "I mean some folks said they were the little birds that looked like English sparrows, and the next fellow said, 'No, they're as big as an eagle'" (Peterson I1, R3). Terry Lockamy, the Agricultural Extension Agent for Cameron County, organized a study group that determined the pesticide ban would cost the county between $125 and $350 million in 1988. Scott Peterson, a cotton grower and irrigation district supervisor who participated in the study group, described the reaction to the EPA's notice:

We looked at the list of pesticides and it was obvious to us in this area that we couldn't grow cotton and corn. . . . We didn't have the technology. There were no other alternatives to these pesticides. . . . There was a lot of concern to start with . . . because we were talking about an economic impact of somewhere between 150 to 350 million dollars to the county. . . . So the first thing that happened was that several folks decided . . . we will just tell them that they can't do that. (I1, R1)

The study group drafted a letter urging fellow growers to contact their congressmen and senators, and a local cotton growers' cooperative mailed it to over 1,000 growers. Senators Gramm and Bentsen and Congressmen Ortiz and de al Garza successfully pressed for a temporary recision of the pesticide ban.

As they investigated further, however, Lockamy and his study group learned that the pesticide ban would not go away but would loom over them again the following year. They realized that their ability to construct long-term plans for the region would be crippled by this threat. Growers could not even plan a year ahead, because the ban could be implemented midway through the growing season, resulting in pest damage that could make a crop in which they had invested significant finances nearly unsalable. Out of this atmosphere of uncertainty a new kind of committee was born. Peterson explained:

It didn't take long before we figured out that we didn't know anything about the endangered species act. . . . Throughout all that, we decided that fighting was not necessarily the answer. . . . So one day there were about four of us sitting in the coffee shop drinking coffee and we decided, "why don't we try to do something positive? Why do we have to be on the defensive all the time?" So we decided to try to put together a group . . . to represent all the folks that would have a concern with the falcon . . . and also with . . . the ability of us to continue to farm. (I1, R1)

The four men drafted a mission statement on a paper napkin then immediately began searching for people who would be willing to join such a group. Lockamy said most people who worked with agriculture turned him down because they were afraid of being branded as traitors. He believed they also were afraid "to sit down at the table with the enemy." When he invited the president of the local Sierra Club to participate, "she declined, but didn't explain why" (I1 field notes). After several months' work the self- proclaimed organizers were satisfied that they had achieved a sufficiently representative membership, and the Agriculture Wildlife Coexistence Committee was born.

The original nine member committee included three cotton grow-

ers and representatives from the U.S. Fish and Wildlife Service, Texas
Parks and Wildlife Department, Texas Agricultural Extension Service,
Texas Department of Agriculture, the Audubon Society, and an
agrichemical company. Membership changed somewhat over time as a
result of professional relocation or personal dissatisfaction with the
group. Both Lockamy (Extension Service agent) and Peterson (a grower)
had been part of the original coffee shop conversation from which the
committee had developed. Peterson chaired the group's meetings, and
Lockamy became the group's (unofficial) facilitator. For this analysis I
interviewed Terry Lockamy and Scott Peterson as well as John Nelson
(manager of a U.S. Fish and Wildlife Service Refuge), Sue Green (manager of Audubon's Sabal Palms Refuge), and others who participated in
committee deliberations but who have not become public advocates of
their process. I also viewed a promotional video that the Cooperative
Extension Service had produced to publicize the committee's success
(Spears and Dale 1995) and read articles written by committee members
and the media. Green, Peterson, Lockamy, and Nelson are featured in
the video as well as in most of the press clippings.

Peterson explained that, after determining the committee's membership, they decided to seek semi-official status by asking the Cameron
County Commissioners Court to "bless this committee as far as the work
that was concerned" (I1, R2). The Coexistence Committee was appointed
as an ad hoc function of county government in February 1988 and held
its first meeting in March. In April members presented official statements
at a local public hearing and at a congressional hearing on the Endangered
Species Act in Austin, Texas. They submitted a final report to the EPA on
31 May 1988. It took two more years and pressure from some unlikely
sources, however, before the EPA acted on their recommendations.

Working Together.   The AWCC had been working for five years
when I first talked with its members. Committee members originally
looked forward to their meetings with dread. According to Lockamy,
"everybody said, 'You can't work with the environmentalists. You
can't work with the farmers. They're unreasonable'" (I1, R12).
Peterson told me that "when we first sat down across the table from
each other it was obvious that most of us were from completely differing viewpoints. And, quite frankly . . . all of us thought that this
was a waste of time; that we would never have anything but just a
dog fight out of the whole situation" (I1, R2). Nelson admitted "feeling pretty skeptical about the whole thing. [He] thought it would be

a big waste of time" (I1, R22). Nobody disputes Green's claim that she was the only member who came to the first meeting with positive expectations. From such inauspicious beginnings a successful collaborative effort was born.

Ultimately, committee members decided that they had not wasted their time. Within less than one year they worked out a solution that "all of [them] could live with": "an environment that the falcon could exist in . . . but also provide a way that agriculture could continue to be an economically viable industry in the valley" (Peterson I1, R2). Nelson attested that the committee "worked out a really neat arrangement there. . . . It worked out fantastic" (I1, R22). He proclaimed publicly that the result "was excellent. . . . We started there and actually worked that one out to where I felt like the endangered species came out of it great—better than they ever would have before. And the farmer felt real good about it too" (Spears and Dale 1995). Green explained: "The whole point here is, we wanted to work together. We've got to have some people who are willing to work together" (I1, R35). She admitted that in order to come to a consensus she had to "give up some things. But we gave it up to benefit the falcon" (Spears and Dale 1995). Both cotton producers and supporters of falcon reintroduction believed that the AWCC's deliberations resulted in recommendations that would lead to an improvement over the previous situation.

After the committee had reached an agreement at the local level, it faced another challenge. Although its recommendations were accepted locally, Peterson explained, the "Fish and Wildlife at the . . . head office in Washington, or whatever, would turn down our ideas. Or EPA would ignore them" (Peterson I1, R6). Nelson took the group's message to the U.S. Fish and Wildlife Service every chance he had. Peterson explained that "after about four years of struggling through this we finally got the attention of the right people" (I1, R6). When Nelson persuaded a regional director to meet with the committee, he "was so impressed with what was being done and with the attitude of all the folks here locally . . . that he began to put some pressure on from the top side" (Peterson I1, R6). From that point the U.S. Fish and Wildlife Service was on the committee's side. The EPA presented another hurdle, which the committee cleared in an unusual way. On 3 July 1989 the agency published a revised proposal for pesticide bans associated with reintroduction of the aplomado falcon. Committee members who read the proposal believed

(accurately) that the EPA had failed to consider their recommendations when constructing its revised opinion but were not sure how
to remedy this oversight. Later that year an official in EPA's Washington, D.C., pesticide section was visiting with representatives of
"one of the environmental action groups [who] were in Washington
doing some lobbying":

> They mentioned to Larry, they said, "There's some farmers and
> some environmental folks and some Fish and Wildlife people in
> the Rio Grande Valley that have been trying for several years to
> work out some solutions and you folks don't listen to them. You
> need to listen to them." . . . I was in a meeting with Larry shortly
> after this happened and Larry said, "I never had anybody from the
> environmental community ever tell me to listen to farmers. . . .
> That kind of rang a bell and I began to go back, and . . . sure enough,
> I found this big thick file there that had all this information from you
> folks. . . . and we began to look at it and decided . . . let's try to
> work with these folks." . . . So what came out of all that was we
> finally were able to offer a solution to provide a relatively safe envi-
> ronment for the falcon and alternatives to farmers that they could
> continue to operate. (Peterson I1, R6)

Lockamy and Nelson also told me that, since gaining the attention
of "people at the top," their proposal had encountered no significant
barriers. The AWCC's proposal for pesticide management became part
of the aplomado falcon reintroduction plan. In 1994 committee members celebrated by assisting with the first major release of aplomado
falcon into Cameron County. The falcon appear to be thriving, and farmers continue to produce cotton.

The AWCC is unique in that it persuaded the appropriate federal agencies to reverse an Endangered Species Act jeopardy ruling
on the basis of a locally generated report. It no longer meets regularly but mobilizes quickly when asked to respond to specific issues.
The group has, for example, initiated discussions between parties
interested in a proposed revision to the county's boll weevil eradication program, facilitated establishment of a coalition to discuss
problems associated with degradation of sea grasses in the local bay
system, and advised the EPA when it was developing a study
prompted by human health issues in the county.

Why Did It Work?   The AWCC has been widely celebrated as a model for grassroots organizing and collaboration. By the time I learned about the committee and met its members, their original conflict had been resolved. The committee's success, however, had taken on almost legendary proportions among the local agricultural and environmental communities as well as state and federal agencies responsible for environmental regulation. The president of the local Audubon Society chapter, a science teacher who had organized the area's first beach cleanup, and two young cotton farmers told me what an incredible woman Sue Green was. A banker, another science teacher who is trying to "develop an ecological consciousness" in her students who live in the *colonia* across the road from their school, and a Texas Department of Health employee in Austin praised Terry Lockamy. When I talked to those who had served on the committee, I was enveloped in a warm, fuzzy cocoon of mutual commendation. They proudly shared stories about how the trust they had developed during the years of hard work had held up since that time. I have interviewed dozens of agricultural producers about conservation issues, and their attitudes toward environmental agencies ranged from overt hostility to grudging acquiescence. I was amazed to hear Peterson's unqualified praise (as well as that of another grower who participated in AWCC deliberations) for the U. S. Fish and Wildlife Service's Ecological Services director. Peterson made sense of this for me by explaining that the director was the person who had met with their committee, had subsequently assisted them in gaining agency support by "put[ting] pressure on from the top side," and who has since encouraged AWCC members to "help others start such coalitions."

Peterson told me a story about a poisoned ocelot (an endangered species native to this area) which was discovered by U.S. Fish and Wildlife Service personnel. After determining that the animal had been a victim of illegal baiting, they called the local Agricultural Extension office (where Lockamy works) with a description of their discovery, including the name of the pesticide used. Peterson proudly told me that "Extension went to all the suppliers and developed a list of everyone that had purchased this pesticide in the last couple of years, turned that list over to Fish and Wildlife, and offered a reward" (I1, R7). My face must have betrayed my surprise, because he went on to explain, "we've really developed a trust here with each other that has really made strides to work out our problems.

We don't hide around behind the trees looking at each other anymore" (R8). I confirmed the story with agency personnel.

All this mutual approbation was a bit disconcerting, especially considering the negative attitudes with which most members had begun their tenure on the committee. The AWCC had no trained mediator. Most members believed that it would be impossible to work with other committee members and did not expect a positive outcome. Two members had to be replaced during the first year. Meetings began in an atmosphere of deep mistrust. There was every reason to expect that the committee would fail to achieve a mutually satisfactory resolution to the conflict. The unusual success of the AWCC illustrates Pearce's (1989) claim that even incommensurate perspectives are "potentially comparable" and that certain practices "facilitate coordination without (necessarily) agreement among the participants" (186). Pearce claims that appropriate intervention in incommensurate conflicts requires "understanding the other, making oneself understandable by the other, and creating, if necessary, a new vocabulary in which 'translations' can occur" (189). The AWCC used the diverse knowledge bases and backgrounds of its members to develop a terministic screen that enabled Cameron County cotton growers, environmentalists, and agency personnel to discover cooperatively, within themselves, capacities that were appropriate for their new situation.

Committee members identified several strategies they used to achieve perspective by incongruity. Lockamy explained that one of the committee's ground rules was deference to each member's expertise, with an accompanying agreement to share information openly. Committee members agreed that agriculturalists would be responsible for bringing information about farming, including what pesticides were used, how they were applied, and economic considerations of various crops and methods. Environmentalists were responsible for bringing information about the falcon's needs, its preferred habitat conditions, and its history. The U. S. Fish and Wildlife Service representative was responsible for providing information about legal limitations, supplementing the environmentalist account of habitat conditions preferred by the falcon, and the agriculturalist account of pesticide applications. Peterson confirmed that "all of us agreed to yield to . . . each other's expertise. In other words, it was very difficult or impossible for me to try to make some determination as to what it would take for a falcon to exist. And it would also be foolish for Fish and Wildlife or the environmental community to try to tell me what it took to grow cotton" (I1, R3). There was no holding back of information. Green explained that, for the process to work, "we had to talk to each other and we had to come in with real information . . . using as much facts as we possibly could upon which to base our information" (I1, R29–30). All committee members professed having learned a great deal from those they had previously regarded as enemies.

The willingness to offer and to accept divergent perspectives did not happen overnight. Lockamy declared that the committee met for a year—Nelson said "six months to a year"—before members trusted one another enough to "drop their fences" (Lockamy I1, field notes; Nelson I1, R22). Lockamy explained that before their participation on the committee they had "created that wall—that callous—y'know that shield that [was] gonna have to be peeled back" (I2, R33). Later he described their experience as "almost like we had to die, then go through the process of grieving before we could work on the problem. It was painful" (I2, field notes). Peterson, who now takes the gospel of coexistence to other communities involved in conflicts between agricultural and environmental concerns, expressed frustration at people's impatience with attempts to transcend old occupational psychoses. He told me that many communities fail at coexistence because they "are still struggling with the fact that you don't automatically and immediately get acceptance" (I1, R7). Nelson explained:

> It takes time to trust each other and quit accusing each other and pointing fingers. You have to come to the point where you're actually listening to the other person and what their views are and understanding them. And then you can move from there. But first of all you've got to get that understanding of what their real problem is. Not what they're screaming and yelling about but what they're really upset about. And if you can get to that then you've got a chance of working on a solution. . . . It takes a certain amount of trust. We're just now starting to get that with a lot of different people, that we've worked with them long enough and they think they believe we're honest enough that we're trying to say what's on our mind and get to the bottom of it and deal with the problem. (I1, R29)

So trust was seen as an essential building block for establishing an understanding of alternative perspectives.

Finally, the desire to seek creative alternatives was discussed by all members. Green, who was optimistic about the committee from the beginning, explained that "finding the right people to put on this committee was important. You can't put in people that are not going to listen to anybody else and are not going to look at any other facts. You've got to put people in there that are willing to listen and talk and to be sincere" (I1, R32). Peterson disapprovingly lumped a wealthy property rights advocacy group with a litigious environmental advocacy group, "who just increase our adversarial situations in Texas," claiming that "if they want it to succeed . . . they have to look for alternatives and that's the key. As long as you can solve it with dollars or with law you're never going to get to the people problem" (I1, R11). When Nelson discussed the importance of accepting alternative approaches, he emphasized the similarity between supposed enemies: "The perception of the enemy is always that they are this huge monster. And once you kind of get to know them a little bit and talk to them, they're no different than anybody else. They just have a little different spin on life" (I1, R30). He argued that, when people realize how much they share, they lose the fear that has blinded them to new alternatives. Lockamy emphasized both the similarities between all humans and the positive value of diversity. He explained that "once [people] get to the table and get beyond the first initial . . . hostile encounter . . . they find out that what they really want out of life is not very different from what the other guy wants" (I2, R68). When discussing the importance of searching for solutions, he argued that "it wasn't the sameness that has made [the United States] strong. It's been the diversity" (I2, R41). Later he added that "working relationships" based on diversity were "extremely powerful" (I2, R82). The committee's diverse membership enabled it to develop a terministic screen that had not been identified previously by any interest group from which members derived their primary sense of identity.

I've had considerable difficulty extracting myself from the fuzzy cocoon formed by the AWCC members, and perhaps this description reflects that mood too completely. Yet these people are no Pollyannas; they still live at the bottom of the Rio Grande. Nelson, who wishes he could spend more time working on successful collaborations like this one and less time "putting out fires," summarizes the value of this experiment when he explains, "the word 'coexistence' was a unique part of the title. I used that to explain it to a lot of people in Fish and Wildlife. We don't have to love each other. It's not about everything's gonna be lovy-dovey, cuz it probably won't. But we can coexist" (Spears and Dale 1995).

One Border Foundation

The One Border Foundation extends the concept of coexistence in a different direction. The AWCC works to facilitate coexistence between humans and wildlife and, within the human species, between environmentalists and farmers. Although One Border limits its efforts to coexistence among humans, the people for whom it serves as an advocate are as distant from the powerful economic function system as are any wildlife. Both organizations owe their existence to local discontent with governmental responses to a crisis. The AWCC eventually received enthusiastic endorsement from those governing bodies, partially because it seems to have resolved a potentially divisive issue. Conversely, One Border, which began as a means for conducting independent research into the anencephaly outbreak around Brownsville, has yet to achieve a harmonious relationship with the Texas Department of Health or the Centers for Disease Control. Another fundamental difference is that membership in the AWCC consists of a wide variety of interest groups, while membership in One Border consists primarily of health professionals. Although AWCC participants came to understand highly incongruous perspectives among themselves, they have been able to mitigate environmental perturbations with minimal alterations to the relations between function systems. One Border, however, advocates a realignment of these function systems which demands a new social configuration. By focusing on the health of people who are alienated from the economic system, the organization offers the possibility of expanding the discussion of development beyond the terms provided by the economic code.

Background.   I went to the Brownsville Community Health Center to interview Carmen de la Cruz Gomez and Rosa Ramirez, two of the most vocal critics of the TDH-CDC birth defects study. Ramirez manages the center, and Gomez was the only pediatrician on staff at the time. A secretary told me that, despite our appointments, Ramirez might not be able to see us that afternoon. She was working on a grant application with an epidemiology student who had to leave the next day. When I said we were flexible and offered to reschedule for the next day, or the day after, she grudgingly made another appointment. Then she explained that Gomez had so many patients that it probably would be impossible for her to talk with me. She was sorry. After I had waited for about an hour, she asked if I would like to see the clinic, which was just next door. The labs and treatment rooms seemed familiar. The waiting room, however, overwhelmed us. The room was jammed with sick people. The low rumble of conversation was punctuated with coughs and wheezes. There were no fish tanks or magazine racks. There were no free walls to lean on. Instead, rows of folding chairs stretched from wall to wall. Every chair was occupied by an adult. A few adults and many children sat or squatted on the floor. When people were called by a receptionist, they collected children and possessions and, stepping over other people's children, made their way to the front desk. One of the adults who had been sitting on the floor quickly slipped into the empty chair. When we left the waiting room at 5:00 P.M., it was still full. By 5:30 most of the office staff were gone. Ramirez, however, remained closeted in her private office until 6:00. When she and the graduate student emerged, they were discussing a problem with a filing cabinet at the satellite clinic. They needed some information that was in the cabinet, but someone had lost the keys. When Jay Todd, the graduate student who participated in this set of interviews, revealed that he could pick simple locks and offered to help, Ramirez immediately confirmed an appointment with her for tomorrow. The next thing I knew, I was following Consuelo Rosario down a rutted road somewhere in Cameron County.

The cabinet contained no confidential records, so, after Rosario had pulled out the data she needed for the grant application, she permitted us to rifle through the files. We spent the evening reading the correspondence eventuated by Gomez's appearances on national television, newspaper clippings regarding anencephaly in Brownsville, and notes regarding the establishment of a nongovernmental organization called the One Border Foundation. Rosario shared Ramirez's and Gomez's belief that state and federal health agencies had long ignored environmental hazards associated with the border manufacturing industry because they were under pressure to support NAFTA. She never had spoken with the news media, however, because she was a student who would someday be seeking employment in those agencies. Rosario explained that ignorance of Cameron County's culture had limited the potential of the TDH-CDC study, which had then led Ramirez, Gomez, and Paula Steiner (a nurse at a local hospital) to press for more carefully targeted studies.

Ramirez's involvement in the anencephalic birth study "started when one of [her] midwives came in for her weekly meeting . . . [and], as she was walking out the door said . . . 'I got a teenager that's about to deliver an anencephalic child'" (I1, R1). Ramirez asked for clarification, and the midwife promised to keep her abreast of any related developments. A few days later Ramirez received a telephone call from someone from the CDC who wanted to talk with her about three anencephalic births that had been reported by a local physician. Their telephone conversation led Ramirez to conclude that the person "didn't know what we were, who we were, or anything." She was worried, because "this guy's coming out of Atlanta, he's a big cheese," and he would be conducting a study in her community (I1, R2). She was further dismayed when she learned of his plans:

> He said, "well, we've got an instrument that we're using. It's the normal protocol. And, um, you know, we'll look at the results after we've finished. . . . We've found there's 21 [moms], and we're going to talk to all of them." . . . Then I asked him if the survey had been translated, and he said, "we've got somebody that's well versed in it that will be asking the questions in Spanish. . . . So then I said, "so how successful have you been with it?" And he said, "well, we've known for about 20 years that it [the instrument] really doesn't work." And I said, . . . "so why do you use it?" And he said, "well, it's protocol you know. We don't make the rules, we just follow them, and you know it takes an act of Congress, literally, to make these changes." And I said, "I see we're behind the times in Brownsville, Texas." (Ramirez I1, R2)

Gomez explained that the "well-versed" person who interpreted the instrument was "a Hispanic female who had zero experience doing interviewing." Gomez "liked her" but believed "she ha[d] no ability to translate an instrument like that" (I1, R16). Steiner, the nurse who had telephoned TDH about the anencephalic births, believed that TDH and CDC had done the best job they could, given the fact that they were from "out of town. They did not know our culture." When she attempted to facilitate connections between them and local health professionals, there was no time available (I1, R16). Gomez echoed Steiner's concern that the study "was done very hastily" (I1, R16). Gomez considered the use of an English-language interview instrument that had not been effective in past studies to be only "the first insult" (I2, R20).

Ramirez maintained that the CDC "didn't know about our [Cameron County's] culture" and did not attempt to learn (I2, R20). Although "they're supposed to become sensitive to the particulars of the area, in terms of health care," she pointed out, the CDC, for example, "didn't know about our *parturas*, our lay midwives" (I1, R21). As several of my informants explained, midwives deliver a large portion (exact percentages are not available) of the infants born in Cameron County. Gomez had "tremendous problems with their lack of understanding with the border. You know, it's like, 'we're feds, we're state employees, we can't cross the border.' Well, what are [they] doing here?" She laughed. "I mean, really, this is one community" (I1, R16).

A final irritation, explained Gomez, was that "any environmental concern that we gave them was just completely ignored" (Gomez I1, R16). Gomez said she tried to "work with TDH. . . . But any time we gave them any information it would be either irrelevant, or not collected appropriately" (I1, R12). She and Ramirez noted, for example, that all the mothers who had given birth to anencephalic infants during the past year had lived extremely near the Rio Grande during the early part of their pregnancies. When they mentioned this concern and provided TDH-CDC with a map, they were told that it was irrelevant to the study. When TDH and CDC began "work on the first draft" of the final report, they sent "select bits and pieces" to the Brownsville clinic. Ramirez started "to panic because they hadn't done any of the environmental stuff. And the person who was in charge of that continued to say that there's nothing wrong with the environment" (I1, R24). Ramirez later discovered that the person responsible for exploring environmental linkages had gone to the state archives: "The state archives show nothing. So her explanation was that if there is nothing in the archives then there's nothing wrong. Okay. And that was the extent of it" (I2, R25). Her concern about the mother's location in relation to the river was irrelevant because the study did not examine potential environmental connections. Rather, it looked to see if past studies had done so.

As part of the data collection phase, TDH and CDC personnel asked Ramirez to provide them with a list of names and addresses for relevant patients as well as any statistics she had on infants born with neural tube defects. Despite her irritation that the patient survey would be conducted with an instrument that did not work, by people who had not even attempted to understand the local culture, Ramirez provided the list. Local activists including Ramirez, Gomez, and Steiner wrung an agreement from those conducting the study to hold an interim meeting in Brownsville to report their progress. The meeting date came and went with no word from either TDH or CDC. A week later Ramirez telephoned their liaison and told him: "I'm really pissed. We really need to get these people on the stick. We have a community that's waiting to burst because, . . . we still are in the dark. They've used us, they've abused us, they've used our numbers, they've used our names and addresses, and we deserve something better than this" (I1, R5). By the time a meeting had been rescheduled, Ramirez was "already working on the One Border Foundation because [independent research was] a really hot potato, and [they felt] like the clinic [would] get in all kinds of trouble if [they went] out after private money" (I1, R6).

Working Together.   Gomez explained that One Border "was set up, hopefully with long-term goals, so that when health needs arose . . . in this community, we would be able to respond with whatever funds we could raise" (I1, R24). Ramirez established the foundation because the TDH-CDC study convinced her that, without local control, human health research conducted in the Lower Rio Grande Valley would not be sensitive to the health of those it studied. After efforts to cooperate with TDH and CDC had failed, she attempted to sponsor independent health research through the Brownsville Community Health Center but discovered that the center was barred from certain activities because of its status as a federal grantee. Gomez explained that the clinic is "a 60 percent federally funded community migrant center. . . . [However,] over the last twelve years of the Republican administration, we've been cut progressively so that we have to seek alternative sources of funding" (I1, R8). The clinic's legal status also posed "real super logistic" problems (I1, R7). Ramirez pointed out that "because we're federally funded we're not allowed to call Matamoros, to go to meetings in Matamoros, or do business with anyone on the other side. . . . And so, we would go on annual leave every time we would go across, and we'd use our own personal cards to call across the river" (I1, R7). This proscription seemed irrational at best. Steiner explained: "we share so much, . . . we need to look at how we can work with Matamoros . . . because if you don't, you always are gonna be in a third world country. We're always gonna be dealing with that, because we're only bringing half the people up" (I2, R23). Another woman clarified that people move both directions between Matamoros and Brownsville. "A lot of people from the States go to Mexico for their health care," she explained, because they "like the care in Mexico better." Others use Mexico's socialized medical system because they "don't have any money" to pay for care in the United States. Conversely, those who cannot "access the care there . . . come over here, [and] a lot of, umm, pregnant ladies would come and deliver over here so that a child would be an American citizen" (Salvador I2, R101–2). She added that "the Brownsville Community Health Center was sending some ladies to have tubal ligations in a hospital in Matamoros, [because it's] . . . a tenth or a fifth of what it would cost here in the United States" (I2, R106). It seemed clear to these activists that their community did not stop at the Rio Grande.

To obtain alternative funding necessitated by cuts in federal support, the clinic relies on "support from the local community." When Ramirez proposed that the clinic should sponsor further research on anencephaly, "those who are a part of the chamber of commerce, the Economic Development Foundation, and county officials and city officials were concerned that we were going to create such a ruckus with the research that the ability to bring in new industry and tourism was going to be killed." Because the clinic "couldn't afford to kill those relationships," she decided to establish a "separate nonprofit organization" (I2, R13). Participation in the anencephaly research, even when supported by One Border, rather than by the clinic, angered some residents. Steiner described an incident that occurred in a "health committee at the chamber of commerce." The chair turned to her and asked: "If they have to do the study on anencephaly why don't they do it somewhere else? Can't they do it in Hidalgo County? They need to do it elsewhere." She nodded at my puzzled expression then added, "And this is a *health* committee!" (I1, R33). Gomez, who was the clinic's medical director at the time, disclosed that a member of the clinic's board of directors had "requested [her] resignation because of the work that we were doing" (I2, R5). She resigned as medical director rather than eliminate her participation in One Border's projects.

One Border is governed by a board of three members. Ramirez, who is the chair, is assisted by Steiner and a local physician. When I first interviewed Ramirez and Gomez, the foundation was approximately one year old and had obtained funding to start two projects. The largest was an independent comparison of anencephaly rates, and the other was a community outreach program designed to educate about and provide increased access to prenatal care (Gomez I1, R25). One Border was trying to work with health providers in both Brownsville and Matamoros on the prenatal care and education project. Ramirez, Steiner, and Salvador, another informant, described how they had integrated nurses, midwives, and other health providers into Brownsville's community outreach program. The second time I spoke with Ramirez she was delighted because she had "just met with people in Matamoros last week," to discuss their attempt to "to duplicate what we're doing on this side [of the border]" (I2, R49). When I spoke with Steiner and Salvador eight months later, the collaboration had been pronounced a success, and the network they had developed was providing the basis for a new project. They were working on a binational health education program to be implemented in both Matamoros and Brownsville. Steiner characterized a related visit with Matamoros educators as "a real eye-opener," because "Matamoros had gotten a little bit further than what we had" in its health education efforts. Steiner, who had expected that Brownsville would "share so much, because they [Matamoros] don't have very much," was amazed by the sophistication of the health education program offered to students in Matamoros schools (I2, R19–22).

Ramirez and Gomez also attempted to work with their counterparts in Mexico on One Border's anencephaly rates study. "The whole anencephaly thing," however, "became very political" (Gomez I1, R25). Ramirez expanded on Gomez's comments about the political challenges they encountered, in an attempt to illustrate the importance of working through an independent organization. One of the weaknesses of the TDH-CDC study, which One Border attempted to remedy in its follow-up, was the failure to examine data on anencephaly rates in Mexico, especially the region surrounding Matamoros. The data, however, were not forthcoming, despite several attempts by One Border participants to procure them. Ramirez finally asked a Mexican colleague to put her in touch with an epidemiologist from Mexico City. Although the epidemiologist did not provide Ramirez with data on anencephaly, she did explain why the data were unavailable: "no one from the Federal Government is going to allow you to do research on the Mexican side from your side of the border, because it will ruin the chances of NAFTA passing" (I2, R27). Ramirez became angry and scheduled a meeting with Texas governor Ann Richards. Governor Richards told her that she had a dinner appointment with Mexico's President Salinas within the next two weeks and would mention the problem to him. The afternoon following Richards's and Salinas's appointment, Ramirez received "an urgent call from some people that had flown in from Mexico City who

were epidemiologists and health officials." She accepted their invitation
to discuss the possibility of sharing information but predicted that "24
hours will pass and I'll get a call from Washington." The next day Ramirez
obtained data, as well as information explaining how they had been
gathered and interpreted, from the team. Later in the afternoon, however, she received a call from "an irate person" in Washington, D.C.,
who demanded: "how dare you meddle in this? This is an international
affair and you have no business making contact. Remember you are
a federal grantee" (I2, R28). Ramirez responded to the thinly veiled
threat by telling the caller that she had been acting as chair of the
One Border Foundation, which was "an independent, not-for-profit organization" (I1, R28).

Ramirez, who has been involved in health care politics for years,
describes the decision-making process in Austin and Washington, D.C.,
as "real skitsy," or "just insane." One Border provides her with a "sanity
point," from which she can take "the logical route" to improving human health at the bottom of the Rio Grande (I2, R66). She sees the
foundation as an opportunity "to start from zero and devise a system to
set up base data for the sake of determining what is going to be safe for
our kids." She laments that this should be so difficult to achieve, when
"we all claim to be Texan, we all claim to be bright, we all claim to love
our country and love our families and love our kids. But when we get in
the same room with each other it's like, let's go for the jugular" (I2, R67).

What They Learned.   All of the women associated with the One
Border Foundation saw it as a vehicle for improving the living conditions in Cameron County and beyond. As they designed and conducted
their own epidemiological research, they acquired increasingly sophisticated mastery of scientific argument, which intensified their original
anger at attempts to minimize their concerns. They also became less in-
clined to value outsiders' versions of reality over their own experiences.
After following the TDH-CDC study, Steiner asked, "how can you separate environment away from y'know health? . . . Because we are all
part of the system that we have to look at together." She considered
the decision not to study environmental pollutants a fundamental
error (I1, R118–21). Salazar seemed more tolerant of outsiders' inability to understand reality. After all, it took residents of Brownsville
and Matamoros "years to realize that we're one community. . . . It's
the same air [on both sides of the border.] . . . I mean we can't say,
'OK, this is the border,' for the water and air and all that" (I1, R107–8).

Given outsiders' ignorance of such basic information, however, she doubted their ability to conduct meaningful research in the region. One of Gomez's most serious concerns "is the growth of unregulated industry without any clue of what's in the environment." After describing a long struggle to obtain environmental monitoring equipment, she indicated its minimalist nature: "what we've got is a pump at the zoo" (I2, R14). When CDC and TDH personnel "come up to [her] and say, 'have you gotten enough attention now?'" Gomez responds, "Well, I hardly think so since all we have is a pump at the zoo" (I1, R29–30). Ramirez responds to their cavalier attitude by telling them: "you can't come down here and be condescending because it doesn't affect you. You don't live here. You've never experienced a child without a brain. You've never experienced the poverty. You've never experienced the mess of the environment. And you can go back to your nice little hole and turn it all around. So don't come to us" (I2, R30).

One Border arose in response to epidemiological research, which is medical research concerned with determining the nature, causes, extent, and methods of preventing diseases occurring in groups of organisms (Christie 1987). Epidemiologists attempt to reconstruct and to infer the effects of doses of a substance from reports of subsequent illnesses and deaths. Commonly, this research takes the form of "population studies" that compare the occurrence of conditions allegedly caused by the substance in question in an exposed population to both their normally predicted occurrence and their occurrence in a similarly constituted but nonexposed "control" population. Taylor (forthcoming) depicts epidemiology as a systematic project seeking to explain and predict the relationship between pollutants and human bodies. He argues that, while epidemiology is cloaked in the powerful myth of scientific objectivity and rationality, its practice involves strategic decisions about formulating research questions, selecting data, and determining appropriate models for analysis. He argues that, in the case of nuclear testing, the contingencies of epidemiological data and positivist criteria for validating claims of association between pollutants and illness converge to support official arguments for sustaining dangerous practices.

My informants argued that similar convergence has justified continuation of dangerous industrial production in Cameron County, where the rhetoric of epidemiology is integrated within a complex network of political, economic, legal, educational, and religious interests that utilize the technological psychosis to perpetuate the logics of pollutant production. One Border participants are not impressed by claims of objectivity. "Why is it okay to include the guy from the public utilities board who says that the water inflow valve to Brownsville, Texas, is nowhere near the *maquiladoras* [in the final report of the TDH-CDC study]," asked Gomez, "and it's not okay to include my statement, standing in front of the inflow valve, pointing at a *maquiladora,* saying 'that's a *maquiladora.* This is the water intake valve'" (I1, R15). Gomez accused TDH and CDC of using the precepts of epidemiology to further "their interests . . . in calming the public, first and foremost." She did not believe they had any interest in conducting an "investigation that might turn up some answers that may be hard to deliver" (I1, R15).

For a variety of reasons the TDH-CDC study did not establish industrial pollutants as a cause of Cameron County health conditions. Because the examination of environmental factors consisted of looking in the state archives for results of past studies, Ramirez refers to the section that reports "no correlation" between neural tube defects and environmental factors as "the environmental research that never happened" (I1, R34). Even if environmental monitoring had been performed, however, this type of association is difficult to establish, because the cumulative effects of many pollutants are not immediately visible, do not yield evidence of their cause, and are affected by other intervening variables (Taylor, forthcoming). For example, because illness in Cameron County's population may be influenced by multiple factors including lifestyle, diet, and heredity, a number of complex influences can combine to affect the probability of any individual's developing a specific set of symptoms. Additionally, safety levels have yet to be set for many of the chemicals used in the Lower Rio Grande Valley. Although "if you fall in a vat of the stuff you're going to die," Ramirez points out that "no scientist has ever risked saying this *will* be hazardous to anybody's health over a period of time" (I2 R60–61). Studies of long-term exposure, at relatively low dosages, are expensive and are difficult to fund. Ramirez does not find this surprising, because "the people that could do that are the people that produce the stuff and they're making good money off of it. Why should they want to stop making money?" (I2, R63).

The TDH and CDC dismissed findings from the Brownsville clinic as "statistically insignificant" because of their small sample size. Gomez believed this argument was carefully constructed to justify a choice not to examine unwanted data. Ramirez and Gomez explained that, during the study, local health professionals thought it would be important to test anencephalic infants or fetuses. They "asked them [CDC] multiple times, . . . 'what do we do with the baby, with a placenta? Give us some guidelines.'" The CDC sent no guidelines, however, and did not follow up on their suggestion to conduct tests (Gomez I1, R12). Clinic personnel "did test just one baby on [their] own. [Yet, after they reported the results to CDC, they] were unable to do it anymore, because it wasn't the proper protocol." The infant they tested showed "breakdown products of benzene, [and] most people didn't even know how to interpret it." The CDC ordered them not to conduct any additional tests and "denied that it was significant at all" (Gomez I1, R13). In a later conversation with Gomez the CDC clarified that the lack of significance was determined because only one baby was tested. "I'm open-minded enough to know that . . . one baby is not significant, but certainly, it's the only positive result that we have today," declared Gomez (I1, R13). She added: "the other thing we picked up on the baby, that we were very concerned about, was five different pesticides. We didn't know what standards we had for pesticides in something that small." When they were again rebuffed by the CDC, they asked "the U.S. Fish and Wildlife Service for an opinion on the levels of pesticide picked up on the infant." Although the agency was unable to tell them whether the levels were inappropriately high, "they were concerned about it." This interchange led to discussions of cooperative studies with the U.S. Fish and Wildlife Service (Gomez I1, R13).

Epidemiological studies also can emphasize viral, genetic, and lifestyle factors as principal causes for illness, reconfiguring the situation as one wherein victims are responsible for their own illness. The TDH-CDC folic acid recommendation illustrates this strategy. Gomez explained that "folic acid was still in the middle of controversy in most scientific journals" when the final report was completed (I1, R22). Further, neither the blood tests nor the questionnaire responses indicated that a folic acid shortage was present in Cameron County's population. In fact, Gomez explained, "zinc deficiency is much more critical among the Cameron County population, and large dosages of folic acid can intensify zinc deficiency" (I1, R22). Ramirez and Steiner added that the traditional Mexican diet provides satisfactory levels of folic acid. Gomez believed that the agency turned to the folic acid recommendation as a means of deflecting responsibility for neural tube defects from society onto individual mothers. The only statistically significant correlation reported by the TDH and CDC was that between socioeconomic class and neural tube defect rates. Gomez also pointed out that "the [folic acid] campaign" is flawed; as she put it, it consists of "see[ing] how many bottles of Centrum we can put out there" (I1, R22). The campaign focused on marketing, with no follow-up and no evaluation component. She concluded her remarks by suggesting that she did not know "if you can find anybody in this community who feels that passing out Centrum vitamins is going to make a huge [difference]" (I1, R22).

One Border members also argued against the validity of comparisons between Cameron County neural tube defect rates and those of Mexico. Both local politicians and scientists emphasized that the anencephaly rates in Cameron County were similar to those of Mexico City. When Brownsville's mayor repeatedly described anencephaly as "a Hispanic disease" (Terrell 1992), Steiner wondered, "are the genetics a part of the transformation of an environmental issue?" (I1, R28). She argued that, although Hispanic populations in Mexico and South America have a higher rate of anencephaly than does the U.S. population, this could be caused by environmental factors as easily as by genetics. Salazar indicated that the only aspect of the situation that was "caused" by the high proportion of Hispanics in the population was the choice not to conduct extensive environmental monitoring. One factor that prevented environmental monitoring was cost, and, "if this anencephaly problem had happened in Austin, they would certainly pour a lot of money in there." But, Salazar asserted, the study was done at minimal cost "because it's on the border" (I1, R16).

Ramirez took the argument further, arguing that the statistics used in the TDH-CDC report misrepresented reality. She had learned, in her forbidden discussion with epidemiologists from Mexico City, that the figures TDH-CDC had presented as constituting the Mexican anencephaly rate "are only, like, the top 10 hospitals in Mexico City—the largest. And it does not include the . . . hospitals or birthing centers along the more highly developed areas" (I2, R41). She added that, if one included rates reported from these institutions, the rate "translates into pretty much what we say in the United States is the norm. . . . So the [Mexican] national average . . . [used in the TDH-CDC report] . . . is based on the population in Mexico City, and on "a very small segment" there (I2, R42). Steiner pointed out that, even if neural tube defect rates from Mexico City provided a valid comparison, the conclusion that the victims' Hispanic heritage caused their higher rates did not necessarily follow. "Mexico City is not the cleanest city in the world either," she charged. Rather, "it's one of the worst environmental areas in the world" (I1, R29–30). "Maybe it's a lot of different causes that are happening. But let's find out what they are," she urged. "Let's don't just say, 'Oh, Hispanic. You're similar to Mexico City. That's the reason'" (I1, R31).

The intuitive connection made by Brownsville residents between human health and the Lower Rio Grande Valley's ecological integrity has been vigorously rejected by politicians as well as by the scientists they employ. These officials have provided bland reassurances about their protection of public health and have invoked the warrants of rationality, patriotism (NAFTA), and racism to suppress dissent. They have characterized associations made by the public as misperceptions and have used technical jargon to intimidate residents with little formal education. One Border's story offers an alternative vision to that provided by government officials and their scientists. It confronts official knowledge claims with a powerful subjectivity that threatens to destabilize traditional perspectives toward development. It threatens, for example, to supplant the economic function system's dominance when it rejects the liberal risk models (which underestimate risk) chosen by industry representatives. Rather than arguing with claims that conservative models (which overestimate risk) could disrupt the functioning of NAFTA or diminish the chances of new industries deciding to locate in the region, One Border changes the fundamental grounds for argument, claiming that economic recovery is not the point.

Even more significant is my informants' replacement of scientific knowledge claims with a different kind of truth. Epidemiology conceptualizes the anencephalic infant as an object existing independently of the scientist and all other persons. It fragments the body into independent pieces, such as "age" and "percent of neural tube development," for evaluation. After codifying the body as bits of data, epidemiology then aggregates it with other pieces in new categories based upon their possession of traits and conditions the researchers have selected. Epidemiology, then, objectifies, codifies, then aggregates bodies to establish universal truths (Taylor, forthcoming). My informants' stories spoof epidemiology by emphasizing the interpretive processes whereby scientists select and use various models that influence the universal truths they discover. Instead of objects, they depict mothers who give birth to monsters and babies who are born without brains. They challenge the economically bounded development story by evoking the complex relationships that exist between nature, ethics, economics, and people. They attest in credible detail to the work associated with sustaining life in Cameron County, with the "Third World grasping at the First" (Gomez I2, R23). Ramirez summarized, the last time I saw her, that One Border's purpose is "keeping people alive down here" (Ramirez I2, field notes).

Commitment to Community

Sustainable development in Cameron County, Texas, presents an impossible disaster or a vast array of possibilities. Its residents have discovered what it means to encourage perturbations between function systems. Members of the Agriculture Wildlife Coexistence Committee redefined sustainable development by collaboratively building a new terministic screen. One Border's members examined the technological psychosis presented by epidemiology and discovered that the emperor had no clothes. Neither case entails total destruction of old perspectives; as Terry Lockamy pointed out, "the farmers still don't want to get in bed with the environmentalists" (I2, field notes). Both, however, entail new commitment to change. Maria Salazar explained that she "was never a fighter before. I mean I was just kind of real meek. . . . But I think we need to be strong so I don't care what they think about me" (I2, R147). Most important, both represent community as coexistence among all dimensions of life.

Understanding the terministic screens that prevent interpenetration between function systems is central to implementing sustainable development in real communities. The stories of sustainability told by Cameron County residents expose old screens, suggesting policy alternatives that encourage system interpenetration. Further, they indicate how fundamentally we need to question our thinking about development. Exploring their diverse approaches to sustainability can help us better understand how symbol systems influence the possibilities for building community among people as well as for preserving opportunities for connections between humans and other life forms.

Chapter 7

Envisioning
Sustainable Development

We are all indigenous to the Earth.

Kai N. Lee 1993a

The rhetoric of sustainable development has linked international negotiators in Rio de Janeiro with participants in public hearings across Alberta, Canada, and residents of Cameron County, Texas. In each case participants struggled to construct a humane system for managing rapidly increasing demands on the environment. If nothing else, these cases indicate that traditional patterns of development require fundamental revision. Sustainable development's presumption of a bounded, rather than infinitely expanding, world may provide a basis for that revision. It offers neither an alarmist vision in which technologized civilization is doomed to immediate extinction nor a complacent arrogance that assumes technology automatically will fix everything. Instead, the concept of sustainable development implies flexible boundaries that are amenable to human ingenuity, which in turn is grounded in nature.

Sustainability offers an attractive alternative to the dichotomy between ecocentric and anthropocentric frames for ethical questions about how humans should live. It encourages us to require that further technological development expand protection for the natural environment in which that development is grounded. Its optimistic vision discourages doomsday predictions and thus protects us from the despair that often leads to inertia. Kai Lee (1993a) explains that sustainability reminds us that "the future of the earth is entwined with the human race—not only in the sense that the earth is our home, not yet in the sense that we can control the planet, but already in the sense that human actions influence decisively the habitability of the world for ourselves and all other species" (4). It offers hope that there will be a tomorrow toward which we should direct our energies.

Lee (1993a) suggests that environmentally sensitive development demands increased understanding of both "the relationship between humans and nature" and "the relationships among people" (8). Rhetorical criticism is one means for exploring the second of these issues. The three analyses presented in this book have shown how analyzing people's talk about development issues helps us understand the complex relationships among those issues. They also suggest that meaningful sustainable development will emerge from localities in which drastic environmental perturbations disturb the typical functioning of those relations.

The cases I explored suggest that sustainable development offers no pat answers to complex questions. It does, however, offer a systematic means for incorporating divergent ethical orientations and political norms into policy decisions. Communication practices both constrain and facilitate attempts to bring these orientations and norms to bear upon political solutions—which vary across time and space, resolving and exacerbating conflicts, promoting and hindering research, and sanctioning a diverse array of environmental policies. Although the case studies do not provide a unified definition for sustainable development, they do offer clues to how we might construct such a definition. They suggest at least three pathways toward sustainable development. First, interactions between function systems and terministic screens impose both positive and negative constraints on sustainable development. Second, sustainable development is most likely to emerge from bounded conflicts. This does not lead to an orderly development program but, instead, to an expanded and increasingly meaningful public sphere. Third, perspective by incongruity can enable those who would implement sustainable development to transcend their differences, rather than merely pretending them away.

Interaction between Function Systems and Terministic Screens

The United Nations Conference on Environment and Development provides empirical support for Luhmann's (1989) caution against allowing a single function system to dominate discussion of an issue. Both the *Rio Declaration* and the speech delivered by President Bush deferred completely to neoclassical economic explanations when discussing environmental protection and human development. Although market transactions do not lead automatically to sound environmental and development policies, the concept of the free market attained mythical dimensions in both documents. This imagery led to a terministic screen wherein "sustainability" was barely visible, being essentially displaced by the concept of (economic) equity. This set of terms had the unfortunate effect of reviving the pre-Brundtland language of rights and responsibilities, within which international discussion reverted to a mutual diatribe of blame between rich and poor nations. Social training can trap people in self-enforcing patterns that direct them toward destructive behavior.

The unfortunate emphasis on economic equity which emerged as the central tenet at Rio de Janeiro reminds us of Burke's ([1935] 1984a) concern that an inappropriate system of human interaction is just as likely to be self-enforcing as is an appropriate one. Sustainable development remains especially susceptible to the erroneous assumption that technology can fix anything. The accommodationist stance taken at Rio can encourage thoughtless development, based on an expectation that a new technology can be found to repair whatever damage may accrue. Lee (1993a) cautions against relying too heavily on technology when deciding how to manage human relations with the earth, pointing out that over the past decades "our science and technology persistently outran our ability to govern our expanding capacity to change the world and ourselves" (4). Sustainability's close association with the traditional development paradigm may encourage reliance on the economic function system to the exclusion of all others, blinding us to past folly.

The Canadian hearings on whether to exterminate all bison in Wood Buffalo National Park illustrate a case within which competing terministic screens produced competing vocabularies. Although speakers for both the Cree and Dene Metis people and Agriculture Canada relied primarily on the scientific function system's code of truth and falsity to frame their vocabularies, they were unable to create compatible terministic screens. Aboriginal speakers' facility in drawing terms from other function systems into their discourse provided them with far more flexibility than most other speakers demonstrated. Whether Agriculture Canada's proposed bison slaughter simply threatened the existence of their society drastically enough to provoke the necessary resonance between function systems or because their culture was inherently more flexible, their use of a "poetic" vocabulary enabled them to highlight the ridiculous aspects of their opponents' "technological" discourse. The poetic terministic screen used by aboriginal participants was not, however, sufficiently flexible to penetrate Agriculture Canada's technological terministic screen. Although the hearings appeared not to change any policy, they sparked additional scientific research into the truth or falsity of relevant taxonomic issues. The aboriginal argument that experience (as opposed to formalized education) provided a better information base upon which to base truth claims revealed the interaction between the science and education function systems to public view. This increased public attention may have influenced an unofficial nonimplementation policy pursued by politicians eager to avoid being removed from office.

Aboriginal insistence that religious questions of eminence and transcendence were central to any decision introduced the troubling notion that science was only one among many functions performed for and by society. This threat to scientific omniscience constitutes the most radical aspect of aboriginal discourse. These members of the nonexpert public claimed that education gained through mundane experience, combined with religious beliefs, provided more appropriate guidelines than science for deciding how to develop the region. They articulated what Campbell and Benson (1996) call "the premodern impulse at the heart of the rhetoric of science, [which] is the . . . effort to reclaim common sense or practical reason as intelligent" (88). Ironically, an impulse that Campbell and Benson characterize as "premodern" facilitates a "postmodern" critique that deconstructs Agriculture Canada's control of the decision-making process .

The system closure that protects Agriculture Canada and the hearing conveners from their social environments, however, clearly includes the seeds of its own disruption. Because a system's most fundamental attribute is self-preservation, opportunities to disrupt ingrained patterns of interaction occur whenever the system's environment intrudes dramatically enough to arouse fear of system destruction. In Cameron County, Texas, some residents have rejected the assumption that market transactions provide both necessary and sufficient criteria for determining what sort of technological development will most enhance their quality of life. They explicitly drew upon multiple function systems when exploring development options. In addition to exploring development from an economic perspective, they explored its legal, educational, scientific, and political implications. The resulting discussion facilitated greater awareness of interpenetration among function systems and exposed the dominant patterns of discourse to public view. Once exposed, the vocabulary that scientists and government officials had used to produce and reproduce their own perspectives became nothing more than a tool that could be accepted or rejected according to its usefulness in a rapidly changing situation.

Emergence from Bounded Conflict

The decision to qualify the term *development* with any modifier implies some level of concern with traditional patterns of growth, which immediately opens the door to conflict between supporters of tradition and advocates for change. Further, sustainable development emerges out of multifaceted, sometimes intractable, conflicts. Most obviously, advocates of conventional economic development face off against advocates of environmental protection. Fractionalization occurs within and across these groups as well. Ecological economists blast neoclassical economics for its failure to include development's environmental costs, nuclear energy proponents vilify the coal industry for degrading air quality, and McDonalds brags that its beef does not destroy tropical rainforests. Waddell (1995) points out that even "within the environmental community . . . there is considerable diversity of opinion about the concept of sustainable development" (209). For example, many environmentalists from developing countries opposed the UNCED's Convention on Biodiversity, claiming that environmental organizations based in the United States and northern Europe crafted it with little regard for its human impact. Issues such as these provide the impetus for people to talk about what they consider desirable and undesirable and to justify their claims. The resulting conflicts can be managed in order to create opportunities for usable conceptualizations of sustainable development to emerge. Possibilities, however, rarely become realities. Those who successfully cultivate a social environment that encourages public involvement in changing public policy do so with a combination of careful management and flexible responsiveness to apparently random occurrences. If, on the one hand, conflict is completely stifled, public discussion never happens. On the other hand, if it spirals out of control, nobody hears what anybody else is saying, and communication fails.

The UNCED proceedings illustrate how an international forum can initiate this debate. Intensive media coverage provided enticing tidbits of information to people from diverse stakeholder groups. Because the coverage linked U.S. participation at UNCED to national politics, even people who rarely concerned themselves with international development or environmental protection issues took an interest. An international audience watched environmentalists hang their heads in embarrassment over George Bush's apparent pettiness. If they grew bored with statistics comparing the financial aid Germany, Japan, and the United States promised to developing nations, there were stories of well-heeled entertainers cavorting at the alternative summit. While environmentalists bemoaned the UNCED's failure to initiate substantive international programs to protect the environment, other groups feared it had done too much. Jasper (1992), for example, warns that "the neo-pagan cult of nature worship, long prevalent in environmental and New Age circles, was formally launched as the new world religion" at the summit (134). The UNCED, he claims, has substantially strengthened the plans for "a UN-dominated world dictatorship" (138). Conflicts spawned at Rio provided grist for numerous quarrels but little basis for an exchange of ideas. The result is similar to an escalating interpersonal conflict in which the disputants are unable to recall what led to their argument in the first place. Despite sustainability's supposed centrality, questions regarding the definition and implementation of sustainable development did not loom large in public discussions of the summit.

On the other hand, certain aspects of the summit were effectively isolated from conflict. The *Rio Declaration* displays none of the angst that *sustainable development* typically has produced in supporters and detractors alike. Instead, it uses the term without displaying any awareness of its internal tension. When that tension threatens to intrude into the principles that will guide international decisions regarding environment and development, sustainability is replaced by economic equity. Given Bush's self-proclaimed focus on his presidential candidacy, he might have probed alternative perspectives within the United States. Instead, he responded to the tension by retreating into the protective custody of a small, relatively homogeneous group of advisors who presented a unified front opposing the very idea of sustainable development. Rather than discussing what sustainability meant or its role in redefining development, the United States proclaimed that no redefinition was needed. There were no grounds for discussion.

I do not, however, intend this as a blanket indictment of either the Earth Summit or of such meetings in general. Benedick's (1991) plea that we not judge the conference by its "immediate results, but by the process it sets in motion" can be extended across both time and space. Jasper's (1992) fears are not totally unfounded, for the newly formed Commission on Sustainable Development might possibly provide a forum for discussion about appropriate implementation strategies and even unlock questions about who gets to participate in the decision-making process. U.S. advocates of sustainable development have taken advantage of the fact that Albert Gore has replaced Dan Quayle in the admittedly powerless position of U.S. vice president. The UNCED led to organizations such as the (U.S.) President's Council on Sustainability, which enables diverse groups, including individual municipalities, to become involved in the debate over their own sustainable development. Although none of these opportunities guarantees the emergence of a vision of development transformed by sustainability, each offers a new possibility that should not be ignored.

The public hearings on whether Agriculture Canada should kill all the bison in Wood Buffalo National Park provided the opportunity for a specific, politically grounded exploration of sustainable development to emerge. Lee (1993a) argues that "finding a workable degree of bounded conflict is possible only in societies open enough to have political competition" (10). The hearings themselves were a response to political competition, for aboriginal residents demanded a chance to voice their opposition to Agriculture Canada's plans. Although no translation occurred across vocabularies, both vocabularies were aired. It was clear that Agriculture Canada envisioned a region that would be managed to facilitate more efficient beef production, while aboriginal representatives envisioned a region that would be managed to facilitate a lifestyle that enabled them to interact with wildlife in a traditional manner and on a regular basis. Despite the differences, the focus was clearly on development. One group emphasized increased production, while another focused on the quality of life experienced by the region's human inhabitants, claiming that the coexistence with relatively independent nonhuman life enhanced that quality. These hearings present a bounded, though not simple, conflict from which usable conceptualizations of sustainable development could emerge.

Members of the Agriculture Wildlife Coexistence Committee in Cameron County, Texas, structured a bounded conflict within which they could work toward sustainable development in their region. They accomplished this by limiting their mission to conflicts between the Endangered Species Act and agricultural interests in Cameron County and focusing their efforts on the conflict over reintroduction of the aplomado falcon. This limitation is not wholly satisfactory, for it ignores the larger issues that make it necessary to implement legislation such as the Endangered Species Act. The committee's success in bringing opposing groups into dialogue may have impacted these larger issues more tangibly, however, than if it had attacked them directly. Limiting discussion so explicitly also ameliorated some of the risks associated with participating in this attempt at jointly defining *sustainable development* for their community. Critics should not underestimate the social and economic risks accepted by anyone who joins such an effort. For example, the U.S. Fish and Wildlife Service employee eventually was promoted, based largely on his participation in the coexistence committee. His supervisors and coworkers used several means to discourage his participation, however, until someone in a position of influence happened to examine the committee's actions and decide they were laudable. The Audubon Society employee was transferred because her participation on the committee was found to compromise her employer's position. Although she was not fired, her options for continued employment with the organization have been severely limited. The Extension Service employee has been lionized by his agency, but he was surprised when someone he had never met recognized him and shouted obscenities about the committee from across an airport lobby. One wonders how committee members might have fared if their efforts had ended in a flurry of lawsuits or in a decision that failed to protect their constituencies' primary interests. The condition of bounded conflict induces people to explore new possibilities before fully committing themselves to the outcomes and seems essential to the emergence of sustainable development.

Cultivating Perspective by Incongruity

If rhetoric is a symbolic means of provoking a sense of community among diverse people, the essential rhetorical characteristic of any community lies less in the psychological motivation of the players than in the strategic situation they face. A set of mutually reinforcing strategic expectations binds that community together, encouraging some responses while discouraging others. In any society patterns of expectations owe less to the creation of laws than to the evolution of norms. The relentless flux of that evolutionary process terrifies some participants, while its leisurely pace frustrates others. Those who would avoid social change use language as a tool to minimize it, labeling choices as clearly "right" or "wrong" based on their continuity with the past. They represent that past in rosy hues that no resident would recognize and explain the value of mundane acts as a means of protecting traditional norms. Others impatiently point out the faults in conventional patterns of living, irreverently focusing public attention on the shortcomings of honored traditions. Burke ([1950] 1969) argues that, if human society existed in a state of complete identification, there would be no motivation to communicate with one another. Because each person is a separate entity, however, complete agreement is impossible. Likewise, if we existed in a state of total alienation, communication would be an impossibility. Reality, he suggests, vacillates somewhere between these extremes, with language providing the most basic tool for charting a course of relative harmony.

The comic attitude advocated by Burke ([1937] 1984b) encourages maximum consciousness of human existence as situated in particular patterns of social interaction. By centralizing the concept of human positionality, the comic frame constructs a social world wherein participants collaborate to revise themselves and their situations. That collaboration is not always friendly, and rarely is it easy. It is distinctively cooperative, however, rather than combative. *Sustainable development* offers a guiding term around which supporters of tradition and advocates of change can organize important community discussions. The concept does not require humans to subordinate their needs to those of other life forms, for development is unabashedly human centered. The coupling of sustainability with development, however, is decidedly incongruous. If we maintain that tension, the concept can provide the comic corrective needed to enable us to lurch into the future without the need to destroy our past. By giving us a terminology for asking old questions in a new way, it enables us to discover new solutions. One of the greatest tragedies of the Earth Summit is that organizers banned most of those voices who could have provided a comic corrective to traditional perspectives. Although many of them spoke at the alternative summit, their input to official discussions regarding the relationship between humans and the rest of the planet was essentially lost. Organizers who began with a terministic screen constructed out of a neoclassical economics vocabulary turned to market economists for a revision and ended up pretty much where they began.

Structures for public participation often function to minimize opportunities to articulate incongruous perspectives. Despite being locked into such a structure, however, Cree and Dene Metis participants in the Canadian hearings offered an entirely new vocabulary to Agriculture

Canada and other hearing participants. They began by rejecting the technologically sterile discourse offered by the chair of the hearings and used by most insiders. Arguments castigating the methodology of a competing scientific claim are the easiest, and most commonly used, technique for refuting claims that involve ambiguities about procedures (Prelli 1989, 144–58). Aboriginal participants could have easily taken this approach, emphasizing methodological weaknesses in the research reports upon which Agriculture Canada relied. They chose, however, to highlight experiential knowledge over technical expertise. They argued that spending one's life with the buffalo produced knowledge of greater validity than reading books about them or examining parts of them under a microscope. Instead of arguing over whether the bison had brucellosis or tuberculosis, they said that it did not matter whether or not they did. Agriculture Canada's justification for killing bison was at best trivial and at worst evil. Tribal elders supplemented the fundamental rejection of technological argument with a further incongruity by choosing to testify in their own languages and use a translator to render their remarks into English. Some of these people were perfectly capable of speaking in English but made the strategic decision to speak in the vocabulary of their own locale.

The new terministic screen placed higher value on local concerns than on those expressed by Agriculture Canada and expressly rejected technological reason as an appropriate basis upon which to make decisions about developing Wood Buffalo National Park. It did not, however, extend to rejecting all humans who had used such reason. Aboriginal participants expended great effort showing other hearing participants how to use the new vocabulary. They retold intensively detailed stories to illustrate what kinds of concerns provided a more legitimate basis for decision making. They related an extensive network of such stories to illustrate how these concerns might be woven together to create a more acceptable development plan that would sustain the relationships they valued. Their performance of the new terministic screen invited scientists and decision makers to explore its space, at least temporarily. The new terministic screen never attained the status of a legitimate alternative within the hearing structure, its vocabulary never appeared in any official statements, and the committee's final decision ignored it completely. The hearings were open to the public, however, which included the press. Television, radio, and print audiences learned that Agriculture Canada's story of Wood Buffalo National Park was only one among many. The story told by Chief Beaver, Mr. LaViolette, Chief Sewepagaham, and others provokes public awareness that an alternate vision for regional development exists. That alternative vision has been implicated in the decision to delay indefinitely the proposed slaughter of the bison.

Cameron County's Agriculture Wildlife Coexistence Committee moved a step further in accelerating the evolution of norms upon which development decisions were based by creating an entirely new terministic screen for discussing development in Cameron County. Members of environmentalist and agricultural interest groups joined together to craft a new vocabulary that enabled divergent interest groups to reconstruct a conflict. The new terministic screen enabled members to envision a future that all members saw as an improvement on their current situation. They used one another's previously alien vocabularies to develop a "perspective by incongruity," which enabled them to revise, without destroying or denigrating, social relations within the community. Because the group's work was so politically sensitive, it was not discussed outside of official meetings, except when the discussion had been cleared previously with other committee members. Although few of the committee's constituents became fluent in the new vocabulary, committee members learned how to translate appropriate aspects back into the terministic screens used by the various stakeholder groups from which they had come. Further, their own reflexivity had been enhanced to the point that they were able to help one another develop translations for stakeholder groups they formerly had perceived as enemies and still viewed as opponents. Committee members put their own linguistic resources at risk to blaze a relatively safe trail for individuals who sought some means for coexisting with other community members.

One Border members followed the same path as the Cree and Dene Metis in their rejection of the sanitized account of development offered by technological experts. They began by constructing a terministic screen grounded in experiential knowledge, rather than technical expertise. Based on their experience, they rejected the atomistic vision of humans existing outside of their natural environment as both stupid and wrong. They then moved to an impious description of epidemiology's interpretive dimension in an attempt to point out that its apparently objective data also were grounded in personal experience. Thus, they indicated that those who claimed the right to make development decisions because of their technical expertise ultimately made such decisions for value-laden reasons. If cultural values were to provide the basis for decisions, the values held by community members most affected by those decisions should dominate the decision calculus. One Border members explicitly demanded that sustaining healthy human life, on both sides of the Rio Grande, was the most basic concern when making development decisions.

The rhetoric of One Border is angry and not conducive to collaboration with others. It does not, however, reject all notions of development. Instead, its members provided an incongruous perspective from which both residents and outsiders can invent a new understanding of current development practices in order to achieve more sustainable, community-validated practices for the future. For example, One Border does not reject the practice of conducting traditional scientific research; its members simply claim the right to influence the decisions about what research questions will be asked. It does not reject the practice of economic development; it does, however, require that the social impact of proposed economic development be evaluated according to its potential interaction with other function systems. One Border's rhetoric is frightening to supporters of the status quo precisely because it demands such a wide-open accounting of development issues. As its name implies, One Border refuses to substitute a political boundary for an ecological one. Members are well aware of the difficulties involved in pursuing development policy at an international level. Yet they refuse to use these difficulties as an excuse to ignore fundamental problems. They use the Rio Grande to focus attention on the concept of boundaries and on the conditions shared by borderlands. They vigorously resist all attempts to set development policy for one side of the border without consideration of the other side. They offer the concept of "one border" as a central term for a new teministic screen that encourages a holistic account of development in their region.

"The Comedy of the Commons"

Science alone cannot solve the complex environmental problems we humans have created in communities around the world. Botkin (1990) points out that the metaphors within which our cultures are grounded pose far more significant constraints to policy than do the limitations of our scientific knowledge. Further, broadly based knowledge of ecological principles that explain environmental problems does not ensure that we will resolve the problems, for "we have become committed in ways both deep and complex to the activities that cause these problems" (Lee 1993a, 5). This does not mean that environmental problems have no solutions. It does mean, however, that solutions depend on some type of social organization, which must be contrived through communication. Without communication, or any way to organize socially, we are unlikely to solve problems. To communicate sustainable development's potential for solving environmental problems, we must account for the increasing complexity of society, simultaneously retaining the complexity within the term *sustainable development*. Kenneth Burke's suggestion to seek "perspective by incongruity" encourages us to conceptualize sustainable development as a comic corrective to our current situation. Niklas Luhmann's claim that competing function systems best capture the complexity of modern society urges us to ensure that our perspective does not rely completely on any single function system.

This book is not an attempt to tell the reader how to implement sustainable development in her or his community. The social problems associated with the emergence of sustainable development are complex and are manifested in highly imperfect laboratories. Rhetorical criticism is not very good at devising programs; it cannot even predict which outcomes of various programs are preferable. Conversely, rhetorical criticism is particularly capable of enabling participants of the rough and tumble political world within which we engage the symbolic struggles about sustainability to envision new possibilities.

Garrett Hardin's (1968) popular phrase, the "tragedy of the commons," suggests that, when natural resources are left available to a public that does not own them as private property, they are wasted. Everyone snatches whatever is available today, with no thought for tomorrow. Uncritical acceptance of this concept has led to the widespread assumption that natural resources are best managed by centralized government control or radical privatization. The UNCED programs designed to encourage sustainable development vacillate between these two options. Environmental devastation discovered throughout much of the former Soviet Union, however, illustrates the folly of centralized governmental control, while the rapid destruction of Amazonia illustrates the folly of radical privatization. Carol Rose (1986) offers an alternative perspective, claiming that some property is best left "open to the public at large," rather than subjected to neoclassical "economic presumptions favoring exclusive control" (717). This "inherently public property" is collectively owned by society, rather than by a private individual or a government

(720). Rose argues that, with such property, the commons is "not tragic, but comedic, . . . because it has been thought to enhance the sociability of the members of an otherwise atomized society" (723). Rose offers roads and waterways as examples of "inherently public property," because they enhance social interaction by encouraging commerce. Such enhancement requires substantial vigor and may result in considerable discomfort, for in our atomized culture "humans recognize interdependence only when it is more inconvenient not to do so" (Lee 1993a, 12). This condition points out the fragile existence of a meaningful public space wherein we may join the debate over development.

Locally emergent sustainable development preserves this space by inducing increased sociability among members of the public who participate in decisions ranging from definition to implementation. We can interpret the natural resources seen as intrinsic to a community's sustainability as its "managed commons, where usage as a commons is not tragic but rather capable of self-management by orderly and civilized people" (Rose 1986, 749). Order and civility need not be interpreted as an absence of conflict. They simply constitute the means for coordinating the conflicts that surely will emerge. Some communities have organized themselves in an attempt to achieve this coordination. For example, Waddell (1995) describes one group's attempt to develop regional plans for sustainable development in Michigan's Upper Peninsula. Members created an expanded conception of sustainable development which drew "upon the knowledge and values of both experts and the non-expert public" (211). Although community members were unable to agree on a traditionally formulated definition for *sustainable development*, fruitful discussions focused on mechanisms for creating sustainability in their region.

Sustainable development offers no program for controlling the commons. It can, however, encourage a new vision that enables us to explore previously unimaginable options for their management. Those options emerge within temporal and spacial boundaries that have meaning and social value for a given community, rather than for the entire world. Participation in sustainable development's emergence enhances the sense of identity within a community, increasing both the value of participation opportunities and the desire to sustain the community. A "comedy of the commons" can develop out of such a vision.

If sustainable development is to provide the political vision to miti-gate technology's "uses and misuses" which Burke ([1937] 1984b, 340) sought, it must be democratized and politicized. Elitists of all political stripes find this prospect terrifying. Environmentalists fear that the "un-washed masses" will sell nature too cheaply; entrepreneurs fear that public hysteria over risk will stifle economic opportunities. A rhetoricized sustainable development, however, will demonstrate the properties Fuller (1993) identifies with a rhetoricized science, in that it will "maxi-mize the distribution of knowledge-and-power, even if this serves to undermine the autonomy and integrity of current scientific practices" (27). This vision of sustainable development promises no certainty and many risks, yet it is entailed in a renunciation of social systems that sustain injustice, domination, and suffering. Peterson and Horton (1995) argue that environmental policy decisions are enhanced when "collec-tive identities and power relationships among [all potential participants] remain open-ended" (161). They argue that, although "the quality of our public discourse is problematic, . . . democratic self-governance would be all but impossible in the absence of that public discourse" (162). Community-based sustainable development offers a realistic hope for recovering the centrality of the public sphere. By regularly infusing that sphere with locally grounded participants, it encourages a healthy skepticism toward technological miracles as well as a dogged determi-nation to make things work.

Sustainable development, as a rhetorical construct, does not offer the perfect solution to our environmental problems. It can provide a mask for traditional development patterns that threaten to destroy hu-man life on earth. We still have difficulty remembering that sustainable development is about coordinating, rather than controlling, the relation-ship between humans and other life forms. On the other hand, it can provide a comic corrective to "business as usual" which does not re-quire total destruction of traditional values. Sustainable development is worthwhile simply because it offers a participatory, community-based means for muddling through our current dilemmas.

Appendix A
Rio Declaration on Environment and Development

Preamble
The United Nations Conference on Environment and Development,
Having met at Rio de Janeiro from 3 to 14 June 1992,
Reaffirming the Declaration of the United Nations Conference on the Human
Environment, adopted at Stockholm on 16 June 1972, and seeking to build
upon it,
With the goal of establishing a new and equitable global partnership through
the creation of new levels of cooperation among States, key sectors of
societies and people,
Working towards international agreements which respect the interests of all and
protect the integrity of the global environmental and developmental
system,
Recognizing the integral and interdependent nature of the Earth, our home,
Proclaims that:
Principle 1
Human beings are at the centre of concerns for sustainable development. They
are entitled to a healthy and productive life in harmony with nature.
Principle 2
States have, in accordance with the Charter of the United Nations and the
principles of international law, the sovereign right to exploit their own
resources pursuant to their own environmental and developmental
policies, and the responsibility to ensure that activities within their
jurisdiction or control do not cause damage to the environment of other
States or of areas beyond the limits of national jurisdiction.
Principle 3
The right to development must be fulfilled so as to equitably meet developmental and environmental needs of present and future generations.
Principle 4
In order to achieve sustainable development, environmental protection shall
constitute an integral part of the development process and cannot be
considered in isolation from it.
Principle 5
All States and all people shall cooperate in the essential task of eradicating
poverty as an indispensable requirement for sustainable development, in
order to decrease the disparities in standards of living and better meet the
needs of the majority of the people of the world.

Principle 6
The special situation and needs of developing countries, particularly the
    least developed and those most environmentally vulnerable, shall be
    given special priority. International actions in the field of environment
    and development should also address the interests and needs of all
    countries.

Principle 7
States shall cooperate in a spirit of global partnership to conserve, protect
    and restore the health and integrity of the earth's ecosystem. In view
    of the different contributions to global environmental degradation,
    states have common but differentiated responsibilities. The developed
    countries acknowledge the responsibility that they bear in the interna-
    tional pursuit of sustainable development in view of the pressures
    their societies place on the global environment and of the technologies
    and financial resources they command.

Principle 8
To achieve sustainable development and a higher quality of life for people,
    States should reduce and eliminate unsustainable patterns of production
    and consumption and promote appropriate demographic policies.

Principle 9
States should cooperate to strengthen endogenous capacity-building for
    sustainable development by improving scientific understanding through
    exchanges of scientific and technological knowledge, and by enhancing the
    development, adaptation, diffusion and transfer of technologies, including
    new and innovative technologies.

Principle 10
Environmental issues are best handled with the participation of all
    concerned citizens, at the relevant level. At the national level, each
    individual shall have appropriate access to information concerning the
    environment that is held by public authorities, including information
    on hazardous materials and activities in their communities, and the
    opportunity to participate in decision-making processes. States shall
    facilitate and encourage public awareness and participation by making
    information widely available. Effective access to judicial and adminis-
    trative proceedings, including redress and remedy, shall be provided.

Principle 11
States shall enact effective environmental legislation. Environmental stan-
    dards, management objectives and priorities should reflect the
    environmental and developmental contest to which they apply. Standards
    applied by some countries may be inappropriate and of unwarranted
    economic and social cost to other countries, in particular developing
    countries.

Principle 12

States should cooperate to promote a supportive and open international economic system that would lead to economic growth and sustainable developments in all countries, to better address the problems of environmental degradation. Trade policy measures for environmental purposes should not constitute a means of arbitrary or unjustifiable discrimination or a disguised restriction on international trade. Unilateral actions to deal with environmental challenges outside the jurisdiction of the importing country should be avoided. Environmental measures addressing transboundary or global environmental problems should, as far as possible, be based on an international consensus.

Principle 13

States shall develop national law regarding liability and compensation for the victims of pollution and other environmental damage. States shall also cooperate in an expeditious and more determined manner to develop further international law regarding liability and compensation for adverse effects of environmental damage caused by activities within their jurisdiction or control to areas beyond their jurisdiction.

Principle 14

States should effectively cooperate to discourage or prevent the relocation and transfer to other States of any activities and substances that cause severe environmental degradation or are found to be harmful to human health.

Principle 15

In order to protect the environment, the precautionary approach shall be widely applied by States according to their capabilities. Where there are threats of serious or irreversible damage, lack of full scientific certainty shall not be used as a reason for postponing cost-effective measures to prevent environmental degradation.

Principle 22

Indigenous people and their communities, and other local communities, have a vital role in environmental management and development because of their knowledge and traditional practices. States should recognize and duly support their identity, culture and interests and enable their effective participation in the achievement of sustainable development.

Principle 23

The environment and natural resources of people under oppression, domination and occupation shall be protected.

Principle 24

Warfare is inherently destructive of sustainable development. States shall therefore respect international law providing protection for the environment in times of armed conflict and cooperate in its further development, as necessary.

Principle 25
Peace, development and environmental protection are interdependent and
indivisible.
Principle 26
States shall resolve all their environmental disputes peacefully and by
appropriate means in accordance with the Charter of the United Nations.
Principle 27
States and people shall cooperate in good faith and in a spirit of partnership in
the fulfillment of the principles embodied in this Declaration and in the
further development of international law in the field of sustainable
development.

Appendix B

Excerpt from Northern Diseased Bison Environmental Assessment Panel

Dr. Novakowski: Yes, I understand you completely, Dr. Bulmer. The first premise that I want to make, you know, is I am not making a judgment on whether it is more appropriate to leave the animals, you know, here as hybrids or whether it is more appropriate to substitute them with wood bison.

The word genetic diversity has been bandied about quite often here, and my interpretation of what genetic diversity is quite different—as an ecologist is quite different from the meaning that is imputed here, which I believe to be an increasing number of species, subspecies or genera in any environment which would add to the richness of either a floral or faunal assemblage. You know, we're not talking about subspecies genetic make-up here. We're talking about numbers of species or subspecies, not individuals.

Secondly, there have been, as you would expect, among scientists who have challenged whether in fact this is—we are talking about wood bison or not, in the Mackenzie Bison Sanctuary, and there have been enough experimentation now, both electrophoretic, other than the penological examinations, to—which indicate there is a great deal of similarity between the Mackenzie population, this population, the Elk Island population, two populations in the United States of plains bison.

That indicates that we haven't got the genetic markers, and which indicates that the genetic markers are not very numerous. Which indicates to me that the difference that produces the phenotypic difference is going to be very, very limited in scope. In other words, to the extent that you may have the same DNA make up in a bison X cattle cross, in a cattelo, and is that genetic diversity? I don't think so.

So what we're talking about here are some—bringing it down to the level which many people can understand and I can understand, and that is that these animals are different, you know, why not say they are and let's get on with it.

Dr. Bulmer: Thank you.

The Chairman: Any other questions? Mr. LaViolette, please.

Mr. LaViolette: Mr. Chairman, I'd like to —I think Dr. Novakowski kind of forgotten some of the members—numbers out of Hook Lake. I think one you forgot was the 18 delivered to Hay Camp, Doctor? Out of Needle Lake

Dr. Novakowski: No, there were—

Mr. LaViolette: You forgot those?

Dr. Novakowski: No no, there were not 18, there were six I believe.

Mr. LaViolette: Eighteen.

Dr. Novakowski: Because they were all put in stalls and suspended.

Mr. LaViolette: You know, it was 18 to start with, probably we lost two or three before we left Needle Lake.

Dr. Novakowski: But those were the sick animals, yes.

Mr. LaViolette: Yes, and as a doctor, and I'm sure you supervised this to go to Hay Camp, what was the reason for so much animals to be left suffering for—the longest one was three months, almost three months?

Dr. Novakowski: I was, you know, I was given treatment regime, and that—in other words, you know, I'm not a veterinarian myself, and I was told what to do and I did it.

Mr. LaViolette: I can't hear you, Doctor.

Dr. Novakowski: I say I was told what to do and I did it.

Mr. LaViolette: But that was a real cruel, cruellest of the Needle Lake, actually.

Dr. Novakowski: It sure was, I agree.

Mr. LaViolette: And I was there when the last one died in April, that never did stretch a leg again. The hind-ends were frozen, hey, almost three months.

So then the other one is didn't the bison for Providence, and the nine you talk about was put in the corral close to Smith, didn't they stay together in the one holding corral in Fox Hole for, was it a year or six months or more?

Dr. Novakowski: No.

Mr. LaViolette: Sure. There was no corral built on Highway 5 here when we were doing this.

Dr. Novakowski: In '65? Yes there was.

Mr. LaViolette: No, it was built after, after we loaded the buffalo for Providence, only after—

Dr. Novakowski: Well, just a minute, that—

Mr. LaViolette: —that corral was built in Highway 5.

Dr. Novakowski: Yeah, but just a minute, that was—

Mr. LaViolette: Come on now.

Dr. Novakowski: That corral was 1965, those are the animals that went to Elk Island Park, which you helped me load at Hay River.

Mr. LaViolette: Yes, but Providence as well. We got some disease animals—

Dr. Novakowski: We didn't keep any animals from Fort Providence, from the Fort Providence group.

Mr. LaViolette: Oh yes. Some people shot some diseased animals, remember? And sneak it out of the corral.

Dr. Novakowski: At the where?

Mr. LaViolette: You wasn't around, maybe. I don't know where you were, but they had shot the diseased animals and took it out to eat, out of Fox Hole corral, but never proven who done it.

Dr. Novakowski: News to me.

Mr. LaViolette: Well you got it now.

Dr. Novakowski: Yeah.

Mr. LaViolette: And they talk about nine outside of Fort Smith here, where the calves taken away as it comes.

Dr. Novakowski: Yes.

Mr. LaViolette: In the slaughter of the nine later years, I was there again, with Dr. Ann Currie. She was there.

Dr. Novakowski: No, I wasn't there.

Mr. LaViolette: I know you wasn't, but Ann Currie was there.

Dr. Novakowski: Yes.

Mr. LaViolette: She managed the slaughter there, and four or five of us and even that small corral was hard to get these animals, because they knew they'd been shot at.

I think somebody mention here today, one of the leaders, you know, the last 500 is going to be hard to get in the Park, which I think so. The experience I had in Hay Camp as well, and that nine buffalo, we shot and butchered in the field there, but what was brought into game warehouse for boning, and the bones, I think, were shipped to the University of Toronto or some place, Ontario, but most of that meat was taken home to use, and nobody ever died from it. But how dangerous, what was brought to the attention of the world actually by the doctors who are dealing with slaughtering all the buffalo.

It's kind of a—out of line for me, because—I don't want to call another doctor a liar again. I called one doctor a liar in Hay River, and he almost went crazy. I guess you're not suppose to call a doctor a liar. So—but there is doctors that can be reasonable and talk to you nicely.

Dr. Novakowski: Well—

Mr. LaViolette: But there's always one, there's always a smart ass, and that I cannot stand.

Dr. Novakowski: Frank, you see the point I'm making is that it's not very easy, you know, and the things that you have brought out were very, very difficult to live with. And the other point I was making was that neither you nor I were really trained for this kind of thing, but we had to do it and we did it. And anybody else who follows us is not going to have it that easy either.

Mr. LaViolette: Well, one thing I'm driving at is when I talk about these nine here and some went to Elk Island Park, remember we flew to Hay River and loaded that on the truck. That was the hottest day of the year, and the point I'm driving at is they delivered that 16 bison to Providence Game Sanctuary. Of course again, go back to the great loss we had in the first trip to the barge, right? I think you spoke about that.

Dr. Novakowski: Yes, that was—

Mr. LaViolette: That was heartbreaking thing.

Dr. Novakowski: —1965.

Mr. LaViolette: Not only for you, for all of us that worked on it.

Dr. Novakowski: Yes, I'm sure.

Mr. LaViolette: So therefore I guess one thing to go back to, what some of the officials of the Territorial Government saying, the Native people they don't care as long as they go out and shoot one or two buffalo a year, they don't care what happens to the buffalo. That never was true from beginning. Before some of these young guys become biologists—

Dr. Novakowski: Nobody asked—

Mr. LaViolette: We're working with the buffalos.

Dr. Novakowski: Nobody asked me. I could have told them.

Mr. LaViolette: And another one is I think the delivering of this bison to the—to Providence, especially Providence. Elk Island Park is different thing. You put 'em in hotel there to stay there. Didn't that come from very great percentage of the disease heard?

Dr. Novakowski: The Fort Providence group?

Mr. LaViolette: Well, both herds.

Dr. Novakowski: Well, they came from Nyarling River.

Mr. LaViolette: Yes, and—

Dr. Novakowski: And the Nyarling River—

Mr. LaViolette: We had the disease in that area?

Dr. Novakowski: Yes, absolutely, yes.

Mr. LaViolette: And then some spent time in the same holding corral there and afterwards, and Providence here, and every doctor here is actually saying was the top quality buffalo, disease-free. Now what I'm driving—they are saying, actually true what they're saying. But I think to restock both Wood Buffalo Park and outside the Park as a group I'm working with, it's Treaty 8 and Metis in Alberta and Northwest Territories, we are working on the bison as one group of bison, whether is in the Park or outside the Park. Now, we don't want to be split up.

I think it was tried today by Renewable Resources, which is a different group of bison in the Northwest Territories, but we are working together as one group of—one herd of bison, between the Park and the Northwest Territories. I hope at least you can understand that. The others don't.

And then I guess to come back to this transfer of the big game, I believe, as far as I know, it's one of the biggest ever undertaken in Canada, outside of musk ox for Russia—they pick them up with big helicopters, I guess, and put them in the plane and haul them away. But I think in your position, Dr. Novakowski, and the Deputy Minister of Renewable Resources, which had a heck of a lot of work into this, had never come up with—actually, always left out, and the people that worked for Jim Bourque, had never used this herd of buffalo was delivered to Providence, come from disease herd.

So therefore I think there's a great job been done, and I think it can be done again, if we ever have to make the decision to do it. That we can weed out the good buffalo and do away with the sick buffalo, but as far as I'm concerned I think we need more time. Somebody mentioned 30 years since the buffalo was closed down. I think buffalo was closed down more or less 70–80 years, from the time the Park is established and so on. So you're thinking about, I would say 50 years before any of the grandchildren, if ever, to shoot a buffalo again.

But what I'm driving at here is do you really approve that this little herd of bison in the Needle Lake area, Nyarling River, with about four little herds we work on, didn't we? And are they actually pure wood bison?

Dr. Novakowski: Well, I think, Frank, I said at the outset that they are different, different in appearance. Different, the term we use is phenotypic, but they're different in appearance, and that is as far as I want to go. Whether they are pure bison or not maybe that doesn't even matter. But they are different looking animal, and we may never have—because of the fact that there's obviously some connection between the transplanted—that is the plains bison, obviously some connection between that and that Nyarling River area, which is at one time wood bison habitat, wood bison territory and there were wood bison in there before 1925.

Mr. LaViolette: Well, I think I can agree with that part.

Dr. Novakowski: So there obviously was some connection because otherwise the animals might not have been diseased.

Mr. LaViolette: In 1925 when the bison were delivered to the buffalo landing above Fitzgerald, that fall I don't know what month it was, it could be August, that fall there was an old trapper, Germain Tourangeau, which I travelled with him for 21 years, he says what we call Wainwright, you call it prairie buffalos or whatever.

Dr. Novakowski: Yeah, that's right.

Mr. LaViolette: They're not really big ones. They already south of Sass Lake by the 15 of November, and from Sass Lake to the location you're talking about where we work is not too far away, and the migration trail, really you probably seen it over and over, that runs beyond Sass Lake, which crosses Little Buffalo—

Dr. Novakowski: It runs on the Ninishute [?] Hills.

Mr. LaViolette: Yes, Ninishute [?] Hills into just south of Sass Lake, into Needle Lake. Now, if this buffalo never been crossed but still the prairie buffalo, which is much bigger than already in a few years—you know, the ones from the south I seen they were very small buffalo.

Dr. Novakowski: They were young buffalo.

Mr. LaViolette: What happens, they just go there and visit, come back, they don't breed in breeding season or what is it? What do you think? You don't want to go further than that either?

Dr. Novakowski: You know, I can't make a prediction on that. The one point that has to be considered is the fact that the earlier transplants from Wainwright were tested, and it is only in the last two years or maybe the last year, where the animals were not tested they were just hauled south. So if you believe that those animals moved when they were released at Buffalo Landing, animals moved west to Sass Lake and so on, these would not have been diseased animals.

Mr. LaViolette: Oh, I guess it not going to get that far, yes.

Dr. Novakowski: Yeah.

Mr. LaViolette: But one of the bison was killed in, I think it was '53 in the Hay Camp slaughter, was branded 33 years previous and nobody knows how old the bison was when it was branded. So I guess some do live quite a long time.

Another thing I don't agree with you is that, you know, the wolf could never kill a buffalo on the prairie. Well, you were sitting so close to me and we haven't seen each other for a long time I didn't want to call you what I called the other doctor the other day, but they do kill on the prairies quite a lot. That I don't agree with you.

Dr. Novakowski: This was strictly in the discussion between you and I, not an issue which I presented at any time. But nonetheless, as I mentioned to you and as is quite plain to me in the past, that most of the kills were in the wooded areas, rather on the prairie, but they're—sure, they're now out in the prairie killing bison.

Mr. LaViolette: I think it's very important, some of this I bring up, especially to the younger people. I'm not—we have to talk to the Panel, all right, but I think it's important to deliver some of this experience to the younger people.

You were here already and doing a lot of travelling, I know you worked until midnight and sleep till noon, but that's your way of life. You still get your hours in.

Dr. Novakowski: How did you know?

Mr. LaViolette: I should know. But during the poisoning of the wolves, you were there when Ralph Cameron was—

Dr. Novakowski: No, I was there with John Tourangeau.

Mr. LaViolette: —Fox Hole and Salt Plains. He had taken a heck of a lot of wolves, because old Billy Schaefer, with his helper, he couldn't keep up to Ralph Cameron hauling in the wolves. He couldn't keep up to skinning the wolves coming in, and he was hauling it a heck of a long ways sometimes, with a dog teams, to the truck And that's when the population of the buffalo kind of creeped up. Of course, we talking back quite awhile now, before the delivery of the bison to the Providence.

So do you believe the wolves are taking a lot of the animals, which helps to bring down the population number?

Dr. Novakowski: Well, in the only testing that we did, or at least that I did, which is where I was involved with Bill, was—and in fact because wolves range widely and they have their own kind of social structure. So you have to know what's going on over a much larger area that we were able to cover with—that's all we were working with, was a vehicle. So it's wher- ever we could drive. But under those circumstances the only thing I had to prove was that wolves do eat buffalo, and they do.

Mr. LaViolette: When there's buffalo around, one thing I hope you can clarify me, they don't only live on rabbits and mice, is that true?

Dr. Novakowski: Not in buffalo territory they sure don't, no.

Mr. LaViolette: Well, that was put to me by some of the biologists in the past, and I was—and again, I think the young people should know. You know, a good bison will weigh 2,000 pound, the average bull will weigh 2600 pounds, on hoofs, and the mice is two ounce, the biggest mice you can get.

Dr. Novakowski: That's a snack.

Mr. LaViolette: So he wouldn't waste time getting mice. I don't believe some biologists, they try to tell me. They prove that by wolf dropping.

I don't think there's enough study been done, why the population of the bison going down. One is—wolves is one. And not so much taken by the hunters to get down that much, and we certainly—we had our own study through the local groups, which was on the tape played in Resolution the other night, or the voice of Roger Brunal. Also a lot of us helped him to prepare that study for that winter, because we didn't believe that all the buffalo was killed off by the hunters, and this was quite a lot of buffalo in the Lowlands then, and especially in Hook Lake, we really aiming at.

And I think something like March 15th or back to the November 15th, we had raised money to get a small aircraft to fly, and I think we estimated probably something 340 buffalo disappeared in the Hook Lake area, and they get talking to trappers of Resolution, which the biggest user of Hook Lake herd, and some are out people here, during that period there was only about 43 buffalo taken for food. And still we been accused, as the hunters and trappers in that area, that we kill too much buffalo. So—and a hell of a lot of wolves.

Dr. Novakowski: So you have 300 animals you can't account for?

Mr. LaViolette: Right. So it had to be wolves.

Dr. Novakowski: Yeah, I can't—you know, I've been away from this so long, Frank, that I can't make any—

Mr. LaViolette: But when you learn something, doesn't it stay with you?

Dr. Novakowski: Yeah, it makes sense. We're talking common senses.

Mr. LaViolette: I asked a biologist one time in Yellowknife, I think that's probably the time that I met you one breakfast there, asking for your report if he has it and this guy didn't have it. Another three biologists that put a heck of a pile of buffalo in pain, to experiment on anthrax in the barn, in the stalls—and the reason I'm talking, Mr. Chairman, I think some of the young people should learn what went on.

They sacrifice over 200 buffalo, young stuff, just to see how they die with anthrax. That's all it was. You're talking about squeeze and gates, yes. There's only one way, the way we use in Needle Lake and Hook Lake. That's the only way, and as they go into the stall, I think it was seven stalls in the barn, specially built stalls in this big barn. Then they inject the disease into it, the anthrax. Then they study how they die.

There was three young biologists there, and they were telling us at dinner table, supper table—of course we kept very quiet, very reluctant to ask them a lot of questions. We couldn't go into that place after we finish it. And they could die from seven hours to five days, and that's a day after day suffering the buffalo, just for these guys to experiment how they die, as far as I concerned. Because later I asked another biologist—the biologists come and go, and—but he had no record of this, these guys making, sacrificing these buffalo.

So I wonder what happens to the experience of each biologist when he dies?

Dr. Novakowski: Well, in this case we are not talking about biologists. Biologists were not involved in this thing at all. It was—

Mr. LaViolette: Well, since you have left I have changed my mind towards biologists, and I have said across Canada and to Ottawa many trips, there should be a bounty on biologists, not on wolves.

Dr. Novakowski: Well, if I can explain this. It was done by the Health of Animals Branch to test the efficiency of the vaccine used for anthrax. There was a real problem there, because the vaccination only lasted, it was ten to 12 months, and if you were going to protect bison from anthrax, which is a different question than we're facing here, then that meant that every year you had to get that same animal back again and give him another shot, and that's impossible. You know, it's logistically impossible and—

Mr. LaViolette: Well, I can understand what you're saying, but I wonder if it was ready necessary to—they should know by now it was necessary to try and cure anthrax. Anthrax come and go.

Dr. Novakowski: Yeah. I'm not—I was not involved in that, and you know—

Mr. LaViolette: But I was around.

Dr. Novakowski: Yeah.

Mr. LaViolette: And I would hate to see the replacement ever takes place, that replacement that use what we can pure wood bison. Therefore, even my great grandchildren will never get a chance to shoot buffalo.

Doctor, a lot of us are hurt by what's going on, for some time two years, about what they want to do with the buffalo is kill them off. Two days, especially last two days here, sitting there listening, I don't have a degree and a doctorate, and so many doctors here the last two days, and to me they all have one thing in mind, is blood and kill off the buffalo that we live on since '56. But a lot of us have used bison long before it opened to us, for survival in the bush as well.

Dr. Novakowski: I know that.

Mr. LaViolette: We had to.

Dr. Novakowski: I would too.

Mr. LaViolette: With all the stupid, cruelty slaughters I have seen, driving buffalo out of Hook Lake, never any come out of Hook Lake because they went back the same night. They tried, but it was—attempt was brought over I think two or three times, across the winter crossing there, and—because I was there next morning and I had a D-8 [tractor] in there to open the road for wherever they want to go, wherever they want to drive them. Some of the bison once come from Nyarling River, past Point Brule, a lot of them got—well, 50 per cent got to the Fox Hole holding corral, but 50 per cent didn't.

Then finally they got so smart they will head for the bush as soon as the helicopter comes, and then again it's for the young people I wanted to know, to let them know. They decide to shoot the buffalo off in Grande Tour, from Nyarling south, and they couldn't move them and there was hundreds of buffalo in there, lots.

I seen the time when I drove into Grande Tour camp, where we used to pick up grub and fuel there, because we're out in the field, we had our caboose, and there was three fix-wing aircraft sitting on the little landing behind Grande Tour, two helicopters at noon hour. When we walk into the kitchen all this government officials, I think they were still federal, they come out there just before noon for pleasure. Then they been flown out to herd, where the herds are, and then they shoot the buffalo for the hell of it just for pleasure. They keep circling with the helicopter, then they kill a bunch, go back, have dinner and fly back to Smith. This is cruelty.

Now, after some of us working there start complaining about this here—and there was already hundreds of them were shot in the prairie, not a knife stuck into them. You know, the reason I'm telling this, I would not want to see any of these young people here to ever see that kind of sight again, that I have seen and my age of people have seen. It's cruelty. We did not point the finger at John Mulfair [?] who was the head of the project. He got orders from Ottawa, like some of the doctors are here, they set this up. There was no game warden ever got in our way that we can raise hell with, because we thought it's not their fault, it's not what they want to do.

Anyway, after we start complaining they brought in about eight or nine skinners with a bombardier from Fort Smith. Dr. Schuket was with them. He's the Canadian Wildlife Service is he or one time?

Dr. Novakowski: Yes he was, yes.

Mr. LaViolette: One time I drove up with a Cat there, and there must have been about 50–60 buffalo laying there, was shot just recently, hour or two before. And the boys will get out—and some of the boys still alive. They get out before Schuket because Schuket is getting old and too slow. They get up to a big cow, beautiful cow, says Doctor, this one has TB, and he will say, we'll go on to the next one. So that buffalo is left alone. But they only skin for two days, and they been shot buffalo there for days, to clean them all out, so nothing left in that area.

That's one of the worst sights to see, and later on, two–three weeks later I was told to bring a squeeze to Hook Lake, metal squeeze. You know, the squeeze to—when you examine the buffalo, and we went in there, Dave King and I walking a Cat from Salt River to Hook Lake, and we were there after again, the helicopters and gunmens. There was one prairie alone, second big prairie just behind Grande Tour, we counted near 80 buffalo in one prairie alone, shot and never stuck a knife into it.

So actually, first of all the buffalo died of anthrax. It just not all be buried, because in the bush you don't find 'em, you don't bury them. That we can't get into the biologists head. They said they buried so much they cure the anthrax. They never cure the anthrax. As a matter of fact, driving the buffalo right after calving in the spring, actually kills a lot of calves because they get away from the mothers and so on. I was there too. And then this such a slaughter for nothing, that brought the bison down. They never cure the anthrax by burying them, they never cure them by giving needles, because any buffalo is walking is not anthrax.

And so the cruelty that had happened, I wouldn't want my boys to see it, and I hope the young people here today, the Native people and the community people that have never witnessed that kind of cruelty again, because it doesn't help.

But I do understand that the Native people, Treaty 8, surround Wood Buffalo Park and looking at the bison as one herd between Hook Lake and the Wood Buffalo Park, as one herd that we are fighting for, and I can understand by involving, seriously involving with the Native people that something could be done and still save some healthy animals to carry on. But to kill, even though the anthrax was fairly heavy in that area, the Hook Lake area, and slaughtering the buffalo to the bumper zone, I guess they would call it now, didn't call it that then, they just going to kill them off.

I think Chief Beaver had brought this up. Even if they done all this, they didn't go out to kill every animal so we have buffalo today. But this is very serious and it's a heartbreaking thing to listen to, is to slaughter all the animals that we live on. And that buffalo, I think I asked you the question today, been here since the beginning of time and you said, no but probably 10,000 years. That's long enough. That's longer than Alberta farmers, you know, 10,000 years, and so the buffalo should have a right in that Park.

Now, for all the millions of dollars that been spent on the Wood Buffalo Park, that is to protect the buffalo. Jim Bourque was on the radio a couple of weeks ago, he says when he first went to work for the Parks as a buffalo ranger, we call them then, he was 18. They gave him a team of dogs and they sent him out to Jackfish River to protect buffalo—I don't know that, he wasn't so light either when we worked together.

But I guess I would say that the reason that I don't want to see pure wood bison used, because some day—all the time we can hunt the buffalo, and Mr. Chairman, I want to thank you for giving me this time and I want to thank Nick for listening to me. Thank you very much.

The Chairman: Thank you, Mr. LaViolette. Maybe one more question, but first of all thank you, Mr. LaViolette, for the questions of Dr. Novakowski. It was very interesting to hear the recounting between the two of you of the history of that operation.

We have some children that I know want to speak this evening, and I'd like to get to them quickly, because I know it's getting late, but Mr. East, please.

Mr. East: Just a very brief question for Dr. Novakowski, if I may, Mr. Chairman. This is a pickup on something that Mr. LaViolette suggested, and I'd just ask for Dr. Novakowski's views on this.

If there was enough time, and this is going back to the feasibility of the salvage option and trying to accomplish it without some of the cruelty that Mr. LaViolette has been describing, in your experience if there wasn't as severe a time pressure, that you had a pretty fair number of years and there wasn't serious financial constraints, that you had perhaps not unlimited manpower and dollars but a fair number of dollars and significant manpower, do you think that the salvage operation that's been discussed on and off over the last couple of days, might be feasible without the kind of adverse effects that have been described?

Dr. Novakowski: I don't believe, with the exception of the time and the financial constraints, if those were not an issue, where you could do this on a gradual basis and you had—and you had found some way to deal with not only the existing disease question but also the latency question, then I am not, you know, hooked on the fact that, you know, it's got to be wood bison in here or nothing. And in fact, it doesn't have to happen that way, if everybody wants to get along.

But I have told you that the tools we have available to us now, which are only the phenotypic rules, the fact that the wood bison look different from the hybrids and from plains bison, if we want to apply that criteria,

that same criteria, yes, we may find some of those animals in Wood Buffalo
Park existing right now at Hook Lake. In fact, very possibly at Hook Lake,
that would meet that criteria, and perhaps that these animals should be
saved.

But all of these other things have to happen first, and I am not in a
position to make that kind of an evaluation.

The Chairman: Thank you, Dr. Novakowski. Take one more question from
Chief Henry Beaver, please.

Chief Beaver: One of the things that you just explained is that you can tell the
difference between a hybrid and plains bison and wood buffalo.

Dr. Novakowski: Yes.

Chief Beaver: Okay, to me a hybrid is like a Metis, isn't that so? I mean, it's a
cross between two animals, which they come in between?

Dr. Novakowski: Okay, they're—

Chief Beaver: Is that correct?

Dr. Novakowski: Yeah.

Chief Beaver: Okay, in this audience can you tell me the difference between the
Dene and the Metis, in this room?

Dr. Novakowski: Not any more than I could tell the difference between any
other human being, that's what I'm saying. That's what I said during my
discussion of this, that the genetic markers are so very few and far between, and we're talking about thousands and hundreds of thousands of
genes interacting, that the genetic question may be a false lead, in that
there's so little difference in the genetic make-up.

Appendix C

Excerpts from Cameron County Interviews

Excerpt from Interview with A. S.

R91: Just a lot of—a lot of kids live with earaches and they don't know any better and they think that's what they need to do until it starts draining and then the teacher notices, then they go to the nurse and y'know by that time it's kind of—it's kind of late to do any kind of preventive and they need to go in and get some work done. Umm we see a lot of umm emotional problems—a lot of emotional problems. Our nurses—particularly in the elem—in the secondary schools are spending a lot of their time in doing—dealing with emotional problems, whether it be suicide or abortions or they think they're pregnant or somebody—a boyfriend. We just had a case—the boyfriend would beat the girl up. Then they don't wanna press charges and it—y'know it's just—it taxes our resources—our manpower resources because it takes a lot of time to do that—to deal with that. And then sometimes it's frustrating because if the girl's not gonna press charges, we're back to square one y'know and he's gonna do it again and again and again. So in that—in that area, we do have counselors in the schools. But a lot of times the students opt to go to the nurse. Umm the nurse y'know takes the time to deal with them and sometimes [?] counselors are away and they—they're academic counselors primarily.

Q: Mmhmm.

R92: Not, umm, y'know counseling counselors—some per se.

Q: Mmhmm.

R93: And then a lot of the time—and I would say, oh, it's a big chunk of time—the nurse is spending trying to, umm, refer students to different agencies. So lots of times we're on the phone forever y'know trying to—okay, this child needs to be seen. They don't have any money. Or they need a tonsillectomy. Well, they don't have any money. They don't qualify for any programs. What are we gonna do? They've gone to the clinic. [?] Y'know it's just—or they're not—they're clinic patients. They don't wanna go—they wanna go somewhere else. And then just . . .

Q: Mmhmm.

R94: Y'know, trying to plug them into a social agency or a medical agency. So I think a lot of the time we're spending just trying to tell the parents, "go here, go there," and they don't have transportation. When they have to go out of town—we had a girl that had problems neurologically and finally was seen at the clinic, and they said, "look, this girl needs to go like right now to Dallas." And, umm, as a matter of fact, I think the mother spent like—I know for a fact she spent a month there.

Q: Mmhmm.

R95: She lived alone. She had little kids. She didn't have—she didn't have a way. The girl was illegal so the nurse had to go and fight the immigration with letters from the doctors so the lady could go there, find some money for the lady to go to Galveston. She had two kids. The nurse ended up taking care of the kids for a month. I said "I [?]." She—y'know . . .

Q: That's heroic.

R96: I mean, yes. I mean I'm thinking, "ah." And she has—all her kids are adopted. She's got about three or four kids, maybe. [?] adopted. So, y'know, it didn't really bother her a lot to have more kids in there, y'know. I mean she's just—I mean a kind hearted person. For a month—that's a lot. And they were little, y'know.

Q: Mmhmm.

R97: She had to go buy diapers and then we tried to get her—I mean y'know it's just a lot of [?]—and Child Protective Services, to see if they could get her at least some money for the food and for the diapers and all this other stuff.

Q: Mmhmm.

R98: So this is the extreme cases. I mean we don't get a case like that every day, but y'know that's—that's what we're dealing with here. It's not like if we had—even in McAllen—I mean if we had a hospital or we had a university or we had in Galveston. In McAllen at least we could drive them over there and leave the—y'know.

Q: Mmhmm.

R99: And have better care. But, y'know, we don't here in the Valley.

Q: So that's I guess—that again, you—I had wanted to ask about particularly how being right here influences kinds of medical . . .

R100: Yeah. It's hard for people . . .

Q: What you have to . . .

R101: It's hard for people to realize that Matamoros and Brownsville is a community, y'know. Just because there's a border—it's still—a lot of people from the States go to Mexico for their health care.

Q: Mmhmm.

R102: And these are the people that can afford—well even, y'know, they can afford, but not maybe that much, or they like the care in Mexico better because that's what they've grown up with and that's what they want, y'know. And a lot of people that don't have any money. Or some can't even, y'know, access the care there or maybe they don't know—they come over here. Umm a lot of—y'know this—and I don't know how much is happening right now, but a lot of, um, pregnant ladies would come and deliver over here so that a child would be an American citizen, y'know.

Q: Mmhmm.

R103: So I think they're—uh if—I mean I—how can you refuse somebody at the border? They're in labor and they say "I need to go . . . "?

Q: Mmhmm.

R104: Y'know, I mean—y'know how can you—I mean I wouldn't.

Q: Yeah.

R105: [?] if I would get sued or what—or finally, y'know, this is a child, this is a person—how are you going to refuse their care?

Q: Mmhmm.

R106: So, y'know, and it is. It's just one community. It—and I don't know. I guess I've touched base with you before, but even the Brownsville Community Health Center was sending some ladies to have tubal ligations in a hospital in Matamoros. And the people from the clinic work real closely with the doctors over there, and so they know that the doctors are good doctors and all that stuff.

Q: Mmhmm.

R107: Because it's cheaper. It's like maybe a third—not even a third, maybe it's a tenth or a fifth of what it would cost here in the United States, y'know, to go into the hospital. Y'know it's expensive to go into a hospital. Just going into a hospital, having surgery and staying a day, or half a day, or whatever and coming out—well they could do that with a tenth of the cost or— yeah—I don't know if it's a tenth, but it was just barely a fraction of the cost. They would go over there and so, y'know—so it was referring from one medical facility to the other. Y'know so we are a community, and we— we need to deal like with those issues. And for a long time, I think even—y'know even the natives here, we didn't wanna have anything to do with Mexico—kind of—but y'know we need to deal with it. It's—y'know it's like the air. Environmentally I mean it's the same air.

Q: Mmhmm.

R108: I mean we can't say "okay, this is the border," for the water and all that. So y'know—and then it was—it took years for us—or for me anyway—to understand that this is y'know one community.

Q: Do you think umm people are beginning to—who especially—at least people who live here—are beginning to realize that more or is it still a problem?

R109: I think so.

Q: When you go to Development Council . . .

R110: Yeah.

Q: . . . and things like that.

R111: Umm not so much at Development Council. I think their—that their motive is more business, more, y'know, the dollars. So I think they need to deal with both. I think it's more the—I see a lot of our nurses . . .

Q: Yeah.

R112: Y'know, I can give you an example. A lot of the nurses y'know, they just—they just so angry at these people that they come over here and they use our resources and y'know—and they just are real, real angry. And I know we see it here. We—and register people and I say, "well you can go across"—of course the public health is not across any more—"but get your shots and they'll charge you a dollar." "Oh no, I have Medicare. I'll go to the doctor." I mean, they're just registering their kids from Mexico. So I mean y'know the abuse is there somewhere—I mean.

Q: Mmhmm.

R113: Some people are real smart in dealing with that and so. And so nurses do get real, real upset and they still don't understand and don't realize that this is one border, that this is one area. They're still [?] "they should go back to Mexico. Y'know they were born in Mexico. They should [?] Mexico."

Q: Yeah. What's the best way to—to—to help people uh understand more?

R114: Well, whenever I talk to them, I say "y'know I understand. I'm a mother. I want the best for my child." So that's—y'know we need to be understanding to the families—that they want what's best for their kids. And that's—y'know, in a humanitarian way, that's the way that I deal with it. Umm, I guess just more education, letting them know, "look, y'know this is the same air we breathe, the same resources that we're using." I don't think a lot of people know that—y'know what we're doing—sending some people over there to have tubal ligations and stuff like that. Y'know it's not a—and I don't know how, umm, at risk the people from Brownsville are when they do that themselves y'know.

Q: Mmhmm.

R115: I mean the medical providers that do that. I mean I just don't know.

Q: So people here get angry because "we're helping people across the border?"

R116: Right. Right. Right. Yeah. Umm, but I think more and more universities are coming in and wanting to go to Mexico—to Matamoros—to see their school of nursing, to see the medical school that they have there. And so I think that's even given us a little bit more—"well, if they wanna know, maybe we should look into it and see what it is that . . ."

Q: Mmhmm.

R117: . . . y'know that they do over there, too." I—y'know I don't know how we could better let people know that.

Q: Well, it's frustrating I'm sure.

R118: Mmhmm. Yeah. And—yeah, that's it. And then when you have somebody that has been here for many years, and their families were from Brownsville and then they can't access the system because they fall in between the cracks.

Q: Mmhmm.

R119: That's even worse.

Q: Umm [?] we asked you what were the most difficult issues that you had to deal with in the schools. What do you think is—in the Brownsville area here—what do you think are the most fundamental issues to be resolved or that we really should y'know focus energies on? Sometimes there are some—some problems that if you get them solved, other little problems get solved down the way. Are there any . . .

R120: Mmhmm.

Q: . . . you see?

R121: Yeah.

Q: In that category?

R122: Umm, emotionally. I think that if we dealt with the problems at the elementary—umm y'know we have a lot of sexual abuse, and we have a lot of problems that the kids—maybe their family's homeless or they're immigrating or whatever, and the kids feel this—this y'know burden because they're going to school and maybe using a different name so that they can—I mean can you imagine . . .

Q: Using a different—why do they do this?

R123: Well, it's an extreme case we had two years ago. This girl in high school was gonna graduate from high school, and I think either she needed a Social Security number or something—I don't remember what was happening. So they finally told the school district that this girl's name wasn't Maria whatever—that actually it was Agora. But her cousin Maria died when she—when Maria was real little, so she assumed this identification so that her parents—so that she could be in school for all those years. Umm . . .

Q: Oh. Oh.

R124: Y'know heaven knows how many cases of that—the kids—we get the kids in school and we need to umm—something happens in school and we need to take them home.

Q: Mmhmm.

R125: You're still digesting that other.

Q: I'm sorry.

R126: We need to, umm—it's an extreme case granted. I mean I don't know how many cases we have, but I know that's an extreme case. But we have an emergency. The child breaks their leg or . . .

Q: Mmhmm.

R127: . . . a laceration or whatever. And we're trying to—to locate the parents. And the child is scared to begin with. And the child has been told "don't say that you live in Matamoros. Don't say that."

Q: Mmhmm.

R128: Y'know so we're trying to do—and so the child here—"well, where's your mother?" "Well, I don't know. Well, she went shopping." Y'know "well where?" And we're trying to get to the bottom so that we can get a parent to be responsible, and the parent is in Mexico and the child lives in Mexico. So how are they gonna tell us until, y'know, a guardian or somebody that's taking—kinda taking care of them here in Brownsville gets—so y'know you're living with that. It gets—I mean, I can't believe a six-year-old being put through that.

Q: Yeah.

R129: Emotionally it's just . . .

Q: Mmhmm.

R130: I mean how can you—how can you get over that stuff y'know? And so you don't deal with this here. And it's gonna be in middle school and then all the problems of growing up and doing—y'know, your hormones and all that and so y'know—and then get to high school and y'know, you just— the problems just kind of accelerate. So I think that if we had a component in the elementaries to deal with a lot of the issues, whether they be because they're homeless or because they—y'know they're trying to cover up abuse, or because, umm, they don't have a parent or whatever—I think y'know that would be so—you need to—to get them mentally healthy before they go into more problems and are able to deal with these issues and they'll have a better sense of understanding. They can deal with these issues. They can deal with the issues of drugs and suicide and girls and boys—y'know whatever.

Excerpt from Interview with C. R.

R10: That's something that I was uh telling [?] before that umm [?] y'know it makes a difference uh when you are from here in terms of—you're not looking at the issue not just in the so-called traditional—I don't even know what the word "objective" means—uh but in the so-called objective manner. And I don't know really what that means. Does it mean that you can detach yourself . . .

Q: Yeah.

R11: And y'know here you have this [?] radical hypothesis and then look at y'know this problem and try in theory to get them together, link them. I don't know. Y'know I know that I am from this community, and I've read the literature. But I also know what's going on in this community as far as how the hypothesis may fit into these particular communities. And the added—the added dimension is that I'm not just a scientist. And Dr. Rocco's not just a pediatrician, but she's also a mother and she's also a person who has chosen to live in this community. And what that means is that we're concerned not just as a pediatrician or a scientist, but as a person who sees her future here. And my grandchildren will live here. And umm—and so when you have to hear and listen to the questions of your children, umm my—I have teenagers who say "y'know how is the environment gonna be for my grandchildren?" So y'know I cannot be so objective when I have also my future and my children's future involved in the question. And that doesn't make uh the questions less valid when the emotions are in them. And I think that's something that needs to be—and [?] in particular an environmental community study that uh—"subjectivity" and "objectivity" are some words that need to be redefined.

Q: Exactly.

R12: Umm in terms of the "detached scientist." What does that mean? Does that mean that he can have—or she can have better methodology? To me, it's the methodology but it's objective. Umm and—but the questions that need to be asked aren't asked.

Q: Mmhmm.

R13: And I think this objectivity comes in where there's—and there are political and economic interests where uh that influence becomes the questions and therefore the methodology that is going to be used. That to me is where this objectivity comes in. Umm and yet both questions are not asked often.

Q: Mmhmm.

R14: Y'know who is being this objective here?

Q: Yeah, we really explored it . . .

R15: Yeah.

Q: So I understand what you're saying.

R16: And y'know—y'know objectivity comes—it's a philosophical position, but it's outdated y'know. I mean it comes from y'know early—y'know 20th century y'know where the objective is.

Q: Yeah.

R17: The positive is basically. Uh it's a philosophical position that believes that basically there is reality out there that can be measured independent of your [?], but which is ridiculous y'know.

Q: Yeah.

R18: Y'know it is ridiculous. And to me it's more honest to say I come to this situation with these questions, and these questions are based on my own historical process.

Q: Mmhmm.

R19: And yet I am honest enough to say I'm going to look at them because of my background and at the same time look at this reality and see how biased or not biased they are. To me, it's more honest to come to a situation and say "I may be biased because of this or because of that" rather than just say "I'm a scientist and I'm not biased." Excuse me. [?] confront yourself. Y'know don't be so [?] y'know.

Q: Mmhmm.

R20: Or, y'know, arrogant.

Q: Yeah.

R21: Y'know, to me it's arrogance. And [?] that academia—because we're made of egos y'know—a place that should [?]. Y'know, how many scientists have such large egos that—y'know, how you have to be rubbing them constantly, y'know. And I mean that's my own occupation, y'know. And I'm supposed to be y'know [?]. *[Tape turned off then back on.]* Yeah. And I think that's—that's where, y'know—we have [?]—even with my professor—y'know, we've had discussions on this issue of [?], because I was talking to you, y'know, about subjectivity. Objectivity is also measured umm in the way one speaks, y'know.

Q: Mmhmm.

R22: I mean if you talk soft-spoken, y'know, and your emotions are not here then [?]. If you speak loud and crazy like me you're not—y'know you're not objective. And to me that's the [?]—y'know that's just the [?]. I mean I like speaking this way, y'know. And I mean, I've been told that—"you just—you just kind of [?] subjective." And I say "why?" "Because you're so loud and you're so passionate, y'know." And I said "well, y'know, I don't want to be cold and detached y'know." And that makes me y'know less of a scientist. I am an epidemiologist y'know—regardless of what you may think. And umm—but you speak with me and this is the way y'know I'll talk. And then you'll go and speak with other persons—and like I was telling you, it depends—depending on who—who you're speaking with, what interests do they have, uh what personal gains do they have, what motives are there behind them y'know. And this doesn't mean that it's good or bad. It's just the way it is. People are gonna come—we [?]—we are social beings. We are the product of, y'know, other people's experiences and emotions and information as well. So depending on who you're speaking with, that—that will tell you whatever. And I think that's something that often times reporting does not bring [?]—y'know the information. Well, this person is not [?] TDH, but this person may want to get ahead and be the commissioner so therefore this person will speak in this manner and say these things.

Q: Mmhmm.

R23: And it's—the public does not understand these things many times. I

really believe that. I mean—and Juan sees that because, y'know, Juan has
learned to look at a global, y'know, picture. But the public many times does
not see this. And of course this person would be saying this because,
y'know, he's representing the Chamber of Commerce y'know and so—that
analysis many times is sort of a tacet understanding that reporter—
reporters have but perhaps people will read between the lines.

Q: Mmhmm.

R24: And it's supposed to be objective. "Well, I've got this opinion from TDH.
I'm gonna [?] from the people y'know." And umm—and yet TDH has a
face to give to the public.

Q: Mmhmm.

R25: So they must present the facts in such and such a way.

Q: Mmhmm.

R26: Umm and I think this is at the crux of the problem that we have had here.
And that TDH has a face and we have continuously been wanting to have
a different face for TDH. And how can we have a different face for TDH
when TDH has that face, y'know.

Q: Right.

R27: So—but we have understood that. Umm we have understood that—
y'know a scientist or so-called educated people. But as community people
we have refused to accept.

Q: Mmhmm.

R28: Y'know that is the difference And we understand that—and this is
nothing personal y'know. We, the people are beautiful human beings. But
bureaucrat—they're representing bureaucracy that refuses, y'know, to look
at a community and respect them.

Q: Mmhmm.

R29: And I think they're trying to give a different face this last month. [?]
Don't quote me [?].

Q: An unidentified source.

R30: Exactly.

Q: Just background information.

Q: [?]

R31: Yeah. [?] This process has been wonderful for me y'know. Umm I mean
to realize that the academic preparations of the [?] has been the most
learning experience for me. No, really. I mean, y'know, theory—just book
theory does not prepare you for community research, particularly for
environmental health.

Q: Yes.

R32: It does not prepare you to deal with the whole political process, the
whole economic implication of—[?] question.

Q: Mmhmm.

R33: Y'know I think that many scientists are very naive. But what kind of questions should you ask? Umm that's the book theory y'know.

Q: Mmhmm.

R34: But when you come face to face, y'know, with actual research umm you're faced with should I ask this question differently so the people will not be too unhappy y'know. Or the semantics of research becomes so— y'know so essential in this—and the diplomacy [?] y'know is [?]. I mean y'know—I mean what we're talking about y'know in meetings that we had with CDC [Centers for Disease Control], TDH and umm Mexican government [?]—CDC was there and Brownsville Community Health Center and some other people were there. And umm we were—we were talking about the facts in terms of the rate for anencephaly for this area for—I think it was from '89 to '91 or so. And what they realized is that the rates were indeed very, very, very high compared to the nation alright. And so we posed the question "should we label this as an epidemic based on these rates?"

Q: Mmhmm.

R35: Whether it's a temporary epidemic, whether it's a [?]—should these go beyond the norm? Should we call it an epidemic? And umm—and the CDC guy said "why?" And I said "well because there is no guidelines in no epidemiology book that tells you about rates and epidemics. It tells you that if a disease is rare enough, then one occurrence could be sufficient to be labeled an epidemic." I said "so it's really based on the politics." Epidemic—epidemiology is such a political field because based on these [?] and recommendations how policy decisions are going to be made. So to label something as an epidemic implies great expense as well.

Q: Mmhmm.

R36: It implies action. And so one must be very careful I guess from a health policy perspective to label anything, y'know, as such. So I said "well, here we have rates that are so tremendous compared to the national rates. Should we call it an epidemic?" Well, no. We should not call this an epidemic. But the question wasn't really, "is it an epidemic or not?" The question is "who is in power to call it an epidemic?" Does the community have a say so in whether this should be an epidemic or not? And of course that's where the—that's when the emotions come into being. Y'know— well, "this is not an epidemic," CDC says, and the community responds by saying "how many more children do you want to see dead?" And this is where the emotions come in because we see children out there , and they see numbers, and see the community has to live with it.

Q: Mmhmm.

R37: Y'know I mean I don't see a child here—and this is not to say that CDC does not see dead children as—y'know, as a rate. But they are "objective."

[?] CDC. They're in Georgia. Here we have to live with the results and the everyday happening of the people worrying everyday about "my god, am I gonna have y'know"—gosh, what do they call an anencephalic monster?

Q: [?]

R38: Oh [?] medical records. I mean imagine that?

Q: [?]

R39: And umm—and we have to see that. I mean we see that. And so it isn't at that moment not just the—the scientific question, "should this be labeled an epidemic?" for political questions, but the emotional question.

Q: Mmhmm.

R40: How many more kids do you want to see before y'know—and that's where the subjectivity of our questioning comes into being at that moment because there we are with emotion.

Q: Mmhmm.

R41: Besides the numbers, y'know. We live here. Y'know and [?] you would see that the emotions flared up on every side because, y'know, we're not just pumping up our numbers y'know. We're talking about people's lives here. We're talking about the future of people in this community. And that's where I guess you would say this objectivity comes into being because the questions are influenced by our emotions, our—by living our everyday lives here. But to me, there is nothing wrong with that. Y'know I mean if other people continue to label, y'know, the great emotional concern as being too subjective, then it's—it's okay, y'know. I don't mind that. I guess I would mind it if somebody didn't give me a job because of that. But then I would appear to be very objective—I need a job, y'know. I'm sure when you talk with Dr. Rocco, you will get a similar version of uh [?] because we have [?] on the inside track so to speak.

Q: Mmhmm.

R42: And we have been to all these sites involved and y'know have seen [?] handle the situations and how we have changed because of this.

Excerpt from Interview with M. B.

Q: What kinds of particular challenges do you face as an administrator?

R1: I would say [?] the border causes—makes this area very unique. And uh Brownsville is almost unique for border areas because—I would say because—I would say there's—this area is isolated enough from other places and we're small enough that we—we still have a large, large concentration of people that don't speak any English at all. And like the majority of the radio and T.V. stations—people have—unless you have cable—are Spanish. And so you could live here and never speak English. Like even if you lived in a border city like El Paso or Laredo, there's—

they're big enough that they have a large—that they uh American or the Anglo influence is real strong even though you—most of the radio stations—T.V.—is English and most of the commerce is done in English. But in Brownsville, that's not the case. Umm my wife works at Haggar Slacks. And she's one of the few people that speaks English. And she speaks—doesn't speak English that well. She's from Costa Rica. So—and a lot of those—a lot of those factory jobs like that—from this side of the border, the majority of the workers don't even speak English. And y'know [?] you go downtown to shop, the more—the majority of the conversations take place in Spanish. So for a student learning—growing up in Brownsville, they don't have that—they're not exposed to the English as much and they don't uh have that need—the strongest need to learn the English—so that—I think that makes our area unique. It's—that—this situation takes place in some of the smaller communities too. Uh and it's reflected in the test scores. Like Rio Grande City is uh the community that's—y'know it's a little bit larger, but it has pretty much the same situation. Their scores are very, very low because they have that language problem. A lot of the commerce, the activities take place in Spanish. So—so that's one big—the language is really a big thing here in Brownsville. And that—that affects all subject areas.

Q: Just because if they're busy learning English, they can't learn something else?

R2: Yes. They're learning—if they need English, y'know they—they can't—any question—even though they have—for example, you could talk to a person and communicate with them and you could y'know have a conversation with somebody and they might have some problems. Now when it comes to taking a standardized test, the language throws them off. One or two words that they're not familiar with throws them completely off. Y'know if you're in a conversation with somebody, you can take things from context and so forth. But when you're doing a one little paragraph or a few sentence question, one or two words can completely throw you off. [?] So—so that's the—that's really the—I think it's a big obstacle to education right here—one of the biggest. Also the high poverty level. Y'know this is really, really a high poverty area. And so y'know just that—that adds all sorts of implications. People having to work two jobs to make up—to survive—low paying jobs, low incomes, large families. There's not the support that you would get maybe in a more affluent community.

Q: [?] say the poverty is a cause for a lot of problems?

R3: Well, you have umm—in the border—a border society is always a very interesting—it's always an interesting place to live because there's—the people that are from this area, the border is kind of a gray line. It's not a firm line. People go back and forth across it. So there's always—there's not a lot of y'know—a lot of things going on in Mexico so there's always being an influx of people into this area, taking up jobs. So there's always that— I'd say that's a big contributing factor to the poverty is the fact of all the immigration people coming in here. And uh I guess that would—that would be the big thing.

Q: Now that—when we came down before—that was before Thanksgiving. Since then NAFTA [North American Free Trade Agreementto] has passed.

R4: NAFTA will improve things in Mexico and it will improve things in the Valley for sure. I mean—I mean it's—it's not gonna be something that happens overnight. But there's already a lot more construction going on. We're looking at y'know new bridges. Uh there's lot of improvements going on. There's a lot more focus on the problems with the Valley. So—so it's definitely helped. I think NAFTA—just the process of NAFTA going through put a lot of uh scrutiny on the Valley and our university for example got a lot more funding than it ever has before. And I think that that has—that had something to do with NAFTA and the focus on Mexico. Uh employment has improved in the Valley area recently. And I think it's continuing to improve. It's—the one thing is though, when you get in a slight—like a boom almost—like we're kind of in maybe a mini-boom— you also have an influx of people from other areas. So I mean it's gonna—there's gonna be a—y'know with this—with NAFTA there's gonna be a lot more problems too because we're in—we're growing at a tremen- dous rate, like 2,000 students a year. And so with that many students coming into the school district, if that population increases that's gonna cause all sorts of problems on our infrastructure. We're already—[?] Rio Grande River. So y'know just [?] Rio Grande River, there's not that much water there. And y'know that's where we get our water from. Our drinking water comes from that river. And y'know that water's not—not the best water in the first place. So there's gonna be good things and bad things associated with NAFTA.

Q: One point that we talked about [?] two of the primary things we were concerned about were environmental [?]. Do you see the health issues as [?] to what happens in the schools?

R5: When you think about that, what do you mean? Just how health is directly affecting the schools? Well they—they do. They do. I mean it's interesting. We used to have uh—y'know funding is coming—we used to have a lot of—a lot of our nurses in the school used to be paid [?] bilingual [?]. And then they cut that—I think that was cut out. And we lost all those nurses. So I mean at one time we only had one nurse and then we had a bilingual nurse who helped out. So we had two nurses, and we had a population of like I think 2,000 students in that school. So that was—that was good. Now we only have one nurse again. And some of the schools y'know have a part-time nurse. So there—y'know there's a lot of things that would help. If things get really bad—I mean if people—population continues to grow and efforts aren't made to address the infrastructure and this population growth affecting the environment, we could have tremendous problems in school because the kids come to us and if they're coming from areas where there's no running water—which some of them do—y'know some of the barrios don't have water or sewage—and so if those areas continue to grow at a fast rate and those students continue to come to us, there will be all sorts of social problems related with that because—just the disparity in—of incomes. I mean it will be like Rio de Janeiro or something. I mean it's—it's heading that way. And it's—there's a lot of places that if they grow too much more, they're just gonna be—just outright slums and they're gonna be—but rural slums. Do you know what I mean? Shanty town type things. And we've gotta make sure that that doesn't happen. We've gotta keep up, umm, like I said, the infrastructure.

Q: Do people see those as working together or do they seem to see them as totally separate?

R6: What—you mean the population growth and damage to the environment?

Q: Mmhmm.

R7: Well I think we see uh growth—y'know growth is seen as a blessing and uh—most business people see growth as positive. They're seeing it that they—that the influx—not so much the growth in population but just generally the growth period helps with the tax base, more industry, more labor, so forth and so on. And it's seen from that way. The environmental damage—people tend to—I think—I don't know—in my opinion they put that off. They tend to y'know—because it doesn't affect them immediately. There's still really nice places to live y'know and there's still nice places—the beach is still real close and it still—not—is still beautiful and so y'know they're not concerned with the nature part of it. A lot of people don't consider scrub to be y'know beautiful—mesquite to—that beautiful so—but there is beautiful things there—interesting things there and a diversity and basically just the system itself has to be supported.

Q: When you say that [?] in general [?] I know you're a science specialist, right?

R8: Yes.

Q: Is that [?]

R9: Yeah, the—the culture here hasn't placed y'know—there hasn't been—there's not a lot of value placed on the environment in the culture down here. And I mean there are people that value it a lot, but there's a large—a large people—[?] people coming from Mexico. Okay and if you have lived here and have grown up in a culture where they've been trying to conquer nature, y'know, and people coming from poverty where they've been struggling against nature for so long, it's hard to make the switch to the idea of you need to take care of it. And there's—the economic advantage to them has always been in overcoming it, not keeping it the same way. Y'know it's—like if you live off—if you were living in an area that didn't have roads, you either walked across a brushland. Getting rid of it seemed to be the nicest thing you could do. Y'know, you could plant stuff. You can walk—y'know you can get somewhere. And so that's a big stretch for a lot of people. And there's always—there's a lot of—hunting here is a big thing y'know. It's always been a big thing to do. Not a lot of—not a lot of [?]. That's changing y'know and that's—that's been a worldwide—I think a worldwide attitude that's slowly changing as people get more educated. But education is the key there in changing those attitudes.

Excerpt from Interview with S. R.

R159: . . . my heart has always been here, but now it's a divided heart [?]. I see what's going on and I just [?].

Q: Yeah.

R160: It's not there. And I know what's going on. I mean it's not as if this is all just recent.

Q: And you've been here. Now you were in [?]?

R161: I was living in [?].

Q: For how long?

R162: Twenty-seven years.

Q: Ok. One of the things that people have—umm people have talked to us about there being a border culture. And a lot of them have talked about how the border culture is different from if you're in the north—in the United States.

R163: Oh yes.

Q: I mean people say you're not in the United States. It's like you're in Mexico. But I'm guessing it's not the same.

R164: It goes both ways.

Q: Yeah.

R165: Right. Like 22 miles is more of a division than people think. Yes, definitely. This is—I have nothing against it. But this is what you call the Tex-Mex culture because it is a mixing of the two cultures.

Q: Mmhmm.

R166: And the ideas, the languages, everything is a combination of both things. The ones that can really [?] are my own boys because since they were born and raised in Mexico—but we used to go up to the United States to Wisconsin every summer.

Q: Mmhmm.

R167: And all three of them had a short period of time living here [?]. The oldest one was here the longest. He finished high school here before he went on to the university.

Q: Mmhmm.

R168: The other two weren't here as long umm but they had enough to get a feeling of it and [?] very definitely is not one and it's not the other and even it's not an exact combination of the two.

Q: What . . .

R169: They had developed their own culture.

Q: Can you describe it?

R170: Ok.

Q: I mean . . .

R171: The language to begin with. They say they speak Spanish here, but they really don't. They speak Spanish and they can understand the Mexican Spanish.

Q: Mmhmm.

R172: But what they speak and what they talk and everything is a very different—it's a Tex-Mex language because they mix words.

Q: Ah.

R173: They don't say umm . . .

Q: What's an example?

R174: Just to give you an example—instead of saying a truck or [?], they call it a [?].

Q: Ah.

R175: Ok. Umm, instead of calling a umm laundromat . . .

Q: Mmhmm.

R176: They put together anything that's E-R-I-A usually is a Mexican something—a cafeteria or whatever. It's "eria"—I know that [?] ending.

Q: Mmhmm. Right.

R177: Well they'll call it a washateria—washateria.

Q: Uhhuh.

R178: "Wash" is English.

Q: "Ateria" is Spanish.

R179: They put at the last part—is Spanish—washateria. Y'know that's the laundromat.

Q: Uhhuh.

R180: So many, many of these words are combinations of English and Spanish. And at first—I know both languages—but when I first came here, I had a little trouble understanding what some of those words meant until I got them into context.

Q: Mmhmm.

R181: So umm . . .

Q: So, even the language.

R182: The language is different.

Q: Mmhmm.

R183: The, umm, customs—you'll see that even the health issues are addressed differently than they would be in Mexico or that they would be in the United States further [?]. Because again it's kind of a combination of do we use a *cuerandera* or do we use the health services in the hospital type thing? They'll make it a combination. I see this time and time again where children have what I'm quite sure is a very [?] a bad injury to the arm and suspect that it might be a fracture.

Q: Mmhmm.

R184: They don't go and have an x-ray done first. First of all they go to the massage. And that's the Mexican style—where they try and massage and see if the bones are . . .

Q: [?]

R185: . . . [?] put them back in place and so forth. And they'll come back and they still don't have that arm in a cast. Maybe if we're lucky, they'll have it y'know with umm a splint.

Q: Mmhmm.

R186: More than often not. So I have to insist that they have an x-ray taken and they'll find the fracture there and then finally give them the cast. But they like to see the Mexican type of thing in some families. And you'll find usually that it's the lower income—lower uh—the poorer people . . .

Q: Mmhmm.

R187: . . . who still uh hang on to those customs, cultural customs [?].

Q: Wasn't your husband a doctor?

R188: He is. Yes.

Q: And he was in Mexico.

R189: Yeah. Mmhmm.

Q: I mean it's not like there's not doctors in Mexico.

R190: Oh, no. Listen. They've got some terrific—the fact is; I shouldn't say this, . . . *[Tape turned off and on again].* But anyway, yes, we do have some excellent, excellent doctors down there. And the people—their families umm—people that have a higher education—they'll use their services.

Q: Mmhmm.

R191: But the grandmother—the matriarch—they say it's a patriarchal society down there. That's not true. It's matriarchal. The grandmother or the—or the old aunt or somebody in that family—usually the oldest woman in that family . . .

Q: [?]

R192: . . . is the one who gives the most incentive to what's going to be done, what kind of choices are going to be made. And that includes health care.

Now if you've got a grandma who says that you still have to wrap up the [?] umbilical cord and all that stuff, you still have to wrap it with these special little things that they have with a coin on it.

Q: Mmhmm.

R193: So they don't get a hernia. If grandma says that, you do it even though you know better because you know it's not gonna hurt the child and [?] everybody happy. Well, there are just little things that you learn along the way that you just go along with it. Now if that same grandmother is already of the group of people who are educated, then you're not going to have that.

Q: Mmhmm.

R194: So you still find even a kind of a combination down there sometimes of some of the old ideas and the new. But here at the border since you have very low income people frequently—not always—but frequently. And I don't . . .

Q: There's a lot of them.

R195: Yeah. And you'll find a lot of those border ideas still are being used.

References

Adler, Jerry. 1992. "A Life and Death Puzzle." *Newsweek*, 8 June, 52.

Agriculture Canada. 1989. *Agriculture Canada's Submission to the Northern Diseased Bison Assessment Panel*. Ottawa, Ont.: Agriculture Canada, 17 November.

Allen, Patricia, and Carolyn Sachs. 1991. "The Social Side of Sustainability: Class, Gender and Race." *Science as Culture* 2:569–90.

Althaus, Dudley, Jim Pinkerton, JoAnn Zuniga, and Carlos Antonio Rios.1993. "River to Ruin." *Houston Chronicle*, 17 October, special report.

Aniskowicz, B. Theresa. 1990. "Life or Death." *Nature Canada* 19(2): 35–38.

Anzaldúa, Gloria. 1987. *Borderlands/La Frontera: The New Mestiza*. San Francisco: Aunt Lute Press.

Austin, John Langshaw. 1962. *How to Do Things with Words*. Cambridge, Mass.: Harvard University Press.

Barney, Gerold O. 1981. "The Global 2000 Report to the President: Entering the Twenty-first Century." Washington, D.C.: Council of Environmental Quality.

Beck, Ulrich. 1992. *Risk Society: Towards a New Modernity*. Translated by Mark Ritter. Newbury Park, Calif.: Sage Publications.

Bedard, Paul. 1992. "Bush Proposes Plan for Planet." *Washington [D.C.] Times*, 2 June.

Begon, Michael, John L. Harper, and Colin R. Townsend. 1990. *Ecology: Individuals, Populations, and Communities*. 2d ed. Boston: Blackwell Scientific Publications.

Benedick, Richard E. 1991. *Ozone Diplomacy*. Cambridge, Mass.: Harvard University Press.

Berry, Wendell. 1977. *The Unsettling of America: Culture and Agriculture*. San Francisco: North Point Press.

———. 1981. *The Gift of Good Land: Further Essays Cultural and Agricultural*. San Francisco: North Point Press.

———. 1990. *What Are People For?* San Francisco: North Point Press.

Blankenship, Jane. 1993. "Kenneth Burke on Ecology: A Synthesis." In *Extensions of the Burkeian System*, edited by James W. Chesebro, 251–68. Tuscaloosa: University of Alabama Press.

Blood, D. C., James A. Henderson, and O. M. Radostits. 1979. *Veterinary Medicine*. 5th ed. Philadelphia: Lea and Febinger.

Booth, Annie L., and Harvey L. Jacobs. 1990. "Ties That Bind: Native American Beliefs as a Foundation for Environmental Consciousness." *Environmental Ethics* 12:27–43.

Botkin, Daniel B. 1990. *Discordant Harmonies: A New Ecology for the Twenty-first Century.* New York: Oxford University Press.

Boxer, Baruch. 1992–93. "Getting Beyond Rio." *Issues in Science and Technology* 9(2): 42–48.

Brandt Commission. 1980. *North-South: A Programme for Survival.* Cambridge, Mass.: MIT Press; and London: Pan Books.

Bridgewater, Donald R. 1989. *Parker Land and Cattle Co.: Epidemiological Report, Western Regional Epidemiologist.* Englewood, Colo.: U.S. Department of Agriculture, Animal and Plant Health Inspection Service, Veterinary Services.

Brooke, James. 1992. "U.S. Has a Starring Role in Rio Summit as Villain." *New York Times,* 2 June.

———. 1992. "Earth Summit Races Clock to Resolve Differences on Forest Treaty." *New York Times,* 10 June.

———. 1992a. "Delegates from Four Nations Warm to a High-Profile Role: Global Powerbroker." *New York Times,* 12 June.

———. 1992b. "U.S. Delegation in Rio Strained and Divided over Policy." *New York Times,* 12 June.

———. 1992. "Bush Attempts to Mend Fences." *New York Times,* 13 June.

———. 1992. "Japan Promises Lead Role in Battle against Pollution." *New York Times,* 14 June.

———. 1992. "U.N. Chief Closes Summit with an Appeal for Action." *New York Times,* 15 June.

Brown, Lester, et al. 1984–96. *State of the World 19__: A Worldwatch Institute Report on Progress toward a Sustainable Society.* New York: Norton.

Burke, Kenneth. 1931. *Counter Statement.* New York: Harcourt, Brace.

———. [1935] 1984a. *Permanence and Change.* Berkeley: University of California Press.

———. [1937] 1984b. *Attitudes toward History.* Berkeley: University of California Press.

———. [1950] 1969. *A Rhetoric of Motives.* Berkeley: University of California Press.

———. 1966. *Language as Symbolic Action: Essays on Life, Literature, and Method.* Berkeley: University of California Press.

———. 1978. "(Nonsymbolic)Motion/(Symbolic) Action." *Critical Inquiry* 5:401–16.

Bush, George. 1992. "Remarks and an Exchange with Reporters Prior to a Meeting with United Nations Secretary-General Boutros Boutros-Ghali." *Weekly Compilation of Presidential Documents* 28 (12 May): 845.

———. 1992. "Remarks on Departure for the United Nations Conference on Environment and Development." *Weekly Compilation of Presidential Documents* 28 (11 June): 1035–36.

———. 1992. "Address to the United Nations Conference on Environment and Development in Rio de Janeiro, Brazil." *Weekly Compilation of Presidential Documents* 28 (12 June): 1043–44.

Caldwell, Lynton K. 1988. "Environmental Impact Analysis (EIA): Origins, Evolution, and Future Directions." *Policy Studies Review* 8:75–83.

Campbell, John Angus, and Keith R. Benson. 1996. "The Rhetorical Turn in Science Studies." *Quarterly Journal of Speech* 82:74–109.

Carbyn, L. N., S. M. Oosenbrug, and D. W. Anions. 1993. *Wolves, Bison and the Dynamics Related to the Peace-Athabasca Delta in Canada's Wood Buffalo National Park.* Edmonton, Alta: Canadian Circumpolar Institute.

Carmin, JoAnn. 1994. "Once upon a Declaration: Tales from the Rio Declaration on Environment and Development." University of North Carolina, Chapel Hill. Photocopy.

Carpenter, Will D. 1991. "Insignificant Risks Must Be Balanced against Great Benefits." *Chemical and Engineering News Forum* 69 (7 Janary): 37–39.

Carson, Rachel. [1962] 1966. *Silent Spring.* Boston: Houghton-Mifflin.

Choquette, Lyle P., E. Broughton, James G. Cousineau, and Nick S. Novakowski. 1978. "Parasites and Diseases of Bison in Canada IV: Serologic Survey for Brucellosis in Bison in Northern Canada." *Journal of Wildlife Disease* 14:329–32.

Christie, David. 1987. *Epidemiology: An Introductory Text for Medical and Other Health Science Students.* Sydney: New South Wales University Press.

Coalition for Justice in the Maquiladoras. 1990. *Compilation of Articles on the Maquiladora Industry in Matamoros.* New York: Interfaith Center on Corporate Responsibility.

"Compromise Reached on Emissions." 1992. *Washington Post,* 9 May.

Conrad, Charles, and Elizabeth A. Macom. 1995. "Re-visiting Kenneth Burke: Dramatism/Logology and the Problem of Agency." *Southern Communication Journal* 61:11–28.

Crutchfield, James P., J. Doyne Farmer, Norman H. Packard, and Robert S. Shaw. 1986. "Chaos." *Scientific American* 255(6): 46–57.

Daly, Herman E. 1991. *Steady-State Economics.* Washington, D.C.: Island Press.

Daly, Herman E., and John B. Cobb. 1989. *For the Common Good: Redirecting the Economy toward Community, the Environment, and a Sustainable Future.* Boston: Beacon Press.

Davis, Donald S., Joe W. Templeton, Thomas A. Ficht, Jan D. Huber, R. Dale Angus, and L. Garry Adams. 1991. "Brucella Abortus in Bison II: Evaluation of Strain 19 Vaccination of Pregnant Cows." *Journal of Wildlife Disease* 27:188–204.

DeForest, Mariah E. 1991. "Are Maquiladoras a Menace to U.S. Workers?" *Business Horizons* 34:82–85.

Devall, Bill, and George Sessions. 1985. *Deep Ecology.* Layton, Utah: Perigrine Smith.

Devroy, Ann. 1992. "White House Scorns Summit Foes." *Washington Post*, 10 June.

Douglass, Gordon, ed. 1984. *Agricultural Sustainability in a Changing World Order*. Boulder, Colo.: Westview Press.

Dunlap, Riley E., George H. Gallup, and A. M. Gallup. 1993. *Health of the Planet: A George H. Gallup Memorial Survey*. Princeton, N.J.: George H. Gallup International Institute.

Easterbrook, Greg. 1992. "Green Cassandras." *New Republic*, 6 July, 23–25.

Ellul, Jacques. 1980. *The Technological System*. Translated by Joachim Neugroschel. New York: Continuum.

Esbjornson, Carl D. 1992. "Once and Future Farming: Some Meditations on the Historical and Cultural Roots of Sustainable Agriculture in the United States." *Agriculture and Human Values* 9(3): 20–30.

Extracts from Statements: Plenary and Summit Segment. 1992. "Commission of the European Community." *Environmental Policy and Law* 22:237–38.

Ferguson, Kathy E. 1984. *The Feminist Case against Bureaucracy*. Philadelphia: Temple University Press.

French, Hilary F. 1992. *After the Earth Summit: The Future of Environmental Governance*. Washington, D.C.: Worldwatch Institute.

Frye, Russell S. 1992. "Uncle Sam at UNCED." *Environmental Policy and Law* 22:340–46.

Fuentes, Eduardo R. 1993. "Scientific Research and Sustainable Development." *Ecological Applications* 3:576–77.

Fuller, Steve. 1993. *Philosophy, Rhetoric, and the End of Knowledge: The Coming of Science and Technology Studies*. Madison: University of Wisconsin Press.

Geist, Valerius. 1991. "Phantom Subspecies: The Wood Bison *Bison bison* "Athabascae" Rhoads 1897 Is Not a Valid Taxon, but an Ecotype." *Arctic* 44:283–300.

Giddens, Anthony. 1979. *Central Problems in Social Theory: Action, Structure, and Contraction in Social Analysis*. Berkeley: University of California Press.

———. 1984. *The Constitution of Society: Outline of the Theory of Structuration*. Berkeley: University of California Press.

Gilbertz, Susan J., Tarla Rai Peterson, and Gary E. Varner. 1994. "Addressing Coastal Challenges through Environmental Ethics Education." Final Report, EPA Assistance ID# MX822144-01-0.

Glacken, Clarence J. 1973. *Traces on the Rhodian Shore*. Berkeley: University of California Press.

Goodland, Robert J. A. 1982. *Tribal Peoples and Economic Development: Human Ecologic Considerations*. Washington, D.C.: World Bank.

Goodnight, G. Thomas. 1982. "The Personal, Technical, and Public Spheres of Argument: A Speculative Inquiry into the Art of Public Deliberation." *Journal of American Forensic Association* 18:214–27.

Gore, Albert. 1992. *Earth in the Balance: Ecology and the Human Spirit.* New York: Houghton Mifflin.

Greider, William. 1992. "How We Export Jobs and Disease." *Rolling Stone,* 3 September, 32–33.

Groenendyk, Kathi. 1994. *Covering the Story: A Rhetorical Analysis of Brownsville's Television Newscoverage.* Master's thesis, Department of Speech Communication, Texas A&M University, College Station.

Guillermoprieto, Alma. 1990. "Letter from Mexico City." *New Yorker,* 17 September, 93–104.

Habermas, Jürgen. 1979. *Communication and the Evolution of Society.* Translated by Thomas McCarthy. Boston: Beacon Press.

Halloran, S. Michael. 1984. "The Rebirth of Molecular Biology: An Essay in the Rhetorical Criticism of Scientific Discourse." *Rhetoric Review* 3:70–83.

Hardin, Garrett. 1968. "The Tragedy of the Commons." *Science* 162:1243–48.

Harrity, Chick. 25 December 1995. "Ahead at National Parks: More Crowds and Blight." *U.S. News and World Report,* 78.

Hein, Cheryl D., and Neal R. Von Zante. 1991. "Maquiladoras: Should U.S. Companies Run for the Border?" *CPA Journal* 61:14–16.

Holling, C. S. 1993. "Investing in Research for Sustainability." *Ecological Applications* 3:552–55.

Ikerd, John E. 1990. "Agriculture's Search for Sustainability and Profitability." *Journal of Soil and Water Conservation* 45(1): 18–23.

International Union for the Conservation of Nature and Natural Resources (IUCN). 1983. *15th Session of the General Assembly of IUCN and 15th IUCN Technical Meeting, New Zealand, 11–23 October 1981: Proceedings.* Gland, Switz.: IUCN.

Jackson, Wes. 1987. *Altars of Unhewn Stone: Science and the Earth.* San Francisco: North Point Press.

———. 1990. "Making Sustainable Agriculture Work." In *Our Sustainable Table,* edited by Robert Clark, 132–41. San Francisco: North Point Press.

Jahrsdoerfer, Sonja J., and David M. Leslie Jr. 1988. *Tamaulepan Brushland of the Lower Rio Grande Valley of South Texas: Discription, Human Impacts, and Management Options.* Washington, D.C.: U.S. Department of the Interior, Fish and Wildlife Service.

Jasper, William F. 1992. *Global Tyranny . . . Step by Step: The United Nations and the Emerging New World Order.* Appleton, Wisc.: Western Islands.

Juffer, Jane. 1988. "Dump at the Border." *Progressive* 52:24–29.

Kelly, Ros. 1992. "Extracts from Statements: Plenary and Summit Segment." *Environmental Policy and Law* 22:226.

Killingsworth, M. Jimmy, and Jacqueline S. Palmer. 1995. "The Discourse of Environmentalist Hysteria." *Quarterly Journal of Speech* 81:1–19.

———. 1992. *Ecospeak: Rhetoric and Environmental Politics in America.* Carbondale, Ill.: Southern Illinois University Press.

Kohl, Helmut. 1992. "Extracts from Statements: Plenary and Summit Segment." *Environmental Policy and Law* 22:230.

Lange, Jonathon. 1990. "Refusal to Compromise: The Case of Earth First!" *Western Journal of Speech Communication* 54:473–94.

———. 1993. "The Logic of Competing Information Campaigns: Conflict over Old Growth and the Spotted Owl." *Communication Monographs* 60:239–57.

Lee, Kai N. 1993a. *Compass and Gyroscope: Integrating Science and Politics for the Environment.* Washington, D.C.: Island Press.

———. 1993b. "Greed, Scale Mismatch, and Learning." *Ecological Applications* 3:560–64.

Lehrman, Sally. 1992. "Genetech's Stance on Biodiversity Riles Staff." *Nature* 358 (9 July): 97.

Leopold, Aldo. 1933. *Game Management.* New York: Charles Scribners.

———. [1949] 1968. *A Sand Country Almanac and Sketches Here and There.* New York: Oxford University Press.

Levi-Strauss, Claude. 1958. *Race and History.* Paris: UNESCO.

Lewis, Paul. 1992. "Storm in Rio: Morning After." *New York Times,* 15 June.

Lincoln, Yvonna S., and Egon G. Guba. 1985. *Naturalistic Inquiry.* Beverly Hills, Calif.: Sage Publications.

Lockamy, Terry. 1988. Agriculture Wildlife Coexistence Committee File. San Benito: Texas Agricultural Extension Service.

Lovelock, James E. 1979. *Gaia: A New Look at Life on Earth.* New York: Oxford University Press.

Lowdermilk, W. C. 1953. "Conquest of the Land through 7000 Years." Washington, D.C.: U.S. Department of Agriculture.

Ludwig, Donald. 1993. "Environmental Sustainability: Magic, Science, and Religion in Natural Resource Management." *Ecological Applications* 3:555–58.

Ludwig, Donald, Ray Hilborn, and Carl Walters. 1993. "Uncertainty, Resource Exploitation, and Conservation: Lessons From History." *Science* 260:17, 36.

Luhmann, Niklas. 1989. *Ecological Communication.* Translated by John Bednarz Jr. Chicago: University of Chicago Press.

———. 1992. "What Is Communication?" Translated by John Bednarz Jr. *Communication Theory* 2:251–59.

Lyotard, Jean F. 1984. *The Postmodern Condition: A Report on Knowledge.* Minneapolis: University of Minnesota Press.

MacDonnell, Patrick J. 1991. "Foreign-Owned Companies Add to Mexico's Pollution." *Los Angeles Times,* 14 April.

Mangel, Marc, Robert J. Hofman, Elliott A. Norse, and John R. Twiss Jr. 1993. "Sustainability and Ecological Research." *Ecological Applications* 3:573–75.

McClintock, John M. 1992. "Cluster of Babies in Texas Born without Brains." *Baltimore Sun,* 19 January.

McCracken, Grant David. 1988. *The Long Interview.* Newbury Park, Calif.: Sage Publications.

McCreight, Major Israel. 1950. *Buffalo Bone Days: A Story of the Buffalo Slaughter on Our Plains.* DuBois, Pa.: DuBois Courier Express.

McHugh, Tom. 1979. *The Time of the Buffalo.* Lincoln: University of Nebraska Press.

Meagher, Mary M. 1989. "Evaluation of Boundary Control for Bison of Yellowstone National Park." *Wildlife Society Bulletin* 17:15–19.

Meyer, Judy L., and Gene S. Helfman. 1993. "The Ecological Basis of Sustainability." *Ecological Applications* 3:569–71.

Michiel, Patrick. 1990. "The Bison Saga." *Nature Canada* 19(2): 29–34.

Mohamad, Mahathir. 1992. "Extracts from Statements: Plenary and Summit Segment." *Environmental Policy and Law* 22:232.

"National Search for Sustainability." 1995. *Panthers Magazine* (May): 5. Penrith, N.S.W., Aus.: Penrith Rugby League Club Ltd.

Northern Diseased Bison Environmental Assessment Panel (NDBEAP). 1990a. *Community and Technical Hearings.* 2 vols. Vancouver, B.C.: Allwest Reporting Ltd.

———. 1990b. *Report of the Environmental Assessment Panel.* Hull, Queb.: Federal Environmental Assessment Review Office.

Odum, Eugene P. 1971. *Fundamentals of Ecology.* 3d ed. Philadelphia: W. B. Saunders.

One Border Foundation. n.d. Brownsville, Tex. Photocopy.

Osborn, Fairfield. 1948. *Our Plundered Planet.* Boston: Little, Brown.

Parfit, Michael. 1990. "Earth Firsters Wield a Mean Monkey Wrench." *Smithsonian* 21 (April): 184–86.

Parsons, Talcott. 1977. *Social Systems and the Evolution of Action.* New York: Free Press.

Pearce, W. Barnett. 1989. *Communication and the Human Condition.* Carbondale: Southern Illinois University Press.

Pearce, D., E. Barbier, and A. Markandya, 1989. *Sustainable Development: Economics and Environment in the Third World.* London: Earthscan.

Peterson, Markus J. 1991. "Wildlife Parasitism, Science, and Management Policy." *Journal of Wildlife Management* 55:782–89.

Peterson, Markus J., William E. Grant, and Donald S. Davis. 1991a. "Bison-Brucellosis Management: Simulation of Alternative Strategies." *Journal of Wildlife Management* 55:205–13.

———. 1991b. "Simulation of Host-Parasite Interactions within a Resource Management Framework: Impact of Brucellosis on Bison Population Dynamics." *Ecological Modeling* 54:299–320.

Peterson, Markus J., and Tarla Rai Peterson. 1993. "A Rhetorical Critique of 'Non-Market' Economic Valuation for Natural Resources." *Environmental Values* 2:47–65.

Peterson, Tarla Rai. 1986. "The Will to Conservation: A Burkeian Analysis of

Dust Bowl Rhetoric and American Farming Motives." *Southern Speech Communication Journal* 52:1–21.

———. 1988a. "The Meek Shall Inherit the Mountains: A Dramatistic Criticism of Grand Teton National Park's Interpretive Program." *Central States Speech Journal* 39:121–33.

———. 1988b. "The Rhetorical Construction of Institutional Authority in a Senate Subcommittee Hearing on Wilderness Legislation." *Western Journal of Speech Communication* 52:259–76.

———. 1990. "Structuring Closure through Technological Discourse: The Mormon Priesthood Correlation Program." In *Communication and the Culture of Technology*, edited by Martin J. Medhurst, Alberto Gonzalez, and Tarla Rai Peterson, 77–94. Pullman: Washington State University Press.

———. 1991. "Telling the Farmers' Story: Competing Responses to Soil Conservation Rhetoric." *Quarterly Journal of Speech* 77:289–308.

Peterson, Tarla Rai, and Christi Choat Horton. 1995. "Rooted in the Soil: How Understanding the Perspective of Land-owners Can Enhance the Management of Environmental Disputes." *Quarterly Journal of Speech* 81:139–66.

Peterson, Tarla Rai, and Markus J. Peterson. 1996. "Valuation Analysis in Environmental Policy Making: How Economic Models Limit Possibilities for Environmental Advocacy." In *The Symbolic Earth: Discourse and Our Creation of the Environment*, edited by Christine Oravec and James G. Cantrill, 198–218. Lexington: University Press of Kentucky.

Peterson, Tarla Rai, Kim Witte, Ernesto Enkerlin-Hoeflich, Lorina Espericueta, Jason Todd Flora, Nanci Florey, Tamara Loughran, and Rebecca Stuart. 1994. "Using Informant Directed Interviews to Discover Risk Orientation: How Formative Evaluations Based in Interpretive Analysis Can Improve Persuasive Safety Campaigns." *Journal of Applied Communication Research* 22:199–215.

Pinchot, Gifford. 1910. *The Fight for Conservation.* Garden City, N.Y.: Harcourt, Brace.

Postel, Sandra. 1992. "Denial in the Decisive Decade." In *State of the World 1992: A Worldwatch Institute Report on Progress toward a Sustainable Society,* edited by Lester R. Brown, Christopher Flavin, and Sandra Postel, 3–8. New York: Norton.

Prelli, Lawrence J. 1989. *A Rhetoric of Science: Inventing Scientific Discourse.* Columbia: University of South Carolina Press.

Rakow, Lana. 1986. "Rethinking Gender Research in Communication." *Journal of Communication* 36:11–26.

Redclift, Michael. 1987. *Sustainable Development: Exploring the Contradictions.* London: Methuen.

———. 1993. "Sustainable Development: Needs, Values, Rights." *Environmental Values* 2:3–20.

Reid, Walter V. 1992. "Bush Biodiversity Policy Risks Dangerous Side Effects." *Wall Street Journal,* 8 October.

Reilly, William K. 1992. "Excerpts from Rio Memo: A Plea for the Environment." *New York Times*, 5 June.

———. 1992. "Extracts from Statements: Plenary and Summit Segment." *Environmental Policy and Law* 22:236–37.

Robbins, Michael W. 1995. "Biodiversity and Strange Bedfellows." *Audubon* (January–February): 4.

Robinson, Nicholas A. ed. 1992. *Agenda 21 and the UNCED Proceedings*. New York: Oceana Publications.

Robinson, Eugene, and Michael Weisskopf. 1992. "'No' Leaves U.S. Isolated at Summit." *Washington Post*, 6 June.

———. 1992. "Europe May Stand United on Emission." *Washington Post*, 9 June.

Rose, Carol. 1986. "The Comedy of the Commons: Custom, Commerce, and Inherently Public Property." *University of Chicago Law Review* 53:711–81.

Rubenstein, Daniel. 1993. "Science and the Pursuit of a Sustainable World." *Ecological Applications* 3:585–87.

Rueckert, William H. 1994. *Encounters with Kenneth Burke*. Urbana and Chicago: University of Illinois Press.

Satchell, Michael. 1991. "Poisoning the Border." *U.S. News and World Report*, 6 May, 32–40.

Schneider, Keith. 1992. "White House Snubs U.S. Envoy's Plea to Sign Rio Treaty." *New York Times*, 5 June.

———. 1992. "President Defends U.S. Envoy in Rio." *New York Times*, 6 June.

Searle, John R. 1969. *Speech Acts: An Essay in the Philosophy of Language*. London: Cambridge University Press.

Selby, Gardner. 1994. "People Want Words Turned into Deeds." *Houston Post*, 2 October.

Selcraig, Bruce. 1994. "Border Patrol." *Sierra* (May–June): 58–64, 79–81.

Socolow, Robert H. 1993. "Achieving Sustainable Development That Is Mindful of Human Imperfection." *Ecological Applications* 3:581–83.

Solow, Robert M. 1991. *Sustainability: An Economist's Perspective*. Woods Hole, Mass.: Marine Policy Center, Woods Hole Oceanographic Institution.

Spears, Randy, and Duane Dale, prod. 1995. "The Cameron County Agriculture and Wildlife Coexistence Committee Case Study." *Enhancing Public Decisions through Public Issues Education*. Video (20 min.). Madison: University of Wisconsin, Cooperative Extension Service.

Stevens, William K. 1992. "U.S. Trying to Buff its Image, Defends the Forests." *New York Times*, 7 June.

———. 1992. "Bush Plan to Save Forests Is Blocked by Poor Countries." *New York Times*, 9 June.

———. 1992. "Lessons of Rio. A New Prominence and an Effective Blandness." *New York Times*, 14 June.

Stone, Richard. 1994. "Proposed Global Network for Ecology Data Stirs Debate." *Science* 266:1155.

Strong, Maurice. 1992. "Extracts from Statements: Plenary and Summit Segment." *Environmental Policy and Law* 22:242–44.

Suro, Roberto. 1992. "Rash of Brain Defects in Newborns Disturb Border City in Texas." *New York Times*, 31 May.

———. 1993. "Pollution-Weary Minorities Try Civil Rights Tack." *New York Times*, 11 January.

Talbot, Lee M. 1989. "Man's Role in Managing the Global Environment." In *Changing the Global Environment*, edited by Daniel B. Botkin, 17–33. New York: Academic Press.

Taylor, Bryan C. Forthcoming. "Shooting Downwind: Depicting the Radiated Body in Epidemiology and Documentary Photography." In *Transgressing Scientific Discourses*, edited by Michael Huspek and Gary Radford. Albany: State University of New York Press.

Terrell, Gaynell. 1992. "Tackling the Mystery That Matters: Anencephalic Births Stir Mixed Feelings at Border." *Houston Post*, 20 August.

Tessaro, Stacy V., L. B. Forbes, and Charles Turcotte. 1990. "A Survey of Brucellosis and Tuberculosis in Bison in and around Wood Buffalo National Park, Canada." *Canadian Veterinary Journal* 31:174–80.

Texas Center for Policy Studies. 1990. *Overview of Environmental Issues Associated with Maquiladora Development along the Texas:Mexico Border.* Austin: Texas Center for Policy Studies.

Texas Department of Health, with Technical Assistance from the Centers for Disease Control (TDH-CDC). 1992. *An Investigation of a Cluster of Neural Tube Defects in Cameron County, Texas.* Austin: Texas Department of Health; Atlanta: Centers for Disease Control, 1 July.

"The Texas Border: Whose Dirt?" 1990. *Economist*, 18 August, 20–21.

Thomas, William L., Jr., ed. 1956. *Man's Role in Changing the Face of the Earth.* Chicago: University of Chicago Press.

Thompson, Paul B. 1995. *The Spirit of the Soil: Agriculture and Environmental Ethics.* New York: Routledge.

Thompson, Timothy N., and Anthony J. Palmeri. 1993. "Attitudes toward Counternature (with Notes on Nurturing a Poetic Psychosis)." In *Extensions of the Burkeian System*, edited by James W. Chesebro, 269–83. Tuscaloosa: University of Alabama Press.

Thorpe, Helen. 1995. "Hype or Hero." *Texas Monthly* (November): 22–24.

Tomaso, Bruce, and Richard Alm. 1989. "Economy v. Ecology: Toxic Wastes from Border Plants Poorly Monitored." *Dallas Morning News*, 1 February.

Ulrich, Hans, and Gilbert J. B. Probst, eds. 1984. *Self-Organization and Management of Social Systems.* New York: Springer-Verlag.

United Nations (UN). 1992. "Convention on Biological Diversity." *Environmental Policy and Law* 22:251–58.

———. 1992. "United Nations Framework Convention on Climate Change." *Environmental Policy and Law* 22:258–59.

United Nations Activities. 1992. "Rio Conference on Environment and Development." *Environmental Policy and Law* 22:204–24.

———. 1993. "Commission on Sustainable Development: First Substantive Session." *Environmental Policy and Law* 23:190–201.

———. 1994. "CSD Holds Second Session." *Environmental Policy and Law* 24:206–25.

———. 1995a. "First Meeting of the Conference of the Parties to the Rio Convention." *Environmental Policy and Law* 25:38.

———. 1995b. "Work in the Second Committee." *Environmental Policy and Law* 25:7–10.

United Nations Conference on Environment and Development (UNCED). 1992. *Agenda 21: Adoption of Agreements on Environment and Development.* Rio de Janeiro: UNCED.

———. 1992a. *Forest Principles.* Rio de Janeiro: UNCED.

———. 1992b. *Rio Declaration on Environment and Development.* Rio de Janeiro: UNCED.

Vranitzky, Franz. 1992. "Extracts from Statements: Plenary and Summit Segment." *Environmental Policy and Law* 22:226–27.

Waddell, Craig. 1990. "The Role of Pathos in the Decision-making Process: A Study in the Rhetoric of Science Policy." *Quarterly Journal of Speech* 76:381–400.

———. 1995. "Defining Sustainable Development: A Case Study in Environmental Communication." *Technical Communication Quarterly* 4:201–16.

Waitzkin, Howard 1993. "Interpretive Analysis of Spoken Discourse: Dealing with the Limitations of Quantitative and Qualitative Methods." *Southern Communication Journal* 58:128–46.

Weaver, Richard. 1953. *The Ethics of Rhetoric.* Chicago: Henry Regnery.

Weisskopf, Michael. 1992. "Outsider EPA Chief Being Tested." *Washington Post,* 8 June.

———. 1992. "Behind the Curve in Rio." *Washington Post,* 11 June.

Weisskopf, Michael, and Ann Devroy. 1992. "Global Leaders Set Course for Protecting the Earth." *Washington Post,* 13 June.

Weisskopf, Michael, and Julie Preston. 1992. "U.N. Earth Summit Opens with Calls to Save Planet." *Washington Post,* 3 June.

"With Climate Treaty Signed, All Say They'll Do Even More." 1992. *New York Times,* 13 June.

Witter, J. Franklin. 1981. "Brucellosis." In *Infectious Diseases of Wild Mammals.* 2d ed. Edited by John W. Davis, Lars H. Karstad, and Daniel O. Trainer. Ames: Iowa State University Press.

Wojcik, Jan. 1984. "The American Wisdom Literature of Farming." *Agriculture and Human Values* 1:26–37.

World Commission for Environment and Development (WCED). 1987. *Our Common Future.* Oxford: Oxford University Press.

Index